5.1.80

R. H. TAWNEY:

The American Labour Movement and Other Essays

This is a new collection of the highly significant, and hitherto inaccessible, writings on labor history by R. H. Tawney. It includes four essays which appeared in remote and specialist organs between 1913 and 1934, and a major, yet little-known study of the American labor movement, written in 1942.

These essays bear Tawney's distinctive clarity of style and precision of analysis. The core of the collection is a 35,000 word essay on "The American Labour Movement," here published for the first time. In this, Tawney describes the changes in American industry which precipitated an explosion in trade union membership and perceptively contrasts American and European unionism.

Tawney's other essays illustrate his wide range of interests, from the alleviation of poverty, and China's political and economic structure in the early 1930s, to an analytical census of occupations in 17th century England.

R. H. TAWNEY:
The American Labour Movement and Other Essays

Edited by J. M. WINTER
University Lecturer in History, University of Cambridge and Fellow of Pembroke College, Cambridge

ST. MARTIN'S PRESS **NEW YORK**

Printed in Great Britain
First published in the United States of America in 1979

ISBN 0-312-02503-3

Library of Congress Cataloguing in Publication Data

Tawney, Richard Henry, 1880-1962.
R. H. Tawney: the American labour movement and other essays.

CONTENTS: The American labour movement.—Poverty as an industrial problem.—The assessment of wages in England by the Justice of the Peace.—The condition of China.—An occupational census of the seventeenth century.

Includes index.
1. Labor and laboring classes—History—Addresses, essays, lectures. 2. Trade-unions—History—Addresses, essays, lectures. I. Winter, J. M. II. Title: The American labour movement and other essays.

HD4841. T35 1979 331.'09 78-26736

ISBN 0-312-02503-3

CONTENTS

LIST OF TABLES

EDITORIAL NOTE

The publication of these essays completes the task begun by Tawney in the 1950s to bring together some of the fruits of his historical work over five decades. It was originally intended that one volume of his historical essays would appear, but rising publishing costs made it impossible to include in it all of Tawney's essays which merited reprinting. Consequently, the recently-published volume, *History and Society. Essays by R. H. Tawney* (Routledge & Kegan Paul, 1978) should be seen as complementary to the present edition. The appearance of a collection of Tawney's essays on themes in labour history should in no way be construed as suggesting a division between his work in economic history and in labour history. On the contrary; there is a unity in Tawney's academic and political writings which cannot be found in the work of other scholars. For an evaluation of Tawney's contribution to the study of history in Britain, the reader is directed to the introductory essay 'Tawney the Historian' which appears in the Routledge edition.

Many friends and colleagues have given freely of their time and advice in the preparation of this edition. I am particularly indebted for assistance and support to Tawney's literary executor, Michael Vyvyan of Trinity College, Cambridge, and to the following people: Joyce Cade, Robert Dare, Geoffrey Elton, Royden Harrison, Henry Pelling, and David Washbrook.

Permission to publish or republish the essays included in this book have been granted from: the London School of Economics for 'Poverty as an Industrial Problem'; the editors of the *Vierteljahrschrift für Sozial – und Wirtschaftsgeschichte* for 'The Assessment of Wages in England by Justices of the Peace'; the University of Newcastle for 'The Condition of China'; the editors of the *Economic History Review* for 'An Occupational Census of the Seventeenth Century'. For 'The American Labour Movement', herein published for the first time, transcripts of Crown copyright records in the Public Record Office appear by permission of the Controller of H.M. Stationery Office.

All of the essays in this edition are not readily available to students. The study of assessment of wages, which was omitted from *History and Society,* is no longer in print, and therefore has been republished here.

INTRODUCTION: Tawney on Labour and Labour Movements

In recent years there has been a movement among some labour historians in Britain to try to broaden the context in which to set the study of past working-class life. This search for new approaches in labour history is in part a recognition of the remarkable scholarship of a generation of historians who have provided an impressive historiographical tradition on which to build. The work of E. J. Hobsbawm, Royden Harrison, E. P. Thompson, and Asa Briggs, to name but a few in modern history, and of Christopher Hill and Rodney Hilton, who have written on earlier periods, has changed the way history is written in Britain. They have proved that the history of popular politics and popular culture is neither a marginal subject nor a source of background material against which to set the more important doings of social élites. The labouring man as an extra in grand historical epics is, thanks to their efforts, largely an historiographical anachronism. In this respect, it was no mean achievement to free the subject from what E. P. Thompson has described as 'the enormous condescension of posterity'.[1]

The recovery of the struggles of working men for dignity and a decent life required close attention to the distinctiveness of working-class institutions and the communities in which they grew. But equally important today is the effort to integrate the history of working-class life into the history of society as a whole. Fortunately, developments over the past decades in economic and social history have made such work possible. Consequently, among the most important challenges in labour history is to find appropriate ways to incorporate in it the insights of valuable studies available in business history, population history, agricultural history, legal history, and in other kindred areas of research.

If any historian would have wholeheartedly supported the attempt to integrate the work of labour historians with that of their colleagues in neighbouring fields, it was R. H. Tawney. Professor of Economic History in the University of London, pioneer of workers' education, Labour party adviser and sometime Parliamentary candidate, pamphleteer and scourge of privilege, Tawney never hid the links between his scholarship and his active political concerns and consequently wrote much about the history of labour and labour movements.

The five essays included in this volume reflect this facet of Tawney's historical and contemporary interests. Their publication is intended primarily to complement the selections of his historical essays and of his political writings which have appeared over the last two decades.[2] With this edition of essays on labour and labour history, we now have in print virtually all the writings Tawney himself wanted to republish.[3]

The second function this collection of essays may serve is to stimulate debate about the future of labour history by reference to writings by Tawney which show how its scope can be broadened effectively. The earliest essay republished here is the inaugural lecture delivered by Tawney in 1913, as director of a research foundation established at the London School of Economics (LSE) through the beneficence of an Indian steel magnate. The title of the lecture, 'Poverty as an industrial problem' tells us something of Tawney's rejection of the contemporary treatment of distress as a matter of individual failure. Instead of focusing on the most destitute, Tawney believed that scholars had to place the problem of distress in the context of what may be described as the chronic state of deprivation of the mass of the working population in the pre-1914 period. Consequently, Tawney directed studies of the health and feeding of school-children, the conditions of the homeworker, and the workings of trade boards established in poorly organized trades.[4] Sixty years later, there is still much to be learned about these problems. Many of them have been neglected in labour history because they concern that section of the working class which on the whole was unorganized—women, children, and adolescents, for example—whose lives consequently have not received the same degree of scrutiny as have those of the politically active minority.

The second of Tawney's pre-1914 essays republished here is a study of the workings of the provisions of the Statute of Artificers of 1563 which empowered Justices of the Peace to fix wage rates. Both here and in his first book, *The Agrarian Problem in the Sixteenth Century,* published in 1912, Tawney tried to show how both Statute and Common Law were used to help protect the livelihood of working men in pre-industrial England. As a socialist, Tawney was pleased to note the revival in the twentieth century of earlier patterns of state intervention in the labour market. But as an historian, he pointed to an important area of legal history in which labour historians are at last beginning to congregate.[5]

The third essay republished here is a careful study of the social structure of Gloucestershire in the early seventeenth century. This work, originally published in 1934, grew out of the analysis made by Tawney and his wife Jeanette of a muster roll of 1608. Here, too, the Tawneys occupy the border country between labour history and neighbouring disciplines in their study of the history of a part of the country they knew well and loved. The essay is a good example of Tawney's contribution to local history and agricultural history, both of which have become increasingly important in the writing of labour history in recent years.[6] The essay still stands, though, as the only extant study of the distribution of property and occupations in a single county in the pre-Civil War period.

The title essay of this volume and the essay on 'The Condition of China' point to another area in which Tawney was a pioneer. The study of the comparative history of labour and labour movements is still in its infancy. Many scholars have pointed out with justification how rooted in local conditions are the institutions working-men have built over time to defend their interests and rights. But it is impossible to know precisely *how* British is the British labour movement without contrasting it with labour movements abroad. The most accessible comparison in this regard is with the American labour movement, but as yet relatively little explicitly comparative history of British and American labour has been published.[7] Tawney's introductory essay on American labour, the occasion for the preparation of which will be discussed below, sketched out some of the lines on which such comparative work could be done.

The form of comparative history suggested in the essay on

China, written after a visit there by Tawney in 1930-31 as guest of the Institute of Pacific Relations and of the League of Nations, is of a somewhat different character. It is now a commonplace that the problem of the peasantry was of decisive importance in the political development of several European and non-European countries. This was not so widely recognized when Tawney wrote this lecture, delivered at Armstrong College, Newcastle upon Tyne in 1933, and his book *Land and Labour in China,* published the previous year. In both Tawney showed well how an historian with some experience of the chequered history of the land question in Europe could provide modest, but nonetheless acute, comments on the rural dimension of Chinese economic and social development.

* * *

To set the longest study published in this volume, the essay on 'The American Labour Movement', in its appropriate context, it is necessary to turn to a little known chapter of Allied diplomacy during the Second World War. Tawney was one of a number of historians who crossed the divide between the academic and diplomatic communities during the 1939-45 war, but he was unique in using the occasion to write labour history. As adviser on 'social and politico-economic affairs' to Lord Halifax, British Ambassador in Washington, Tawney demonstrated the usefulness to British diplomats of regular, informed advice about the industrial and political character of American trade unions and about their ties with British trade unions. Since such questions are incomprehensible without an historical dimension, Tawney was able to provide a valuable service to Lord Halifax and his staff during the period surrounding America's entry into the Second World War.

That Tawney would be in a position to provide this assistance certainly was unforeseen when war broke out in 1939. He had visited America several times before the war, the last occasion being during the spring of 1939 to lecture at the University of Chicago.[8] After an earlier visit, he produced for American readers a short history of *The British Labor Movement.*[9] After the European war had begun, he wrote a letter to the *New York Times,* later published in expanded form as a Macmillan War Pamphlet entitled *'Why Britain*

Fights'. This essay was a moving call to Americans to join in the common struggle against fascism. Tawney knew that to counter the 'Colonel Blimp' image of British society, a statement of war aims had to incorporate a commitment to social reform. 'If Great Britain is to rally other peoples and inspire her own', he wrote in words reminiscent of those he used during the First World War, 'she must prove by her actions, not merely by words, that she is no insular egoist or imperial profiteer, but the champion of causes which touch the hearts of all mankind'.[10]

The response to Tawney's appeal brought his work to the attention of the Minister of Information, Duff Cooper, who set in motion the chain of events which led to the writing of the essay on American labour. On 17 June 1941, he wrote to Tawney to ask him to accept the post of labour adviser to Sir Gerald Campbell, director-general of the British Information Service in the United States. His function would be 'to maintain contact with American Labour and the Labour Press, and with Government officials in Washington concerned with Labour matters'.[11]

Cooper had been informed that Tawney had just accepted an invitation to lecture at the University of Chicago on the occasion of its fiftieth anniversary, at which time he would also receive an honorary degree. Cooper hoped that Tawney would accept added responsibilities while in America. After a meeting with the minister, Tawney accepted the appointment, but only reluctantly. He pointed out that among others, Francis Williams, former editor of the *Daily Herald,* was 'better qualified than myself to do publicity work in the United States'. Tawney added that he was not a good speaker, and had no experience of handling the press, but 'I do not feel that I can refuse the invitation in war-time'.[12] He did make his acceptance conditional on the appointment of a trade unionist approved by the Trades Union Congress to work with him. He also asked to retain the right to withdraw from this work after six months, and to have permission for his wife to accompany him to the United States. The first condition was the most important, and it shows Tawney's recognition of the difficulties he would face in America. Only the appointment of a trade unionist, he insisted, would 'ensure that British propaganda had the entreé into the American Trade Union Movement, which I, by myself, should find some difficulty in securing . . . All sorts of doors would be closed, or opened only with resistance, even to a person whose connexion with the Labour Movement is as long as my own'. Attlee's parliamentary private secretary, Arthur Jenkins of the Miners' Federation, was one of the men Tawney had in mind.[13]

Duff Cooper was unaware that Tawney was being considered by the War Cabinet for a much more responsible job in America than that of Press Officer in New York. To one Foreign Office official, Tawney was 'too heavy metal' for such routine journalism.[14] Clement Attlee, then Lord Privy Seal, agreed. He suggested that Tawney should go to Washington as adviser to Lord Halifax.[15] Tawney must have been taken aback somewhat when Duff Cooper wrote to him on 16 July 1941 that the job he had previously accepted was 'one which I frankly think will be hardly worthy of your abilities and record'. Consequently, he was passed on to the Foreign Office, where he was told on 25 July 1941 that his services were needed in Washington. He learned that Attlee, Anthony Eden, then Foreign Secretary, and R. A. Butler, Under-secretary of State at the Foreign Office, thought that he was the ideal choice as a 'person of high standing and qualification who could assist the Ambassador in developing close and unofficial relations with the New Deal element in the United States'.[16] Tawney could hardly have turned down this second offer. With the same proviso that he retain the right to reconsider his position after six months' service, he and Jeanette Tawney set off for the United States via Lisbon on 18 September 1941. He was given permission to fulfil his commitments in Chicago, and took up work in Washington at the end of October 1941.

There were two reasons why Tawney was considered suitable for such advisory work. The first was that his credentials as an opponent of appeasement were impeccable. His angry open letter to the *Manchester Guardian* in the aftermath of the Munich settlement left no doubt as to where he stood in the fight against fascism.[17] The same could not be said of Lord Halifax, who had been Foreign Secretary under

Chamberlain and then under Churchill, who had removed him to Washington as Ambassador in December 1940. He could hardly represent the common cause of working-men in Britain and America against the Nazi menace. Tawney, in contrast, could do so with force and eloquence, as Attlee had learned from over thirty years' association with Tawney in the Workers' Educational Association (WEA), LSE, and the Labour Party.

The second reason why Tawney was chosen was that he was one of the few men who both knew enough about American and British labour to advise the Embassy in Washington and who were free enough from trade union politics to make that advice critical and independent. No one could think that Tawney's opinions derived from personal or political loyalties. This may help to explain why Ernest Bevin, Minister of Labour, kept clear of Tawney's appointment. Bevin probably foresaw, as well, the inevitable conflict which would face a man who tried to plant one foot in the field of labour and the other in the field of diplomacy.[18] If he failed, none the worse for Bevin, who did not interfere in the appointment of Tawney as a translator between trade unionists in Britain and America and between both and American and British diplomats.

Tawney saw the point of having a man attached to the British Embassy in Washington who did not speak with a Civil Service accent. But his doubts about his suitability for the work were more than mere humility. He was over sixty, and was unaccustomed to the social burdens of the diplomatic world and to the extremes of the American climate. In addition, he felt reluctant about leaving England at a time when educational reform was once more a political possibility. Moreover, his academic responsibilities were not easily shouldered by others. The WEA relied on his judgment and made incessant calls on his time, which exasperated Tawney, but no one else could fill his shoes.[19] The LSE had been forced to leave London for Cambridge during the Blitz, and the task of keeping the School going was not an easy one. The *Economic History Review* was also going through a difficult period hit by a shortage of paper, of subscribers, and of contributors, who were otherwise engaged.[20] Tawney could not easily suspend his commitments for ill-defined diplomatic work. He knew that his position was too vague to permit his easy integration into the Washington Embassy; hence his insistence on retaining the right to withdraw after six months at the job.

Still, there was no labour attaché on the diplomatic lists in Washington, and Tawney was prepared to try to fill the gap. But to underscore his independence from the 'traditional Foreign Office line', he accepted the title of 'counsellor' rather than that of 'attaché'. He believed (mistakenly) that the title of 'counsellor' was a more informal designation and that it would help him establish contacts with labour leaders suspicious of diplomats in general and of British diplomacy in particular. The Foreign Office were prepared to permit Tawney to choose his own title, which did not imply their commitment to the creation of a permanent niche for a labour specialist.[21]

The last thing that Tawney came to do in the United States in 1941 was to write history. But in the course of one year, this is precisely what he wound up doing. Tawney would not have written his essay on American labour had not the general secretary of the Trades Union Congress (T.U.C.), Sir Walter Citrine, come to the United States in 1942 to try to establish an Anglo-American-Russian trade union committee. Citrine's visit came out of discussions with Molotov and other Soviet officials in October 1941 in Russia about how to extend Anglo-Russian trade union collaboration during the war. After Pearl Harbour, it seemed natural for Citrine to begin discussions with American trade unionists about establishing a joint Allied labour committee. The only questions were which Americans to approach and in what order? Citrine had informed the Russian delegates on the Anglo-Russian trade union committee that the leaders of the American Federation of Labor (A.F. of L.) had to be consulted first, mainly because the T.U.C. had had an unbroken record of 'continuous relations for the past forty years' with the A.F. of L.[22] Of course, Citrine never intended to ignore or exclude the recently-formed Congress of Industrial Organizations (C.I.O.), but he felt that he could not turn to the C.I.O. before he had reached agreement with her arch-rival, the A.F. of L. With this order of priorities established, Citrine came to the United

States in the spring of 1942.

That is when the trouble started and when Tawney's usefulness to the British Embassy and to the Foreign Office was demonstrated. With his intervention in the handling of negotiations between Allied labour organizations, Tawney's standing in an Embassy not too familiar with labour politics rose virtually overnight. Five days prior to Citrine's arrival, Halifax had submitted to the Foreign Office a highly critical report on Tawney's work at the Embassy. In his first six months, 'neither the Foreign Office nor Mr. Attlee have had a word from Professor Tawney either by way of letter or report on Labour matters'. While the Ambassador recognised the virtues of the appointment of a labour adviser, he told Eden that 'what would be perhaps most useful and more suitable here than Tawney whose appeal is rather to university intelligentsia type would be an official of the Ministry of Labour or a man of Civil Service type who has been in close and sympathetic touch with Labour and labour questions'.[23]

Eden took up the matter with Bevin in late May. The Foreign Secretary complained that Tawney had not 'furnished much information on the complicated but highly important Labour situation in the United States'. Since 'the supply of this is really the crux of the matter', Tawney had failed to do more than adorn the Embassy's staff list.[24]

The Foreign Office knew that prior to the Citrine mission, Tawney shared their appraisal of the minimal value of his diplomatic work. In two letters intercepted by the Censor and reproduced by the Foreign Office, Tawney voiced his doubts about the wisdom of staying on in Washington. To Tom Jones, a friend of forty years' standing and former secretary to the Cabinet, Tawney wrote:

> My own work—if it can be called work—does not come to much. I received no guidance from the F.O. in London as to what I was supposed to do here except that it was hoped that I should establish contact with 'New Deal Groups'. I imagine I have done that to some extent, but it does not come to much when it's done. The Embassy was even less helpful. Halifax, whom I respect, was agreeable; but I asked in vain Sir Ronald Campbell—personally a nice fellow—for suggestions as to what, if

> anything, they wanted done. The fact is, I think, that they were in the dark as to why I had been sent out.

His speeches to university groups may have done some good, but he lacked up-to-date knowledge of British conditions and technical expertise on such questions as air-raid precautions. But more importantly, Tawney told Tom Jones, in words very similar to those used by Eden,

> I regard as my chief failure here my lack of success in establishing intimate relations with the Trade Union Movement. Possibly I ought to have concentrated attention on that and refused other speaking engagements. But there is no Labour Movement here, in our sense—of a body of people with a general conception of social policy, and though I have made the acquaintance of a good many Trade Unionists, I have not succeeded in being invited to talk to Trade Union gatherings or to advise on Trade Union policy. I think that a British Trade Unionist would have an entrée which an 'intellectual' does not.[25]

Tawney reiterated these doubts two months later in another intercepted letter, this time written to M. M. Postan, Tawney's former student at the L.S.E., then Professor of Economic History in Cambridge and editor of the *Economic History Review.*[26] But by the time Postan had received the letter, Tawney was embroiled in the handling of Sir Walter Citrine's visit, the complications of which were puzzling to those unaware of the history of American labour.

Citrine's approach to the A.F. of L. got nowhere. Their deep anti-communism, which their British colleague largely shared but was prepared to shelve for the duration of the war,[27] made the idea of collaboration with Russian trade unionists virtually anathema. And since Citrine had foresworn formal contact with the C.I.O. until the A.F. of L. could be persuaded to join the proposed trade union committee, he had no real chance to realize the aims of his mission. The only result was to complicate further the delicate negotiations, in which President Roosevelt had a hand, to try to arrange the semblance of a wartime truce between the hostile factions of American labour in the period leading to the Congressional election of 1942.

The possible political implications of trade union diplomacy were what interested Lord Halifax in the subject sufficiently to ask Tawney to prepare several memoranda on American labour. These were intended to help him and his staff to feel somewhat more confident when approaching the minefield of labour politics. Tawney produced four papers before he left Washington in September 1942. The longest of them is the essay on the American Labour Movement. It was written rapidly for diplomats who wanted a guide for action in an area on which they knew relatively little. As such, Tawney's essay was an unqualified success.

In all his writings on the American labour movement submitted in 1942,[28] Tawney stressed the necessity, indeed the inevitability, of formal recognition of the C.I.O. as the equal of the A.F. of L. The latter organization could not contain the forces for change within American labour, which had grown rapidly since the mid-30s, and whose character was something of a mystery to the British Foreign Office. Tawney believed that Citrine had played into the hands of the A.F. of L. whose executive acted as if they could shut their eyes and make the C.I.O. disappear by a sheer act of will. This conflict Tawney explained to diplomats baffled by the whole affair. His attitude to the obstinacy of the A.F. of L. leadership is shown clearly in the following letter he wrote to Beatrice Webb in July 1942. Tawney claimed to be perplexed by the A.F. of L:

> They are a mixture of toughness and timidity which reminds me of the shadier sort of businessman or political boss. That, in fact, is what they are. All their worst qualities were revealed on the occasion of the recent visit of Citrine. . . . He asked no one here about the situation before he arrived, and asked me very little after he had done so. If he had told the American Federation of Labor that there were other pebbles on the beach besides themselves, that in the event of their playing rough, he would do the same, and that he intended in any case to ask the C.I.O. to join the committee, which they would certainly do, he might have got somewhere. That is the kind of language the American Federation of Labor understand, and they would probably have come to heel. As it was, he delivered himself into their hands by letting them see

> that he regarded their co-operation as essential. Once they grasped that, they blackmailed him without mercy, refusing to join a committee containing the Russians, and actually threatening him with their displeasure if he made any official approaches to the C.I.O.[29]

Tawney's views on the need to grant an independent status to the C.I.O. were given all the more force in diplomatic circles because they were consistent with what was taken to be President Roosevelt's line on the matter. Sir Ronald Campbell believed that the President was behind the peace initiative of Philip Murray, the President of the C.I.O. It was all the more important, therefore, to prevent Citrine from interfering in FDR's industrial strategy.[30] This may have been an exaggeration of Citrine's ability to exacerbate the tensions within American labour, but it is easy to see why his actions were worrying to diplomats at the time.

This difficulty quickly became a matter for higher authorities to resolve. Eden sent Tawney's memorandum to Attlee on 19 August 1942 with a full endorsement of its recommendations.[31] Citrine had to be restrained from attending another meeting with the A.F. of L. set for mid-September, at which he was more than likely to run into another stone wall. Although in discussion with Citrine at the Washington Embassy, Tawney and Halifax had made the case for an even-handed treatment of the C.I.O., Citrine seemed intent, in Eden's view, on treating the C.I.O. as an illegitimate offspring of the A.F. of L. 'It seems a pity', wrote Eden, 'that when we have a person of Tawney's calibre in Washington to advise on Labour matters, that advice is ignored by distinguished representatives of British Labour who visit the United States.'[32]

Eden's case, which was Tawney's, was fortified by evidence from other quarters. Sir Frederick Leggett of the Ministry of Labour was reported as having said that 'the soreness of the C.I.O. was affecting output in industries in the United States producing munitions for us.' The American Ambassador in London, Winant, who would not have spoken without approval from Washington, referred to Citrine as 'an over-zealous obstetrician'.[33] Philip Murray himself told the British Embassy that 'the visit of the British T.U.C. delegation in September will certainly be the subject of attacks at the C.I.O. convention to be held in November.' The Embassy view was that 'anything of the kind will of course be taken up by the Press with results on Anglo-American relations that will necessarily be grave.'[34]

Three days later, on 31 August, Eden wrote to Churchill, setting out the story and explaining why it was necessary to get Citrine to postpone his imminent departure for the United States.[35] With Churchill's support, Eden instructed Harold Butler of the Foreign Office to see Citrine in London and request a postponement of his mission. Citrine replied that he did not know what the fuss was all about, and did not want to offend the A.F. of L. by initiating any postponement.[36] After reassurance that this request came from the highest sources, Citrine reluctantly agreed to put the matter to the General Council of the T.U.C., which would meet in Blackpool the following week.[37] On 14 September, Citrine wrote to Eden to confirm the decision to seek a postponement of the visit of the T.U.C. delegation until after the November elections. He did so, he told Eden, 'with considerable reluctance and with a strong feeling that the matter has been unduly influenced by representatives of the British government in Washington in whose competence to give advice on this question they [the T.U.C.] have little confidence.'[38]

Citrine was angry enough to state his annoyance publicly at the T.U.C. annual conference in Blackpool. Before replying, Eden took up the matter at the War Cabinet, which supported him and approved his action.[39] The following day, in Parliament, Eden was asked about Citrine's criticism. The Foreign Secretary stated that 'In labour matters, Lord Halifax has had the benefit of the advice of Professor Tawney. The Government are fully satisfied as to the soundness of the advice which His Majesty's Ambassador gave them.'[40] This was not an adequate answer for Emanuel Shinwell, who asked whether Eden appreciated 'that even Professor Tawney, with all his intellectual attainments, is hardly the proper person to decide on matters affecting Trade Union organisations? Would it not be appropriate to have someone on the spot capable of interpreting the minds of both the British trade union movement and the American trade union movement?' Eden chose not to press the matter further, probably on the assumption that Tawney's credentials spoke for themselves.[41] With this not very ominous exchange, the Citrine affair rested.

Citrine was not prepared though, to give up his attempt to form his trade union committee because of one setback which he attributed to Tawney's malevolent influence. Even after Tawney had retired from the diplomatic field, Citrine returned to the United States and met the same stone wall of opposition. The A.F. of L. was adamant about having nothing to do with Russian trade unions, which they believed did not deserve the name.[42] One month later, Citrine met Murray and the C.I.O. executive in Washington. Once again, he got nowhere. The following verbatim exchange between Murray and Citrine is the best evidence of the soundness of Tawney's analysis of Citrine's handling of American Labour. Citrine refused to budge from his view that the A.F. of L. deserved preferential treatment in his negotiations. To this—

> Murray: Personally I am tired of being kicked around like a Trade Union waif in this field of international labour collaboration. It is the only place where [we are] being booted around at the moment and I have no disposition to inject myself into the discussions which you are having with the A.F. of L. Both you and they in the field of international labour collaboration can do just as you damn well please.
>
> Citrine: Will you repeat that, Mr. Murray?[43]

The general secretary of the T.U.C. never managed to bring together in one organization the labour leaders of the major Allied powers. Throughout the war, the Anglo-American (or T.U.C.—A.F. of L.) committee ran strictly parallel to the Anglo-Russian committee, and no exercise in persuasion could make them meet.

Tawney predicted the outcome of Citrine's mission because he saw that it was based on an insufficient appreciation of the sources of the A.F. of L.—C.I.O. split. Many fuller studies and specialist works on this aspect of American labour have appeared since 1942,[44] but as an introductory sketch of the American labour movement when the great schism was at its worst, Tawney's essay is a remarkable achievement, an unintended and happy by-product of a minor episode in the diplomacy of the Second World War.

NOTES

All works published in London unless otherwise noted.

1. E. P. Thompson, *The Making of the English Working Class* (1963), p. 12.
2. R. H. Tawney, *The Attack and other papers* (1953); Rita Hinden (ed). *The Radical Tradition* (1964); R. H. Tawney, *History and Society* (ed. J. M. Winter, 1978).
3. From lists in the possession of Tawney's nephew and literary executor, Michael Vyvyan, of Trinity College, Cambridge.
4. See Tawney's prefaces to A. Greenwood, *The Health and Physique of School Children* (1913); M. E. Bulkley, *The Feeding of School Children* (1914); A. L. Bowley and A. R. Burnett-Hurst, *Livelihood and Poverty* (1915); and V. de Vesselitsky, *The Homeworker and her Outlook* (1916), as well as his two books: *The Establishment of Minimum Rates in the Chain-making Industry under the Trade Boards Act of 1909* (1914) and *The Establishment of Minimum Rates in the Tailoring Trade under the Trade Boards Act of 1909* (1915).
5. Cf. D. Hay *et al., Albion's Fatal Tree* (1977).
6. Cf. J. Obelkevitch, *Religion and Rural Society* (Oxford, 1976).
7. Two notable exceptions are: J. F. C. Harrison, *Owen and the Owenites in Britain and America* (1966); and H. J. Habakkuk, *American and British Technology in the Nineteenth Century* (Cambridge, 1967).
8. British Library of Political and Economic Science. Tawney Papers, Box of Lectures in Chicago.
9. (New Haven, Conn., 1925).
10. *Why Britain Fights* (New York, 1941), p. 46.
11. Public Record Office. Foreign Office Papers (F.O.) 371.26185.A5521. Duff Cooper to Tawney, 17.6.41.
12. F.O. 371.26185.A5521. Tawney to Duff Cooper, 7.7.41.
13. *Ibid.*
14. F.O. 371.26185.A4679. Undated minute, probably by Harold Butler.
15. *Ibid.*
16. F.O. 371.26187.A6429. F. T. A. Ashton-Gwatkin to Derek Hoyar Millar, 7.8.41., in a discussion of the circumstances of Tawney's appointment.
17. *Manchester Guardian*, 23.3.38.
18. F.O. 371.513.A7044. Minute dated 4.1.42., by Neville Butler about Tawney's report on Citrine.
19. Rhodes House, Oxford. Creech Jones Papers. ACJ 6/2 f52. Tawney to Creech Jones, undated.
20. F.O. 371.30700.A2657. Tawney to M. M. Postan on the problems of the *Economic History Review*, whose dire financial straits were to be bailed out by the Rockefeller Foundation.
22. Trades Union Congress Library. General Council Minutes, 28.8.41, 3.9.41, 11.11.41, 28.1.42, 25.2.42. British Library of Political and Economic Science. Citrine Papers, 4/9 and 4/10 on Russian negotiations.

23. F.O. 371.30700.A4137. Cable of Halifax to Eden, 29.4.42.
24. F.O. 371.30700.A4657. Eden to Bevin, 27.5.42.
25. F.O. 371.30669.A4406. Tawney to Tom Jones, 22.3.42. The Foreign Office official who minuted the intercepted letter thought that Tawney may have expected his letter to be read by his superiors and included information in them that he wanted passed on, somewhat circuitously, through channels.
26. F.O. 371.30700.A2657. Tawney to Postan, 26.5.42.
27. Citrine papers, 3/7, Citrine to Duff Cooper, 7.7.41.
28. 1) F.O. 371.513.A7044. 'Report by Professor Tawney on Sir Walter Citrine's Visit to the United States', 20.7.42.
    2) F.O. 371.513.A8009. 'Labour and the Congressional elections', 12.8.42.
    3) F.O. 371.30701.A8560. 'A note on the relations between the A.F. of L. and C.I.O. and between the British and American labour movements', 3.9.42.
    4) F.O. 371.30700.A9007. 'The American Labour Movement', 19.9.42.
29. British Library of Political and Economic Science. Passfield Papers, II.4.M.123, f.225. Tawney to Beatrice Webb, 5.7.42.
30. F.O. 371.30700.A7378. Cable of Sir R. I. Campbell, chargé d'affaires in Washington, to Eden, 9.8.42.
31. F.O. 371.30700.A7378. Eden to Attlee, 19.8.42.
32. F.O. 371.30700.A7378. Eden to Attlee, 19.8.42.
33. F.O. 371.30700.A7518. Minute of H. Butler, 26.8.42.
34. F.O. 371.30700.A7967. Cable of Halifax to Foreign Office, 27.8.42.
35. F.O. 371.30700.A8035. Draft letter, Eden to Churchill, 31.8.42.
36. F.O. 371.30700.A8035. Cable of H. Butler to Halifax, 1.9.42.
37. F.O. 371.30700.A8035. Citrine to Eden, 3.9.42.
38. F.O. 371.30700.A8035. Citrine to Eden, 14.9.42.
39. Public Record Office. Cabinet Papers 6527 War Cabinet 123(42), 10.9.42.
40. F.O. 371.30701.A8254. Copy of Parliamentry exchange, for which see Hansard's Parliamentry Debates, 1941-2, Vol. 383, 11.9.42, Cols. 530-1.
41. Col. 531.
42. F.O. 371.34153.A1991. Halifax to Foreign Office, 21.2.43.
43. F.O. 371.34153.A2116. Transcripts of Citrine's meetings with the A.F. of L. on 27.1.43 in Miami and with the C.I.O. on 13.2.43. in Washington.
44. For a more up-to-date survey see H. Pelling *American Labor* (1960), and on the A.F. of L.—C.I.O. split, see W. Galenson, *The C.I.O. Challenge to the A.F.L.* (Cambridge, Mass., 1960).

THE AMERICAN LABOUR MOVEMENT (1942)*

I Introductory

The year 1942 marks the close of the most critical decade in the history of the American Labour Movement. A specialist in industrial questions, who visited the United States in the later twenties, found much, no doubt, to interest and instruct him; but a layman might be pardoned if he accepted the view, pressed on him with pride from more than one quarter, that geography, history, American economic conditions, and American psychology had combined to create a society immune to industrial tensions of the same gravity and persistence as distracted Europe. That opinion, though no longer the old confident dogma, survives as a ghost, the strength of whose emotional appeal it would be an error to underestimate. The world of reality has gone the other way.

The economic turning-point was the depression; the political landmark the election of the first Democratic President since 1920. The first was not a matter merely of curves changing trends, nor the second of the conventional swing of the political pendulum. Both were symbolical of larger issues than those apparent on the surface. They confounded ideologies, as well as Wall Street, and their moral was as disturbing as their practical significance. The seven years which ended abruptly in the dust and ashes of October 1929 had been, in spite of two brief recessions, a miracle of equable progress. To a large body of American opinion, prosperity, self-perpetuating and ever-increasing, had become something not far short of a religion. Mr. Hoover, with his new beatitude, 'a chicken in every pot, and two cars in every garage', had been the high priest of the faith; the leaders of business, with the Republican party as their vehicle, its most redoubtable champions. The discredit of that creed and its prophets

*Public Record Office, Foreign Office Papers, F.O. 371.30700.A9007, 19 September 1942.

meant, not merely one more of the recurrent oscillations by which an established order maintains its stability, but the collapse of a régime. The absence of violence concealed the full magnitude of the change from observers at a distance; nor were the particular measures which sprang from it so novel to Europe as they were to America. It marked, nevertheless, the opening of a new era. A dominant class was thrust aside. The social philosophy represented by it, if not discarded, lost its hold. It passed from the attack to a nervous defensive.

The full effects on the world of industry did not immediately reveal themselves. Labour's chief weapon is organization; and organization, to be stable, needs time to grow. The Government, on its side, was confronted by the Depression with a multitude of tasks which could not wait. Its first major essay in Labour policy did not stand, and the Act which has proved most decisive was not passed till 1935, nor endorsed by the Supreme Court till 1937. To one who looks back, however, from the vantage-ground of today it seems clear that, in the middle thirties, a watershed was crossed. There was an unprecedented increase in the number of organized workers; and hitherto, at least, that tide has not turned. The advance in the public status of Labour was equally significant. Industrial relations, till then almost exclusively the province of the states, became the subject of Federal Legislation at once novel and important; were handled by the Courts on principles not easily to be reconciled with those previously laid down by them; and received a more intelligent treatment, not only in serious economic literature, but, at times, even from some journalists. The effect of these changes was to create a new body of self-conscious interests, and a political mentality which, if not new, now numbers its adherents by millions, instead of by thousands. The consequences of both have been heightened by the military exigencies and economic strains of the last two years. Today they meet the observer at every turn.

The President, Congress, and half-a-dozen Departments are constantly occupied, from their different angles, with Labour questions. The merits or demerits of Labour policies; the personalities of Labour leaders; the relations of Labour organizations with employers, with the Government and—not least—with each other, have enjoyed the notoriety conferred by Gallup polls, and are probably the domestic topic most canvassed in the Press. Much discussion has been aroused by the decisions on Labour cases of the War Labor Board, and, to a less extent of the Courts; while demands for the amendment of existing Labour legislation have been urged and resisted with an acrimony not diminished by the approach of the Congressional elections. Labour, on its side, has not been silent. It has declared, through its responsible leaders, that it stands solidly behind the President; has bridged chasms in its own ranks—whether temporarily of permanently cannot yet be known—which till recently seemed too wide to be spanned; has officially renounced strikes; and has advanced its own programmes of industrial mobilization. To judge the real influence of a movement by the limelight turned upon it is always an error, and doubly erroneous where limelight is cheap; but, when the blaze of publicity has been duly discounted, the advance in the standing of Organized Labour since the last war still remains impressive. Then it was a factor to be taken into account, and, when need be, consulted. Now it is recognized as one of the major powers in American life, whose attitude and behaviour may well be decisive. If innovations in military technique are one reason for the contrast, the alteration in the balance of social forces is a not less important one.

The crisis struck the United States at a time when American society was undergoing a process of rapid readjustment—a process far from yet completed, and deplored by powerful groups, even when they acquiesce in it. That coincidence of a violent external shock with severe internal strains has proved, as was to be expected, of no small importance. The war has allayed some animosities, but it has sharpened others. It has heightened the importance of the Labour movement, but it has multiplied its tasks and increased its responsibilities. It has turned issues which formerly were important into matters of grave public urgency, and has complicated old problems on the way to be solved by the addition of new problems, the solution of which is not yet in sight. The time to strike a balance has not yet come; but the part which American

Labour will play during and after the war has been largely determined by an organization crystallized, and a mentality fixed, before it began. The peculiarities of both are, therefore, a matter of topical interest. The purpose of the following pages is not to attempt a full-length study of the American Labour Movement, but to indicate briefly the point at which it now stands, and to explain how it comes to occupy a position so different from that held by it in the recent past.

II The Trade Union Revival of the Thirties

Some American Trade Unions are of respectable antiquity; but as a national movement, with a continuous life, American Trade Unionism is much younger than British. It dates, at earliest, from 1886,[1] and as a practical force, from the later nineties. From that time, it grew steadily, but unsensationally, down to 1914, then almost doubled its membership during the war years, and reached its first peak in the boom of 1920. After a long period of stagnation in the twenties, it was hit hard by the depression of 1929, and appeared in 1933 to be going rapidly downhill. But it has experienced in the last nine years a remarkable revival. Today it is more powerful, whether judged by membership or by public standing, than at any previous period in its history.

(i) Trade Union membership today

The membership of American Trade Unions[2] in 1940 was 8,642,000, nearly three times that of 1933 and over 60 per cent above the previous peak year of 1920. Down to the latter part of 1941 the conversion of industry to war purposes was extremely slow; but it meant an influx of workers into occupations which lent themselves readily to organization. Trade Union membership, accordingly, continued to increase. At the turn of the year, 1941-2, it was put by the Department of Labour at approximately 11,000,000.[3] The number of wage-earners in industries other than agriculture was, in 1941, about 24,000,000, and the number of clerical and salaried workers in offices and stores about 7,000,000.

The 8,642,000 trade unionists existing in 1940 amounted to 27 per cent of that total of 31,000,000, and the 11,241,000 existing in 1941-2 to 36 per cent, by which date, however, the total itself had somewhat increased, so that the estimate of 33 per cent given in the journal[4] of the Department of Labor is probably nearer the mark. By the latest date, therefore, for which figures are available, approximately one in three of the workers in industrial and clerical employment were members of unions. Different industrial groups vary widely, of course, in the degree to which they are organized.[5] Coal-mining stood in 1940 at the head of the list, with 90 per cent of its workers enrolled in trade unions. Next came water transportation (including the various maritime unions and dock-workers organizations), with 80 per cent, steam railroads with 60 per cent, metal-mining with 55 per cent, and manufacturing (including construction and railway shops) with 35 per cent. Owing to the expansion of the munitions industries in the last two years, the last figure would, in all probability, be substantially higher today. Trade Unions have added over 2,000,000 to their membership in the last two years. Even though growth at that rate is not likely to continue, previous experience suggests that a continual increase is to be expected while the war lasts. Trade Union membership in 1919 was 54 per cent above the level of 1914. If, during the present war, it rises in the same proportion above the level of 1940, it will at the end of it be over 13,000,000, or more than 40 per cent of all industrial and clerical workers. In reality, the proportionate increase to be anticipated in the present war is larger than in the last. Owing to the changes which have taken place in the intervening period, the trade unionism of today rests on far firmer foundations than did that of 1914. Unions are in a better position, therefore, than in the past to seize the opportunities which the crisis will offer them.

(ii) The obstacles to the growth of Trade Unionism

The heightened importance of Trade Unionism, which these figures reveal, is a recent phenomenon. It is the result of changes both in the economy of the United States and in the trend of public policy. The former were for long less decisive than might, at first sight, have been expected. It is impossible, of course, to overestimate the significance of the conversion of the United States from the predominantly agricultural nation of the nineties into the industrial colossus of today.

The structure of American society, the geographical distribution of the population and the environment in which the majority of it passes its life, the place of the United States in a world economy, the political psychology of large sections of the American people, have all been transformed by it. Modern industry involves the concentration of economic power, and in America such concentration is seen at its height. Counter-organization is the wage-earners' response to it. The growth of Trade Unionism would have been impossible without the Industrial Revolution which preceded it. That movement once launched, it could not permanently be prevented.

It could not be prevented, but it could be held in check. In the United States two factors for long weighted the scales against it. The first was economic. As a determining force in national life, capitalist industry in America is not only younger, but much younger, than in Great Britain. Seen by foreign observers, it was a giant who strode from strength to strength. But, while the rapidity of its development in the present century has been extraordinary, the special characteristic of American technique is its efficiency measured in terms of output, and the increase in manufacturing productivity[6] per worker was not accompanied by a corresponding increase in the number of workers employed in factories. Down to the end of the last century agriculture was still America's largest single industry, and even in 1930 accounted for over one fifth (21·5 per cent) of the employed population. The personnel of manufacturing and mechanical industries, mining, and transportation and communications doubled in the same period, but it still amounted in 1930 to under 40 per cent.[7] Nor was that all. The United States is a system of regional economies. The manufacturing industry of the country is somewhat highly concentrated, and the distribution of the wage earners dependent upon it correspondingly uneven. In 1941, about three quarters of them resided in the area east of the Mississippi and north of the Ohio and Potomac Rivers, only one other region, the South Atlantic states, having as much as 10 per cent of them. There are immense tracts, as extensive as Great Britain, France, and Germany combined, where it is hardly an exaggeration to say that factory industry is known only by its products, and where the mentality which industrial capitalism produces is an alien intruder on an earlier type of civilization, hardly intelligible to those living under the latter, and disliked by them when understood. In such circumstances, the influence of Labour is not widely diffused, as in countries where few villages are a hundred miles from a coal-mine, but localised. Trade Unionism is not yet generally accepted as one of the national institutions, but is at once a power in certain regions and anathema outside them. Thus the balance of industrial and agricultural interests in America remained for long less uneven than the prestige of the United States as an industrial Titan might cause to be supposed. Movements originating in the former were qualified and restricted by the counterpoise of the latter.

The restrictions on immigration imposed after the last war had strengthened the position of the American wage-earner, but their immediate effects on organization had been negligible. The progress of Trade Unionism was retarded, not only by the slow rise to preponderance of the groups to which it appeals, but for another and more important reason. In most countries there has been a period in which Organized Labour has had to struggle hard for the right to exist, in the face of legal disabilities and organized repression. In the United States, that period was abnormally prolonged, and the methods employed were of a ruthlessness elsewhere unknown. British trade union law is a labyrinth in which lawyers, as well as laymen, have sometimes lost their way. American Trade Union law was till recently a jungle, and not one jungle, but nearly fifty. Stated summarily, its effect, as it stood down to 1932, was that the mere fact of combination did make illegal an act which would be lawful if done by an individual, and that trade unions, therefore, were free to exist, provided that they did not trench on rights of property or other civil rights, or come into conflict with Federal or State legislation. That freedom, however, was somewhat narrowly restricted. It was qualified by the Common Law doctrines as to conspiracy and as to the illegality, with certain exceptions, of acts done in restraint of trade. The effect was that the law, while not forbidding trade unions, might be, and frequently was, held to forbid, the majority of methods which trade unions employ. These Common Law disabilities, which had obvious analogies in the decisions of British Courts before, and—to a less degree—after, the legislation of the seventies, did not stand alone. American trade unionists were confronted by three additional dangers. The first consisted of the Acts passed by State legislatures and the decisions rendered by State tribunals. The second was the Sherman Act of 1890, aimed primarily at capitalist monopolies, but so drafted as to be capable of being interpreted as to include trade unions in its general prohibition of 'every contract, combination or . . . conspiracy in restraint of trade or commerce', and so interpreted by the Supreme Court in some celebrated cases. The third was the surprising liberality of the Courts, both State and Federal in granting injunctions on particular acts done by trade unions in furtherance of trade disputes. In the light of some of the decisions given and injunctions issued during the twenties, more than half a century after the British Act of 1871, the trade unionists of the period might be pardoned if they doubted whether there was any form of organized action, from the much-debated 'closed shop' to the mere calling of a strike, distributing of strike-pay, or even 'in any way interfering with the operations of the complainants' business' which might not be held to be illegal.

The failure to modify venerable legal doctrines in the light of the changed social realities to which the law had to be applied did not prevent the development of trade unionism, but it certainly obstructed it. It meant that organization failed to keep pace with the rapid development of a manufacturing country. The effects of the legal precariousness of the position of Organized Labour were heightened by the policy towards it pursued by the world of business. The mentality which prompted that policy reached its zenith in the decade before the Great Depression. It was a curious mixture of credulous idealism and exaggerated apprehension. The seven years 1923-9, in spite of brief contractions in 1924 and 1927, were by general consent, the golden age of American capitalism. The value of the factory output continued to rise till it attained the high-water of 1930 with a figure some seven billion dollars above that of any previous year, and not reached again in the following decade. Profits and wages were both increasing. A new era of continuous prosperity was supposed to have begun.

It became almost an article of faith that the United States had been guided by Providence to a secret—'the American plan'—by which general and increasing well-being would be guaranteed in perpetuity. The one cloud on the horizon was not the crisis which was to bring the deluge, for no one foresaw it. It was the mischievous activities of agitators who menaced social stability, by organizing workers to harass employers with demands injurious to business, instead of co-operating with them. Apart from the law, which was freely and successfully invoked against trade unions, the industrialists' counter attack assumed two forms. The first was the establishment of company unions,[8] which ostensibly conferred upon workers some of the benefits of association, without exposing them to the danger of seduction by organizations not controlled by the firm. The second was the mobilisation of force to destroy trade unionism.

It is natural that industrial magnates, like humbler persons, should desire complete freedom to act at their own discretion, untrammelled by the rules of a rival authority. To decline to admit the right of such an authority to require them to listen to its views, is the first line of defence against its possible encroachments. For that reason, the refusal to 'recognize the Union' has been, as long as that course is practicable, an important weapon in the armoury of business. It was freely used in the United States. But conditions peculiar to America—the extraordinary concentration of economic power; the tendency, natural in a new country, for towns which grew up with a developing industry, to become the franchise or private jurisdiction of the corporation controlling it; the traditional individualism of American life; the restrictions on the action of State authorities and the Federal Government imposed by the Constitution and enforced by the Courts—combined to facilitate a more ruthless offensive against Organised Labour than was possible in Europe. Hence the tactics most characteristic of American employers were not merely the resistance to the demand that they should negotiate with trade union representatives, but the attempt to crush Trade Unionism. The details of the methods employed, ranging from blacklists and 'yellow-dog' contracts to the employment by large firms of corps of spies, service men, and private armed police, reinforced, when the State authorities were favourable, by state police and troops, together with an arsenal including clubs, gas-bombs, rifles and machine-guns, have been set out in the cold precision of official documents, and it is needless to recapitulate them. It is not an exaggeration to say that the attempt to destroy Trade Unionism by corruption and intimidation was for some decades a settled policy on the part of not a few of the recognized leaders of American business. Violence on one side provoked violence on the other. Serious industrial disputes, especially in the heavy industries, tended rapidly to pass into a condition not always easily distinguishable from civil war.[9]

(iii) The new legal status of Trade Unionism

The legacy of the period of persecution is not yet exhausted. It survives in the atmosphere of almost feverish tension which envelops the relations between employers and employed in certain industries and areas, as well as in the rigour of the precautions against action on the part of industrialists to undermine collective bargaining which Unions insist on including in agreements. Judged by its immediate results, the policy of repression was so far successful that, at a time of exceptional prosperity, when economic conditions were favourable to a growth of trade unionism, the membership of the movement as a whole remained stationary or declined. But it had one result which no one then foresaw. It meant that, when the crash came, and the business aristocracy of the past was retreating in disorder all along the line, its treatment of Labour shared the general discredit which attached to it and all its works. The social policy which emerged from the crisis took its colour from that fact. It was directed, not merely to grappling with the immediate problems of the emergency, which brooked no delay, but to ensuring that the most formidable of the weapons which the old régime had used to keep the workers in their place should be locked safely out of reach.

The legislation of the New Deal was highly complex. It dealt with a variety of different problems from currency, banking and investment to social services, provision for unemployment and agricultural distress. The final verdict still remains to be given, and this is not the place to attempt a survey of it as a whole. As far as Trade Unionism is concerned, its characteristic features were two. In the first place, a Federal Labour policy was in itself a novelty. Until the thirties Labour legislation had been left almost completely to the States. Congress, it is true, had enacted protective legislation for certain special groups, such as railroad employees, seamen, dock and harbour workers, labourers and mechanics on public construction work, and persons employed in the District of Columbia. These categories of workers had been, however, exceptions, the nature of whose employment clearly relieved federal legislation with regard to them of any possible taint of constitutional impropriety; and, when federal intervention had gone further, and attempted to prohibit child-labour in manufacturing and extractive industries, it had encountered the restraining hand of the Supreme Court, which promptly invalidated the two Acts concerned. Now the situation abruptly changed. The Federal Government took the initiative. It not only enacted various measures establishing the rudiments of a social security or social services system, but dealt with the major issue of the right of workers to organize and bargain collectively through representatives chosen by themselves, which had been the sphere in which the whole weight of judicial decisions had been thrown most persistently on the side of the utmost possible contractual freedom for the employer. For the first time in the history of the United States there arose a body of national statutory law, defining the rights of trade unionists, and creating administrative organs whose duty it was to ensure that those rights should be protected.

That departure was one of sensational importance. It extended at one stroke the area of Federal jurisdiction to embrace a vast province of complicated economic relations, from which hitherto it had been excluded. The content of the legislation was more remarkable still. When, in Great Britain, the question of the legal status of Trade Unionism was taken up by Governments, no attempt was made either in 1871, or in 1906, or in any subsequent enactments, to compel employers to deal with trade unions or to protect trade unionists against coercion by employers. Parliament confined itself to removing the more crippling restrictions on the activities of associations of workers imposed by Statute and Common Law, and to conferring upon them a definite legal status, while leaving it to them to compel employers to negotiate with them, and to enforce the observance of agreements made, as and when their own strength enabled them to do so. The first of the American Trade Union Acts of the thirties—the Norris-La Guardia Act of 1932—proceeded on the same lines. It was intended primarily to reverse a long series of decisions which had reduced trade unionism to impotence by holding even its most normal and necessary activities to be illegal on the ground that they were in restraint of trade, and, in particular, to check the abuse of injunctions based on that elastic doctrine. It specified nine common types of trade union activity which might not be enjoined by the courts, laid down that persons engaged in a labour dispute should not be judged guilty of a conspiracy by reason of doing in combination any of the acts in question; amended the law of agency by enacting that no federal court should hold any member or officer liable for unlawful acts committed in the course of a labour dispute by any other member or officer, in the absence of proof of actual participation or ratification; and defined a labour dispute in terms so wide as to sanction, not only national, but sympathetic, strikes. The second line pursued by the trade union legislation of the thirties was more original. The Norris-La Guardia Act, like the British Acts of 1871 and 1906, had been designed to safeguard the right of trade unions to exist and function against an attitude on the part of the courts which reduced them to impotence even in the case—in the America of 1932 a highly improbable one—of the majority of employers in an industry being disposed to deal with them. The short-lived Section 7a of the National Industrial Recovery Act of 1933, and the National Labour Relations Act of 1935, popularly known as the Wagner Act, attacked the subject from the opposite angle. It was intended to make it impossible for employers to refuse to negotiate with trade unions, and to crush them by economic duress or physical coercion even when, as after 1932, the law allowed unions to carry on their activities.

The National Labor Relations Act was declared constitutional by the Supreme Court in April 1937, when it was held that manufacturing involved inter-state commerce, though only after drastic proposals for the reorganization of the judiciary had been advanced by the President. Its authority since that time has been unquestioned, and it is today much the most important law relating to Labour in the United States. Its approach to the problem of industrial relations was determined by the weakness—now much less marked—of American trade unionism, and by the tyrannical practices of American employers. It has no parallel in any European country; but it owes something to earlier American examples, and was not the bolt from the blue denounced by its critics. During the last war, two federal agencies, the War Labor Policies Board and the War Labor Board, had temporarily enforced the principle that employers were not entitled to interfere with the right of workers to organize; and the Railway Labor Act of 1926, which was upheld by the Supreme Court in 1930, had prohibited 'interference, influence or coercion' designed to hamper trade unions, with the result that most categories of railway workers were strongly organized, and that that industry conducted its affairs in comparative freedom from the methods of barbarism which disgraced some others. The Act of 1935 was influenced by those precedents, as well as by the National Labor Board established under section 7a of the N.L.R.A., the Railway Labor Act of 1934, and the considerable number of boards which in 1933 and 1934, when the country was swept by a wave of strikes, were created by the Executive in particular industries; but it attempted to improve on these earlier experiments. It emerged as a comprehensive measure governing all industries throughout America in which trade unionism existed.

The assumption of its authors was that tolerable relations between workers and employers were impossible, except on a basis of collective bargaining; that the industrial autocracy of the past must, accordingly, be ended; and that, with that object, the state must not merely permit trade unions to exist, but must, when necessary, compel employers both to negotiate with them and to refrain from practices designed to obstruct or undermine them. The purpose of the Act, therefore, was not to mediate in industrial disputes, but to ensure that workers had complete liberty to organize and that employers dealt, in good faith, with their organizations. With that end in view, it established a National Labor Relations Board, composed of three persons unconnected with either side, and charged with two main functions. The first duty of the Board is to prevent employers from engaging in any one of five 'unfair labour practices' enumerated in the Act, the second to hold elections among employees to ascertain what union the majority desire to be designated as the organization to bargain on their behalf. To enable the Board to perform its task, large powers were conferred upon it. It can appoint such central and regional officers, and make such regulations, as it may deem to be necessary; can subpoena witnesses, require the submission of records, and enforce compliance with requests for information by order of a court of law. In the event of its deciding that an employer is guilty of an 'unfair labour practice', the Board has power to issue an order requiring him to cease and desist, and to petition for its enforcement any federal circuit court of appeals. 'Unfair practices' include almost every kind of action by which employers had attempted to deter their workers from joining a union or to penalize them for doing so. Interference with employees in their efforts to organize; interference with, or financial contributions to, any labour organization; discrimination, as regards conditions of employment, between trade unionists and non-unionists; the discharge of employees on the ground that they had given testimony under the Act; the refusal to bargain collectively with the elected representatives of the majority of employees, are among the practices outlawed. Any employee or trade union official, who believes that the Act has been violated in any of these respects may file a complaint with the Board's Regional Director, or, if his object is to secure an election to determine representatives, may lodge with him a petition to that effect. If the official concerned finds that there is a *prima facie* case, he issues a charge against the employer, and hearings are then held before one of the Board's trial examiners who can either dismiss the case or recommend the action to be taken. In the event of the employer refusing to comply, the matter goes to the Board at Washington, which can then issue the appropriate order, followed when necessary, by an appeal to a federal court.

The mass of business which descended on the Board, when in October 1935, it got to work, and which greatly increased on the Act being upheld by the Supreme Court, is a measure of the need which the Act was passed to meet. In the first five years of its existence, from October 1935, to November 1940, the National Labor Relations Board handled approximately 30,000 cases, involving just under 6,500,000 workers, a figure not far short of two thirds of the total number of employees in the manufacturing industries of the United States. Two thirds of the cases were concerned with various forms of discrimination against trade unionists, including the refusal to engage in collective bargaining with trade union representatives. The remaining third arose from petitions for elections to determine what organization the majority of workers desired to represent them.

The numerous and difficult problems to which the administration of the Act gave rise, much complicated as they were, by the feud in the ranks of Organized Labour described below, cannot here be discussed; but it is important to notice the reactions to the new policy of the classes most directly affected by it. Some employers—a minority—seem to have welcomed the Act as the end of a nightmare. More—probably a majority—acquiesced in it with reluctance, but worked it in good faith once it became law. The first attitude of others, again, appears to have been one of indignant incredulity, which faded only with the decision of the Supreme Court, and not always then. Accustomed to regard themselves less as businessmen than as petty sovereigns, and trade unions, not as representing interests with which negotiation was a matter of mutual convenience, but as enemies to be crushed, they were unable at once to acquire the mentality required for the prosaic business of bargaining as to wages and working conditions. They continued, therefore, to carry into the new régime the social habits of the old; dismissed as preposterous the suggestion that they should sit round a table with 'agitators'; maintained the machinery of repression whose use was now illegal; and countenanced on occasion, even as recently as 1941, a resort to the methods of the jungle which they had learned in their youth. Meantime, the mechanism of the law was grinding slowly forward. The Board issued its orders, and the Courts enforced them. Company unions, if initiated and maintained under the influence of employers, were dissolved. Elections were held in plants where few formerly had ventured to express their views above a whisper, and showed, in most cases, large majorities in favour of representation by independent organizations. Mr. Ford, who—incredible though it seems—appears to have persuaded himself that he ruled by love, discovered, to his astonishment, in 1941, that two thirds of his employees preferred the automobile workers' union to him. As a consequence of that process of gradual education, attacks on the legislation of 1935 show some signs today of changing their target. The old hatred of Trade Unionism is still strong in influential quarters, nor can it yet be said that the principle of collective bargaining has won general acceptance. It is still possible for the head of a great firm to denounce the Wagner Act as involving the control of industry 'by agents and commissions, which . . . impose one-sided, inconsistent rules and regulations; regulate, control, indict and punish management; prevent industry from purging itself of subversive workers and unpatriotic leaders; destroy contracts; and even nullify the right of free speech', and to sigh for the golden age when 'labor relations were a local matter between men and management'.[10] In spite, however, of such outbursts, recent criticisms of the measure by the business world tend, on the whole, to be less doctrinaire and more realistic than those of the past. They increasingly take the form, not of indiscriminate denunciations of collective bargaining and metaphysical rhapsodies on the beauties of free enterprise, but of strictures on particular provisions of the law, and specific proposals for removing its defects. When that ground is taken, it is possible for serious discussion to be, at any rate, begun.

The effect of the National Labor Relations Act, not merely on Trade Unionism, but on the American attitude to all labour questions, has been profound. It is not an exaggeration to describe it as a watershed in the social history of the United States. A situation in which, while industry rapidly expanded, and the wage-earning population grew—though more slowly—year by year, employers redoubled their efforts to prevent Labour in their own country from creating the protective institutions which, in similar circumstances, it had created in every other could hardly, in any case, have been permanently maintained. It survived as long as it did partly because of the prestige with which the prosperity of the twenties clothed the leaders of industry and finance, partly because the mass of the population shared the fruits of progress, partly through the success of the anti-union campaign of employers and the courts. The Depression destroyed the first two bulwarks; the third, though it survived them, was not strong enough to stand alone. With the philosophy of Big Business discredited by the debacle, and an Administration in power in Washington which, for the first time in American history, looked with favour on trade unions, the release of the forces long dammed up was to be expected; and a rush into organization in 1933-4 added 21 per cent in twelve months to the number of organized workers. But neither employers nor judges had changed their attitude. Even before the N.I.R.A. was destroyed by the Supreme Court in May 1935, the former were mobilizing for a counterattack, and some courts were supporting them. By that time the tide, which had run for two years in favour of Labour, showed signs of turning. It was a question whether the ground won could be held, or whether, as ten years before, the gains of the revival would not be swept away. It was the National Labor Relations Act which supplied the answer. It stabilized the situation. It put the power of the Government behind collective bargaining and gave Labour firm legal foundations on which to build. In that sense, the American Labour Movement of today is the creation of the State.

The most obvious of the effects on Trade Unionism of the backing which the Act conferred is shown by the figures of trade union membership set out above. In 1937, a year of good trade, the number of organized workers was half as much again as in 1936. The increase was not a flash in the pan, but continued, though at a slower rate. Four years later, towards the end of 1941, at the moment when the United States was about to enter the war, the figure had risen by another 48 per cent. It was then over three times that of 1933, and over twice that of 1936. So rapid a growth was a doubtful blessing, of the disadvantages of which something is said below. But the rush into organization, which took place when the obstacles impeding it were removed, and still more the stability shown by the new Unionism of the day, were facts of great significance, of which both American business and foreign observers will do well to take account. They conclusively refuted the allegation, so often heard in the preceding decade, that Trade Unionism was an alien importation, which could not take root in the healthy soil of America.

The psychological and moral results of the new status acquired by Organized Labour were as striking as its numerical growth. For the first time, outside certain privileged groups, workers could bargain with their employers on terms of something like equality. For the first time, the workman who was dismissed for holding opinions disapproved by the management could secure redress. For the first time, it was made an offence for firms to deprive employees of their livelihood merely on the ground that they declined to sign contracts not to organize, refused to become members of tame organizations financed by their masters, or exercised the ordinary rights of freedom of speech and meeting. For the first time, in short, the Government and the Courts treated the rights of the wage-earner as not less entitled to protection than those of the property-owner. The revolution which the end of undiluted industrial autocracy involved passed almost unnoticed abroad, but it was a revolution none the less.

In cities dominated by a few great firms, where thousands of families had led their working lives under the control of dictators, sometimes benevolent, sometimes the reverse, but always irresponsible, men were henceforward subject to rules which they had taken part, through their representatives, in making, and which would, when necessary, be enforced by the power of the law. It is not surprising that some of them, who had seen that transformation take place almost over night, should have believed that trade unionism could do more than it can. Nor, once the ice was broken, did reform stop there. Apart from other measures of social amelioration, such as those making provision for health, old age, unemployment, and the welfare of children, apart also from state legislation modelled on the Federal Act of 1935, three further Acts were passed, of which two concerned trade unionism directly, and the third indirectly. The Walsh-Healey Act of 1936 provided that, in the case of every federal contract of $10,000 or more, the contractor should sign an agreement to observe certain minimum labour standards, including the 8-hour day and 40-hour week, no child labour under 16 for boys and 18 for girls, compliance with the health and safety laws of the State where the contract is to be carried out, and the payment of not less than the 'prevailing rates' of wages. The Byrnes Anti-Strike-Breaking Act of 1936 forbade the importation of blacklegs from one State into another to take the place of strikers; and, on this measure being nullified by a federal court, Congress re-enacted it in 1938 with the necessary amendments. Finally, the Fair Labor Standards Act of 1938 laid down minimum conditions of employment for all workers producing goods which enter into inter-state commerce. It fixed statutory minimum rates of wages; established wage-boards for the determination of rates above the statutory minima; fixed a standard working week—after the lapse of two years, 40 hours—all work in excess of which was to be paid at the rate of time and a half; and made illegal the employment of children under 16 in any occupation, and between 16 and 18 in any declared by the Children's Bureau of the United States Department of Labor to be detrimental to their well-being.

(iv) The Rift in the Movement

The sensational growth of Trade Unionism, which took place in the thirties, was accompanied by unanticipated changes in the structure of the Movement. It was the occasion, in particular, of an internal rift, which has had a profound effect on the subsequent history of Organized Labour, and the consequences of which are far from exhausted. The aspect of American Trade Unionism which has attracted most public notice in the last five years is the conflict between the two federal organizations, the American Federation of Labour and the Congress of Industrial Organizations, which between them command the allegiance of rather more than nine tenths of the trade unionists in the country. The personalities of the rival leaders, the inconvenience caused by jurisdictional disputes, the advantage to be gained by playing off the two parties against each other, the easy target which a domestic quarrel within the Trade Union Movement offers to critics who detest the principle of Trade Unionism, have caused the subject to assume a prominence which is apt to seem to the foreign observer disproportionate to its real significance. The fact remains, nevertheless, that the conflict touches industrial politics at every turn. In the past it has strengthened the hands of the enemies of Organized Labour, and offered endless opportunities for intrigue to its false friends. Today it makes it difficult for American Labour to carry the weight which should belong to it in the organization of the economic side of the war effort, to co-operate effectively with the Labour Movements of other countries, or to play its full part in the work of such organizations as the International Labour Office. If the feud continues after the war, when the market, which is now in favour of Labour, may have turned against it, the result for American trade unionism may well be a disaster.

Into the origins of the quarrel it is not necessary to enter.[11] Its immediate occasion was the existence of large masses of workers, clamouring to be organized, and a sharp division of opinion within the A.F. of L.—then the sole federal organization in the field—as to the policy to be pursued in organizing them. The traditional procedure of the A.F. of L. was to draft such new recruits into 'federal labour locals', organizations containing a mixed multitude of workers of many different occupations, and directly affiliated with itself, which served as waiting-rooms or clearing-houses, pending the allocation of the individuals concerned among their appropriate craft unions. It had recourse to that expedient, in accordance with precedent, at the crisis of trade union history in 1933 and 1934; but it ran into difficulties not previously encountered. The mere numbers of the applicants eager to be enrolled in unions; the uncertainty of the craft affiliations of not a few among them; the fact that whole plants, some of them with more than 50,000 employees, had been organized *en bloc;* and that workers swept into the Movement on a wave of solidarity were indignant at the suggestion that they should be pigeonholed, separated from their fellow-workers, and in due time sorted out in deference to the claims of craft organizations whose very names were unknown to them, combined to create an unmanageable situation. As in Great

Britain in 1914, recruiting offices and cadres were overwhelmed by the rush to enlist, with the result that a unique opportunity appeared likely to be lost. The trade union revival seemed about to peter out in a wave of disillusionment.

At that critical moment, events took a new turn. The A.F. of L., though predominantly composed of craft unions, had long contained some organizations of a different type. The United Mine Workers of America, the Amalgamated Clothing Workers, and certain other societies, were organized on an industrial basis. They had experienced the effects of the new zeal for trade unionism, and had found no difficulty in grappling with it. Their leaders now took the initiative in urging that the workers in the mass-production industries, which both supplied the largest number of potential recruits to trade unionism and were least susceptible of organization by the conventional methods, should be enrolled in industrial unions. This proposal to create a New Model Army aroused some alarm among generals with a vested interest in a different tradition. In response to protests from the workers concerned, the Executive of the A.F. of L. had already gone so far as to combine federal locals in certain industries, such as automobile and aluminium manufacture, into 'national industrial councils'; but it still reserved the right to interfere in the organization of these unions and to distribute certain auxiliary workers in them among the craft unions by which they were claimed. It did not at once reject the proposal to sanction the formation of industrial unions; but, composed as it was—and is—of presidents and vice-presidents of craft unions, who saw their organizations excluded, were the suggestion carried out, from a new and fruitful field, and possibly condemned to lose some of their existing members, it could not be expected to welcome it.

The A.F. of L. Convention, which met at San Francisco in 1934, went some way to meet the advocates of a new policy. It passed a resolution which called attention to 'the change in the nature of the work performed by millions of workers whom it has been most difficult or impossible to organize into craft unions', and instructed the Executive, in order 'to meet this new condition . . . to issue charters to national or international unions in the automobile, cement, aluminum, and such other mass-production industries as in the judgment of the Executive Council may be necessary to meet the situation'. At the same time, it accompanied this statement of principle with significant qualifications. It declared that 'craft organization is most effective . . . where the nature of the industry is such that the lines of demarcation between crafts are distinguishable'; laid down that the jurisdictional rights of existing unions must be respected; and provided that, with that object, 'the American Federation of Labor shall for a provisional period direct the policies, administer the business, and designate the administrative and financial officers of the newly organized unions'.[12] In the following year the Executive complied with the resolution to the extent of conferring charters on two organizations of workers, the United Automobile Workers and United Rubber Workers,[13] in industries of the type mentioned, but excluded certain skilled craftsmen and maintenance employees, as under the jurisdiction of other unions. In the 1935 convention, a minority report[14] by the Committee on Resolutions protested against the interpretation placed by the Executive on the resolution of the preceding year. It disclaimed any intention of 'taking away from national or international craft unions any part of their present membership, or potential membership, in establishments where the dominant factor is skilled craftsmen coming under a proper definition of jurisdiction of such national or international unions'. It insisted, however, that 'In those industries where the work performed by a majority of the workers is of such nature that it might fall within the jurisdictional claim of more than one craft union, or no established craft union . . . industrial organization is the only form that will be acceptable to the workers or adequately meet their needs', and demanded 'a clear declaration of the American Federation of Labor', recognizing 'the right of these workers to organize into industrial unions and be granted unrestricted charters which guarantee the right to accept into membership all workers employed in the industry or establishment without fear of being compelled to destroy unity of action through recognition of jurisdictional claims made by national or international unions'.

The resolution founded on that report was defeated, and matters moved rapidly to a crisis. A few weeks after the

Convention, on 10 November 1935, it was announced that the leaders of eight unions affiliated with the A.F. of L., who were convinced that industrial unionism was the only possible basis for organizing the mass-production industries, had met and formed the Committee for Industrial Organization, not as an independent body but as a propagandist agency within the A.F. of L., 'for the purpose of encouraging and promoting the organization of the unorganized workers in mass-production and other industries upon an industrial basis'.[15] In February 1936 the Executive of the A.F. of L. ordered its dissolution; and finally, in August of the same year, after attempts to settle the matter by conference had produced no result, suspended the ten unions then affiliated to the Committee on the ground that the latter was a 'dual organization', an action which was subsequently upheld by the next Convention.[16] Negotiations for the restoration of unity were begun on the initiative of the C.I.O., which by that time had over 3,000,000 members, in October 1937, but proved abortive, as did also those undertaken in March-April 1939, on the suggestion of the President.[17] In November 1938, the C.I.O. changed its name to the Congress of Industrial Organizations, adopted a permanent Constitution, and set out on its career as an independent federation of American trade unionists.

So much for the facts. Their interpretation is still the subject of controversy. As far as the immediate occasion of the quarrel is concerned, the crucial issues are plain enough. In the first place, the constructions placed on the resolution of the San Francisco Convention by the A.F. of L. Executive and the unions subsequently suspended were radically different. The former held that it sanctioned industrial unionism among mass-production workers, but only on condition that craft workers in the industries concerned continued to be parcelled out among their respective craft unions. The latter thought in terms, less of mass-production workers, than of mass-production industries, and, while agreeing that plants where skilled craftsmen predominated should be organized on craft lines, took the view that the solidarity of the newly-formed industrial unions would be fatally impaired, were small groups of craftsmen liable at any moment to be separated from their fellow-workers in deference to the jurisdictional claims of particular craft unions. The truth is that the resolution itself was not a model of lucidity. In attempting to satisfy both groups of interests, it affirmed a principle, and then surrounded it with qualifications, which, if strictly interpreted, went far to stultify it. The Old Unionism of the A.F. of L. emphasized the qualifications, the New Unionism the principle. It is not surprising that they fell out.

Once controversy became acute, a second issue intervened. The C.I.O., as originally conceived, was what would be called in England a Minority Movement. Its intention was, not to secede from the A.F. of L., but to carry on propaganda within it for the extension of its own version of trade unionism to unorganized industries. All Minority Movements are annoying to the leaders of established organizations, who see in their mere existence a criticism of themselves. The A.F. of L. was quick to take alarm. In spite of the declaration of the C.I.O. that its object was to bring unions organized by it into affiliation with the A.F. of L., the President of the A.F. of L. warned it, within a week of its formation, that it was suspected of the sin of dualism, and laid down that a minority outvoted at the Convention was not entitled to press its point of view except at subsequent Conventions. The C.I.O. repeated that its object was to secure the affiliation of additional unions to the A.F. of L., denied that its aim was to raid the membership of any existing union, and not unnaturally asked how any minority could be expected to have a chance of inducing the Convention to modify its policy if it were prohibited from carrying on an educational campaign. Believing that the A.F. of L. Executive was dominated by a small inner ring, which manipulated the Convention in accordance with its own interests,[18] the newly formed Committee was indisposed to forego the opportunity of appealing, over its head, to the rank and file of the Movement.

These clichés of controversy are common form in all countries. The question which matters is that of the realities behind them. The statement that the split in the Labour Movement is primarily an affair of personalities may at once be dismissed. Personalities have been, of course, important, as they still are; but they are a surface matter. The view that the C.I.O. would have collapsed had it not been for the recognition accorded by the National Labor Relations Board to the unions belonging to it is equally unfounded. The Board, in determining what union should be treated as representing the workers in any given case, acted, as it was bound to do, in accordance with the preference of the majority revealed by an election, and the fact that C.I.O. unions gained by its decisions merely means that such unions were frequently preferred by the majority of workers. In reality, by April 1937, when, with the decision of the Supreme Court, requests for elections to settle the bargaining unit became numerous, the C.I.O. already had over 2,000,000 members. There is more to be said for the opinion that the vital issue was between craft and industrial unionism; but thus baldly stated, it also is misleading. Each of these expressions covers more than one type of organization, and the experience of other countries shows that a prolonged feud, as distinct from occasional friction, between them is not inevitable. In actual fact, the A.F. of L., as has been stated above, included before the rupture some industrial unions, and the C.I.O. includes some, though not many, craft unions today. The real causes of the trouble lay deeper. They consisted in the nature of American economic development in the preceding twenty years, and in certain features of American trade union organization which made it difficult for it to adjust itself to a new industrial situation. They were, in fact, impersonal, and most of them would have existed, if the individuals in both groups commonly blamed for the conflict had never been born. If that truth were remembered, much acrimony would be avoided, and a settlement would be nearer than it appears to be at present.

The most striking feature of American industrial development for more than twenty years before the split in the trade union movement was the rapid expansion of the metal and machine-making industries. The most striking feature of the American trade unionism of that period was the weakness of the hold which it had on those industries. Between 1910 and 1920 the numbers of workers (inclusive of labourers) in blast furnaces and steel-rolling mills grew 35·1 per cent; in automobile factories 676·3 per cent; in other iron, steel, and machine-making factories 34·6, and in that group of industries as a whole 54·7. The number of electricians grew by 133·1 per cent, of workers making electrical machinery 334·1 per cent, and of those in miscellaneous manufacturing industries, including rubber, 106·5 per cent. The Trade Union Movement of 1932, on the eve of the push into organization and of the crisis which was to divide it, appears to have been almost untouched by these developments. It derived its main strength from two sources. The first was the building trades, which in that year accounted for more than a quarter, 26·4 per cent, of all American trade unionists, and which were the backbone of the A.F. of L., supplying it with actually 29·5 of its members. The second was transport and communications, with 26·7 per cent, of which the largest block consisted of railway-workers, the majority of whom belonged to the Railway Brotherhoods, but including also a large body of postal, street-railroad and transport workers. Then came, at a long distance, clothing workers (7·1 per cent); clerical workers (5·2 per cent); workers in mines, quarries and oil (5·0 per cent); workers in printing, publishing, and allied industries (4·9 per cent); workers on iron, steel, metals, and machinery (4·9 per cent), domestic and personal service (2·2 per cent), musicians (2·2 per cent); public service (1·8 per cent); food and kindred products (1·7 per cent); textiles (1·6 per cent); and a miscellaneous body of small organizations, none of whom amounted to as much as 1·5 per cent of the total.

It will be seen, therefore, that two industries, building and transport, accounted in 1932 for more than half the trade unionists in the United States. Iron, steel, other metals, and machine-making contributed only some 5 per cent of the total, and the manufacturing industries as a whole less than one quarter (23·5 per cent). In 1932, the United States was in the depths of a depression, and trade unionism, of course, was feeling its effects. But trade union membership has shown no significant increase during the period of abounding prosperity in the twenties, and in 1932 it was still only 8·3 per cent below the level of the boom year, 1929. The depression may fairly be held accountable for that decline, but obviously it cannot have been the cause of the preceding long stagnation. It is difficult to resist the conclusion that trade unionism had failed to keep pace with the practical realities of industrial development. The causes of its stagnation in the twenties, when economic conditions should have favoured its growth, have often been discussed, and something on that subject has been said above. But, in the light of the distribution of trade unionists between different industries, its failure to grow is not a matter for surprise. The industries in which trade unionism was strong were, with some exceptions, such as the clothing trades—a special case—not those which were expanding rapidly. The industries whose swift growth made them most representative of the New America were not those in which trade unionism was strong.

The consequences of that situation for American labour were extremely serious. A mass of unorganized workers, many of them subject, as in the steel and automobile industries, to outrageous oppression, steadily piled up. Previous attempts to organize them had been made, and had failed. New attempts were being made in 1932, with not much greater success. When, at last, in 1933, the economic crisis, the political upheaval and the beginning of the New Deal, ended the period of stagnation, the problem of coping with a flood of new recruits to trade unionism presented a genuine difficulty. In Great Britain, where a similar, though smaller, problem had arisen, it had been solved by one or other of the methods described in the fourth part of this essay. There had been, of course, some friction, caused by the competition of different unions for members, but there had been no split in the movement. Craft unions and industrial unions are equally affiliated to the Trades Union Congress, co-operate without difficulty, and would be horrified by the suggestion that they should blackleg each other for the benefit of employers. The obvious course in the United States was the same. It was to enrol in existing unions those willing and qualified to join them, and to establish new organizations for the remainder—the great majority—who could be organized only on an industrial basis.

That policy had been formally endorsed by the A.F. of L. convention of 1934, which had not only admitted, but proclaimed, the desirability of encouraging, industrial unionism. At that point, however, a difficulty arose which has its source in the peculiarities of American trade union organization. It was not merely the fact that the backbone of the A.F. of L.

had always been craft unionism, and that the Executive was predominantly composed of the officers of such unions. It was still more the conception of trade unionism which some of them held. The view of a union as the owner of a labour monopoly, to be jealously protected, not only against attacks by employers, but against the encroachment of fellow trade unionists, is deeply engrained in the older sections of the movement, and is particularly strong, for obvious reasons, among members of some craft unions. It is fortified by a feature of American political psychology which must have struck all observers. The reverence for the sanctity of contractual rights, which reached its height in the English political thought of the later seventeenth and eighteenth centuries, is stronger today in the United States than in the country of its origin. It is enshrined in the Constitution, and is not without influence in humbler spheres of life. One expression of it is found in consequences which are supposed to flow from the practice of the A.F. of L.—a practice taken over by the C.I.O.—of 'chartering' unions. It is necessary, of course, for unions to avoid, as far as possible, unnecessary overlapping, and for the Federation to which they belong to decide what societies it will recognize as constituting its membership. The system of 'chartering', however, as applied in practice, goes far beyond those simple formalities. The Charter confers on the union concerned exclusive rights of jurisdiction over the workers in a given craft. These rights are lucrative, since members mean fees. They form, therefore, a formidable vested interest, to be defended *à outrance* against all intruders. In some cases, they appear to be regarded almost as a piece of private property, any menace to which excites in their beneficiaries the same indignation as is aroused among other property-owners by the threat of confiscation.

That attitude is natural, perhaps, in the parties whose interests are threatened by an innovation. What is more surprising is its endorsement, as a matter, not merely of convenience, but of principle, by the Federation itself. A clause in the Constitution of the A.F. of L. provides that 'no charter shall be granted by the American Federation of Labor . . . without a positive and clear definition of the trade jurisdiction claimed by the applicant, and the charter shall not be granted if the jurisdiction claimed is a trespass on the jurisdiction of existing affiliated unions without the written consent of such unions'. The question what new departures in trade union organization constitutes a 'trespass' on existing rights, is, of course, a difficult one; and it would have been reasonable for the A.F. of L. to urge the need for a careful adjustment of boundaries in individual cases. That practical and prosaic attitude did not satisfy it. It did not appeal to mere expediency. It did not argue that overlapping was, so far as possible, to be avoided, or that conflicting claims should be settled in an accommodating spirit. It took its stand on high grounds of legal theory. It argued that the Federation, by the mere fact of its formation, and by its action in granting charters to unions then existing or subsequently established, had entered into a solemn contract with the societies in question, which, whatever the situation that might arise, it could not subsequently set aside or modify.[19] In an economic world which had changed out of recognition in a generation, and was changing beneath its eyes, it invoked, or allowed its legal advisers to invoke, a Social Contract theory of its origins and obligations which, if consistently applied, would appear to preclude it from embarking on any new departure that any union chartered by it may choose to regard as prejudicial to itself.

The merits or demerits of these doctrines need not here be discussed at length. Whatever is to be said for them they combined with other factors to produce one result which bears directly on the still unended conflict in the ranks of Organized Labour. If trade unionism is to be a living force, it must be capable of adjusting itself to the changing realities of the economic system. The impression of an observer is that, at a time when such changes were taking place with exceptional rapidity, American trade unionism, as represented by the A.F. of L., suffered from a certain stiffness of the joints, which made the adjustments required almost impossible to effect. The attempt to induce it to find room for a larger number of industrial, as well as craft, unions, was made. Though given a qualified approval by the Annual Convention of the A.F. of L., which is the final authority, the effort broke down, because it appeared to threaten the vested interests of existing organizations. Except on the view that workers who desire to be organized have no right to any voice as to the type of organization in which they are to be enrolled, that state of things was clearly indefensible. The formation of new industrial unions, and later, when their sponsors were suspended by the A.F. of L., the conversion of the original Committee into a separate Federation, were the direct result of it. In view of these facts, to describe the C.I.O. as that bugbear of trade unionists, a 'breakaway' organization, is unrealistic. The great majority of the members whom the unions affiliated with it enrolled had not previously been trade unionists; nor, on the statement of the A.F. of L., itself, was it likely that they could be organized on any but an industrial basis. In the main, therefore, the C.I.O. neither withdrew members from existing unions, nor made members of persons whom existing unions could have hoped to recruit, but cultivated a field which had hitherto been neglected. The feud in the American Labour Movement remains highly regrettable. The greater part of the membership of the C.I.O. unions, however, represents, not a deduction from the membership of unions affiliated to the A.F. of L., but an addition to the total number of American trade unionists.

III Organization and Methods of American Trade Unionism

The last date for which data permitting a full analysis of American trade unionism is available is August 1940.[20] Since then, the membership of the movement has substantially increased, and the relative importance of the different elements composing it have undergone some change; but, details apart, the features which characterized it then distinguish it today. Of the 173 trade unions at that time in existence, 75 had been founded before 1900, 54 between 1900 and 1929, and 44 from 1930 onwards. It is not surprising, therefore, that the last generation of economic development should have left a deep mark on the American Labour Movement. These societies were, and still are, of the utmost diversity in scale, organization, and policy, from old-fashioned craft unions with a few hundred members, to amalgamations embracing a large body of allied crafts, and industrial unions with memberships of over half a million. It is customary in works on American trade unionism to divide them into three groups, consisting of (1) unions affiliated to the A.F. of L. (2) unions affiliated to the C.I.O. (3) independent unions, which are connected with neither. That classification does not provide a reliable clue to the constitution and methods of any particular society; but it is not wholly arbitrary, since the unions included in (1) and (3) are predominantly of a different type from those in (2), and it may conveniently be followed here. Some of the larger problems suggested by the American Labour Movement will be considered later. Before, however, turning to them, it is desirable to offer a bird's eye view of the Movement as a whole, as it was in August 1940, by presenting a dull catalogue of facts as to the dimensions and organization of the three groups composing it.

(i) The 'Independent' Unions

The societies in the last category need not detain us long. They consisted in 1940 of some thirty-one unions, with an aggregate membership[21] of 643,100, of which twenty-six were craft, or amalgamated craft, unions, and two were organized on an industrial basis. Most of these organizations were small, twenty-three having under 20,000 members apiece, and thirteen under 5,000. Different branches of the public service, particularly the postal service, accounted for eight of them, and manufacturing industries for four, the total membership of the former being 187,300 (29·1 per cent of the total) and of the latter 41,800 (6·4 per cent). But the stronghold of independent trade unionism was, and still is, transport and communications; and the backbone of trade unionism in that group of industries consisted then, as now, of the Railway-workers, in particular of the Brotherhood of Railroad Trainmen (146,000), the American Federation of Railroad Workers (86,000), the Brotherhood of Locomotive Foremen and Engineers (70,000), and the Brotherhood of Railway Signalmen (60,000). These four societies accounted in 1940 for well over one half the total members of the unions not connected with the A.F. of L. or C.I.O. The first three form, together with the Order of Sleeping-Car Conductors (97,000), which belongs to

A.F. of L., the well-known 'Big Four' of the American railway world.

Railway trade unionism in America has a stormy past; but, to judge by its recent history, that age is behind it. Several causes have combined to give the larger societies of railwaymen a position and policy of their own, which deter them from throwing in their lot with either of the two great federations. Engaged in work which demands a somewhat high degree of physical strength and mental alertness, and which requires, in the case of some important groups, several years of training, the railwaymen have been able to dispense with insistence on the 'closed shop', and, at the same time to build up powerful organizations, which include a proportion of workers ranging from approximately two thirds in the service as a whole to over 90 per cent among the Trainmen. Possessing, again, unlike most American trade unions, a somewhat elaborate benefit system, they are disposed by that fact to a policy of caution and stability. Both the companies and the Government on their side, have been anxious to avoid stoppages, with the result that the former, sometimes with unofficial pressure, recognized the unions and negotiated agreements with them, at a time when it was still the fashion for employers in important industries to regard trade unionism as a pest to be stamped out. Finally, Congress has tended to treat railway labour as a special case. The first eight-hours Act for adult men was passed in 1916, under the threat of a strike, for the benefit of railway-workers. From 1898 onwards, a series of Acts, successively invalidated by the Supreme Court, had attempted to make it an offence for employers to victimize railwaymen for trade unionism, and the Acts of 1926 and 1934 brought the struggle to a conclusion. The former prohibited under penalties 'interference, influence, or coercion' by railway companies; the latter provided that the majority of any 'craft or class of employees' should determine by vote the organization to represent them, and established a National Mediation Board of three members to superintend the administration of the law.

With these circumstances in its favour, railway trade unionism has been able in recent years to stand above the battle. The Brotherhoods have practised an enlightened egotism; and, while acting together at moments of crisis, have remained aloof from the rest of the trade union movement, for fear of becoming involved in disputes in which they have no direct concern. They have avoided strikes, taken no active part in the conflict between the A.F. of L. and C.I.O., and relied, to win their victories, on collective bargaining, backed by powerful organizations and large financial resources. They offer a classical example of successful trade unionism of the type which is concerned solely with professional interests.

(ii) The American Federation of Labor

The American Federation of Labor is the oldest of the federal organizations produced by trade unionism in the United States. Founded in 1886, it grew steadily in the next fifteen years, and by the turn of the century was firmly established. It reached the peak of its influence in the latter years of the last war; and, down to the expulsion of the important group of societies which sponsored the Committee for Industrial Organization, included virtually all the trade unions in the country, with the exception of the small group of independent organizations already described. In 1934, the last year in which the A.F. of L. reigned alone, over four fifths (84 per cent) of American trade unionists belonged to organizations affiliated to it. With the growth of the C.I.O., the proportion has fallen; but in August 1940,[22] it was still over one half (51 per cent), and stood at 48 per cent at the end of 1941. The half-century of history behind the A.F. of L.; its large membership; the importance of some of the organizations connected with it; and, not least, its tenacious adherence to certain simple principles, which are held to be peculiarly representative of American economic conditions and of the American mentality, combine to make it a power. The long suit of the American Labour Movement is not internationalism; but such slender international connexions[23] as that Movement permits have hitherto been established through the American Federation of Labor.

The societies belonging to the A.F. of L. represent all varieties of size and organization, and most types of industry. Of the 108 unions affiliated with it in August 1940, 31 possessed less than 5,000 members each, and 62, or well over half, under 20,000; while 4 had between 160,000 and 200,000 and 5 between 200,000 and 400,000. As already stated, craft, or amalgamated craft, unions have always been its backbone, and industrial unions accounted in 1940 for only 13 of the total. That fact, in its turn, is connected with the nature of the occupations which give the Federation its special character. It was, and remains, weak in the extractive industries, which contributed less than 1 per cent of its total membership. It was not noticeably strong in the manufacturing industries. In the production of heavy or durable goods, it was, indeed, noticeably weak, drawing from it only about 11 per cent of its members. It was better represented in the non-durable goods, or consumer goods, industries; but, even there, almost four fifths of its 862,700 members (19·2 per cent of its total membership) came from three groups of industries, the clothing trades, food and drink, and printing and paper. Apart from them, its main strongholds were three, transportation and communications (17·8 of its total membership); professional, government and personal service (18·1) and—above all—the building trades (24·8 per cent). Each of these groups comprised some large societies, and a few very large ones. The six numerically strongest unions in these three groups, two in each, accounted for 30 per cent of the total membership of the Federation, and the three groups together for 60 per cent.

The organization of the A.F. of L. is—at least on paper—somewhat complex. The Federation consisted in August 1940, of (1) 108 National and International Unions; (2) 1,450 Local Trade and Federal Labor Unions; (3) 49 State Federations, and 816 City Central Bodies, plus 4 Departments and 720 Local Department Councils.[24] The two latter are primarily a matter of internal administrative convenience, the Departments—of which the four now existing serve the metal trades, building trades, railway employees, and unions using labels on their products—being, in effect, clearing-houses established between allied unions to deal with matters of common concern. The City Centrals are bodies consisting of the representatives of local unions, and correspond to the British Trades Councils; and the State Federations are, in turn, bodies representing the City Centrals and trade union locals (*Anglice,* branches or lodges) throughout a state. Federal labour unions are organizations composed of workers of varying occupations, which are not represented strongly enough in the locality for it to be possible to establish separate branches consisting exclusively of workers of a particular craft or industry. Federal trade locals are branches composed of members of a given craft for which no national trade union yet exists, and which for that reason are affiliated directly to the A.F. of L. These two types of organization represent, therefore, a provisional arrangement, since it is hoped in the first case, that members will increase sufficiently to make possible the establishment of a separate branch for each craft, and, in the second, that national organizations will, in due course, be established, which branches in different crafts can join. Of the National and International Unions no explanation is needed, except to say that International Unions are unions with branches in Canada as well as in the United States.

The functions of the Federation are of two main kinds. It is concerned in the first place, with serving its constituent bodies directly, by carrying on propaganda, disseminating economic information of a kind useful to trade unions, supplying speakers and organizers, issuing charters, settling, or attempting to settle inter-union disputes, assisting unions, financially and otherwise, in their struggle with employers, and generally maintaining and strengthening the internal organization of the Movement. In the second place, it has the duty of protecting the interests of the Movement as a whole. It watches for symptoms of attacks to be made upon it, and meets them when they become more than threats. It handles, through its various committees, a large mass of technical subjects; keeps its eye on all bills introduced into Congress, and arranges for opposition to those injurious to Labour; mobilizes and expresses opinion on legal and political matters of importance to trade unionists; and represents the Movement *vis-à-vis* Congress and public Departments, such as the Department of Labor, the National Labor Relations Board, and the War Labor Board. In both these respects the Central Office of the A.F. of L. is more active than that of the General Council of the British Trades Union Congress, employs a larger staff of officers, and incurs an annual expenditure—the equivalent, in 1940-41, of something over £450,000—which would make the eyes of the latter drop out of its head. Nor, in spite of the growth of a rival federation, is there any signs of the claims on it diminishing. Not only has the expansion of the munitions industries in the last two years been accompanied by a considerable increase in the number of trade unionists, but the trend of policy during the last decade has been such as to confront the trade union movement with new tasks and problems. The age of undiluted individualism is now over, and the policy of the Federal Authorities affects labour at every turn. It is inevitable that a body representing over 4,000,000 trade unionists should find the work on its hands increasing year by year.

The A.F. of L. is not a unitary organization, but a loose Federation. The autonomy of its constituent societies is among the themes most frequently stressed by its officers, and the inability of the central body 'to interfere with the internal affairs of . . . national and international unions' is even pleaded as an excuse for the refusal to take steps to put an end to scandals which gravely compromise trade unionism as a whole. The Annual Convention, which, according to the constitution of the A.F. of L., is its final authority, is composed of delegates from national and international unions, and from the other affiliated groups. As, however, the delegates sent by the unions number one for every 4,000 members, and as each of them has one vote for every 100 members or major fraction of 100, while each of the other groups sends only one delegate, who casts only one vote, it will be evident that the real power in the convention is wielded by the former. The domination of the A.F. of L. by the larger unions is still further strengthened by the composition of the Executive, and by the part which it plays in the affairs of the Federation. Exercising control between conventions of the finances of the Federation, deciding the objects on which money shall be spent and what unions shall receive organizing assistance, having the federal locals directly under its thumb and influencing indirectly the City Centrals and State Federations, dealing with all the major issues which require immediate decision, the Executive has acquired the power which falls naturally into the hands of a body which meets at short intervals, and has its fingers on the day-to-day business of a society. The personnel of the Executive is a curious illustration of the power of the machine in all

America organizations, including those which are most eloquent in lip-service to democracy. It consists of the President and Secretary/Treasurer of the Federation, together with some 13 to 15 members elected annually by the Convention; but the hold which the officials of the great national Unions have on their members, and their bargains with each other, make democratic formalities of minor importance. In practice the Executive is composed of the President, Vice-Presidents, and former Presidents and Vice-Presidents of the more powerful Unions, elected almost automatically and holding office year after year. It is, in fact, an oligarchy.

(iii) The Congress of Industrial Organizations

The circumstances which led to the foundation of the Congress of Industrial Organizations have already been explained. It grew, and is still growing, rapidly.[25] In August 1940, it consisted[26] of 34 national unions, and eight Organizing Committees on the way to become National Unions; together with 32 State Industrial Union Councils, and about 110 City, County, and district Industrial Union Councils. It differs markedly from the A.F. of L. in the scale and structure of the organizations affiliated with it, as well as in the industries which are its strongholds. The small societies with under 20,000 members, which form half the A.F. of L. affiliates, were and are much less prominent in the C.I.O., 16 of the organizations affiliated to it having 50,000 members and upwards, and the 4 largest, with more than 300,000 apiece, accounting for approximately half its total membership. Nearly two thirds of the unions connected with it were in 1940 industrial unions, and the remainder consisted of amalgamations of crafts.

Finally, as far as its hold on different occupations was concerned, the C.I.O. was weak where the A.F. of L. was strong, and strong where the A.F. of L. was weak. It had no members in any of the building crafts, and none on the railways, while the 90,000 members of the Transport Workers Union, a C.I.O. affiliate, were not a quarter of those in the A.F. of L. Teamsters' Union alone. It had only 131,000 members in all the service unions together, compared with 793,000 belonging to the A.F. of L., and was hardly represented in the long list of minor crafts which supplied the A.F. of L. with its multitude of small unions. The chief territories of the C.I.O.

were in 1940 two. The first was the raw material industries, which supplied it with nearly a quarter (23·7 per cent) of its total membership, and where it reigned almost alone, dominating the mining industry with 600,000 workers in the United Mine Workers of America, but also being strong among the ore-smelters and oil-workers, as well as in the processing and packing of agricultural products. Its second main province was manufacturing, which accounted for 58·7 per cent of its total membership, compared with 30·8 per cent derived from that source by the A.F. of L. In the consumer goods industries it could point to the Textile Workers Union, with 314,000 members (8·6 per cent), and to the Amalgamated Clothing Workers (7·1 per cent), as well as to vigorous organizations of leather and rubber workers. Its special stronghold, however, was the industries concerned with the production of durable goods. Iron, steel, metals, and machinery accounted for well over a quarter (28·1 per cent) of its total membership, and the durable goods industries as a whole for 37·4 per cent. Its character is largely determined by these facts. It is predominantly an organization of industrial unions in the extractive and mass-production manufacturing industries.

In social outlook and policy, there are somewhat marked contrasts between the C.I.O. and the A.F. of L. In matters of structure and organization the younger Federation has borrowed freely from the older, and the resemblance between the two is, in these respects, sufficiently close to make unnecessary a detailed account of the administrative machinery of the C.I.O. The local industrial union councils of the latter, like the local trade and federal labour unions of the A.F. of L., are a form of interim provision for bodies of workers for whom no national organization as yet exists, and who, accordingly, are directly affiliated to the parent organization. The State, County District, and City Councils, which also have their analogies in the A.F. of L., are primarily propagandist and organizing bodies, which spread light as to the new unionism in different areas, co-ordinate C.I.O. activities within them, and represent C.I.O. policy in the field of local government and public affairs. The only piece of machinery which can be called a new departure—the Organizing Committee—was a response to the special circumstances in which the C.I.O. began its career. Some of the mass-production industries, which it was its chief function to organize, were not ripe for the establishment of an independent union. Hence Organizing Committees, financed at first by other Unions, and later by the C.I.O. itself, were created to carry on the preliminary task of persuasion and agitation till the time should come when the birth of a new, autonomous, union should make their work unnecessary.

Judged by British standards, the C.I.O., like the A.F. of L., is liberally staffed. The problem of maintaining contacts between the Centre and outlying districts, which, in a country so vast as the United States, confronts all national bodies, is specially serious in the case of a young organization with new worlds before it still waiting to be organized. The C.I.O. attempts to meet it by employing something over fifty regional and sub-regional directors, field representatives, and organizers assigned to particular unions or areas. The work of its central office, which also is not starved of personnel, is of much the same kind as has already been described. Like its rival, it is faced by the necessity of defending trade unionism against attack in a society where the activities of Organized Labour—and, indeed, the mere fact of organization—are still regarded with suspicion. Matters arising from the administration of Labour laws and legislative proposals designed to cripple trade unionism occupy much of the time of its officers and committees. In that respect, it does not differ from the A.F. of L.; but it has not suffered, as in the past did the latter, from an inherited suspicion of State action, and it would probably be true to say that it has devoted somewhat more attention to formulating proposals for reform, as distinct from parrying blows. In addition to concerning itself, like the A.F. of L. with amendments to the Fair Labor Standards Act, with the substitution of a federal system of unemployment insurance for the 48 state systems at present in existence, and with the enactment of a unified old age pensions system, it has put forward a scheme for the reform of the tax system, has prepared a comprehensive programme of legislative reform, and has pressed the proposals for war-time industrial reorganization associated with the name of its president, Mr. Murray.

The constitution of the C.I.O. is still on its trial. It was adopted less than four years ago at the second Convention of the Movement held in November 1938, when what had been the 'Committee' for Industrial Organization was converted into the 'Congress'. It refers to the circumstances out of which the movement arose in a clause which states that its object is 'to extend collective bargaining and to secure for the workers means to establish peaceful relations with their employers by establishing unions capable of dealing with modern aggregates of industry and finance'. In other respects, it conforms in its general provisions to the standard American plan, except—an important exception—that it expressly prohibits discrimination against any worker on grounds of race, creed, colour, or nationality, and that it provides for a somewhat high scale of contributions from the constituent unions, with the result that the Centre is strengthened by the command of substantial resources. Final authority is vested in an Annual Convention composed of delegates of national and international unions, organizing committees, local industrial unions, and local industrial councils. The Executive Board is composed of one member from each affiliated national or international union and organizing committee, plus the President, six Vice-Presidents and Secretary. In the C.I.O., therefore, as in the A.F. of L., power rests predominantly in the hands of the National Unions. In one respect, however, there is an important difference between the Executive of the two bodies. That of the former is small, consisting, with the officers, of only some seventeen persons. In the C.I.O. it is large, since each union and organizing committee must be represented on it, and they include at present, with the officers, as many as forty to fifty persons. So numerous a body has its disadvantages; but it is unfavourable to the settlement of policy by hole-and-corner understandings between a few dominant personalities. It offers some measure of security against the rule of the machine, which is the curse of American public life.

(iv) The Methods of American Unions

a. Friendly benefits and social activities

Organization is a means, not an end. Its object, as far as Labour is concerned, is to enable a body of wage earners, by acting as a unit, to attain results which are incapable of achievement as long as they act as isolated individuals. The expedients employed for that purpose are of considerable diversity; and the effect of trade unionism, both on trade unionists themselves and on the general public, depends largely on the nature of those which are most generally invoked. Before, therefore, attempting to form any estimate of the successes and failures of the American Labour Movement, it is necessary to touch shortly on the methods to which it has recourse.

In that matter, American trade unionism had trodden a beaten path. Till recently it regarded with suspicion the policy of protecting the workers' standard of life by legal enactments, which occupies so prominent a place in the programme of European Labour Movements, and, even today, in spite of the experience of the last decade, it lays less emphasis upon it than might have been expected. With that exception, however, most, if not all, of the methods which it employs are common to the two continents. Benefit schemes, apprenticeship systems, and other arrangements for regulating the entry to the trade or industry, and, of course, the determination by collective bargaining of minimum standards of wages, hours, and working conditions, are in operation in the United States, as in Europe. Some of these devices, however, are less important in the former than in the latter, and others more important. As a consequence, though the ingredients which go into the pudding are much the same, what comes out of the oven has a different flavour.

Friendly benefits, though they have a place in the American Trade Union Movement, play no great part in it. Certain Unions, for example some of the Railway Brotherhoods, were founded originally as benefit societies, and have preserved that feature; while the conservative craft unionism of the eighties, which led to the foundation of the A.F. of L., also caused some unions, including the Cigar-makers, of which Gompers was president before he became the first secretary of the Federation, to look favourably on benefits as contribution to caution and stability. But the high wages of American workers, their objection to paying any but low dues, their traditional individualism, and—more recently—the belief among societies belonging to the C.I.O. that benefits are an obstacle to a militant trade policy, have checked the development of that side of Trade Unionism. The C.I.O. unions have no benefit arrangements; while in 1940 only 64 of the 108 unions then affiliated to the A.F. of L. were reported[27] as possessing them, 64 then making payments for death, 22 for sickness, 14 for unemployment, 12 for old age, 13 for disability, and 39 for miscellaneous objects. Certain social activities, of a kind unknown or unusual in Great Britain, are carried on by some Unions, such as the Union Health Centre maintained in New York by the International Ladies Garment Workers Union, the valuable educational work done by the same body, the provision for health and recreation made by the Amalgamated Clothing Workers in Chicago, and the apartment houses erected by the same union in New York. Such departures, however, are too few to be regarded as more than isolated ventures by exceptional societies; and the experiments in Labour Banks, which at one time made some stir, had left by 1940 only four survivors. Useful work in the field of adult education is done by some Unions, either independently or in co-operation with outside agencies; but the number of Unions who take their educational responsibilities seriously still seems to be small.

b. Apprenticeship and Admission to the Trade

When one turns from these miscellaneous social functions to consider the economic policies of American Unions, one encounters a variety of expedients, the relative importance of which differs widely in different occupations. It may by noted, in the first place, that certain devices, which at one time played a large part in British Trade Unionism but are now of quite small importance in it, still figure among the practices of some American trade unions, and are even more prominent in discussions of the subject. In the United States, as in Great Britain, the earlier protagonists of trade unionism were not the new class of factory operatives, but the workers in the older handicrafts. Such craftsmen were imbued with the doctrine that their trade was their property, to be protected, as in the case of other professions, by limiting the numbers of those entitled to engage in it. Since the great industry, and the organizations of employees dependent on it, developed later in America than in Britain, that tradition survived in the former longer than in the latter and, even today, is more strongly represented in the American than in the British trade union movement. It is most conspicuous in the building trade unions, which are the backbone of the A.F. of L., and in some of the small craft societies which also are associated with it. The degree to which today it finds practical expression in strict apprenticeship rules, and in insistence on high admission fees as a condition of entering the union and practising the trade, is commonly much exaggerated. The former are not important, since it appears that few employers engage as many apprentices as union rules allow.[28] It is probable, however, that the latter gives rise to occasional—and, in some occupations, more than occasional—abuse, which not only are objectionable in themselves, but offer an easy target to critics of trade unionism.

c. The Boycott and the Union Label

A second set of policies, rarely employed in Europe, but long in use in the United States, must also be regarded as the product of the local conditions in which American trade unionism developed. It is concerned not, like the measure just mentioned, with placing a group of workers in a strong position for bargaining with their employers, but with the sanctions by which a bargain, once made, shall be enforced. In conditions in which trade unionism is represented by small local societies, whose members form part of the public which buys their products, the attempt to maintain standards of employment by bringing influence to bear on purchasers is a course which readily suggests itself, and, provided that the market is sufficiently definite to admit of being approached, may even in less favourable conditions, be not without utility.

That appeal to the sovereign consumer is the basis of the 'white lists' of fair employers issued, for example, by some of the British printing unions and by a larger number of American unions; but it has assumed in the United States two further forms. The first, the boycott, or attempt to deprive 'unfair' firms of custom, by persuading dealers to refuse to sell their products and the public to refuse to buy them, was condemned in 1908 in a famous decision by the Supreme Court,[29] and is now, except for small local disputes, of little more than historical interest. The second, the union label, affixed to products made under trade union conditions, continues to be employed by some sixty or more national unions, and is supported by the A.F. of L., which has established a union label department, for the purpose of encouraging a concerted policy among the societies concerned. Such an expedient may attain a measure of success in consumer-goods industries, such as the various branches of the clothing and provision trades; and it is presumably the fact that several of such trades were organized before the heavy industries which explains the attention still given to it. But, as mail-order business supersedes the local market, the attempt to put pressure on consumers becomes increasingly obsolete even in occupations of that type; while, in the industries producing raw materials, capital goods, semi-manufactured products, and the vast mass of commodities which pass through a number of different hands before they reach those of the final consumer, the policy of diverting orders, instead of, or in addition to, withdrawing workers, is obviously futile. If tolerable conditions of employment are to be established in these industries, the only possible method is a collective agreement between the union and the employers, and the only possible sanction for the observance of the agreement is a concerted stoppage of work.

d. Collective Bargaining

Collective bargaining with a view to the establishment of minimum standards of wages, hours, and conditions of employment, is everywhere the foundation of trade union policy. Of the struggle to establish that right in the United States, and of the bitter resistance to its recognition offered by American employers, something has already been said. The rapid progress of trade unionism in the last few years, the changes in industry now taking place under the impact of the war, and the small degree to which American employers are themselves organized, make it impossible to determine with accuracy how far collective bargaining is at present in operation. According to a recent article by Miss Florence Peterson, of the Bureau of Labor Statistics of the Department of Labor,[30] the proportion of workers covered by collective agreements at the end of 1941 was 55 per cent in mining. manufacturing, building and construction work, and transport; less than 10 per cent in wholesale and retail trade, personal service, clerical, technical and professional occupations; and 30 per cent in the country as a whole. The objection felt by important groups of employers to negotiating with unions is by no means dead; but the growing shortage of workers caused by the expansion of the munitions industries, the desire to avoid stoppages of work in war-time, and the pressure exercised by the War Labor Board, have combined to place Labour in a strong position. A long list of important firms was organized for the first time in the latter half of 1941, and that process did not cease on December 31st. It is probable, therefore, that the figure of workers employed under collective agreements is substantially higher today than it was at the end of last year, and that it will further increase during the continuance of the war.

The technique of negotiation is much the same in all countries; but the agreements which emerge from it in America differ in three important respects from their British analogies. The first is a matter of the geographical area covered, the second of the number of firms which are parties to them, the third of the provisions and content of the agreements themselves. Even—to deal with the first point—in a small country like Great Britain, local negotiations, in the case of trades like building, which have strong local attachments, were for long the rule; and the reluctance of the mine-owners to deal on wage questions with the Miners' Federation, instead of, or in addition to, the County Associations, was one factor in the bitter struggles which distracted the British coal industry in the twenties. America is less a country than a continent. Its climate and resources vary widely from region to region; while contrasts of natural conditions are crossed and complicated by the racial and social divergences between north and south. In such circumstances to make a collective agreement covering the whole of an industry throughout the whole of the United States—applying to the shipyards of the West as well as of the East, to the textile mills both of North Carolina and of New England—is obviously, whatever allowance may be made in its terms for local differences, a problem whose solution is by no means easy. The difficulty appears, nevertheless, to be less formidable in practice than it looks on paper, and to be on the way to be overcome. The Central Officials of a Union, who have negotiated an agreement in one area, naturally attempt, in negotiating one in another, to exclude divergences which are not clearly necessary. A union, again, may require, as does the United Automobile Workers Union, that any agreement made by one of its regional directors shall be submitted to it for ratification, and may refuse to sanction more than a limited variation between the wage-rates of different areas. On the whole, it appears that the effect of organization has favoured, as would be expected, a larger measure of standardization.

The second peculiarity of collective bargaining in the United States is less familiar and more important. It is a matter of the procedure by which agreements are negotiated. The foreign observer, accustomed to arrangements under which an agreement reached by half a dozen to a dozen representatives on each side of a table is applied almost automatically to hundreds or thousands of businesses, employing anything up to half a million or more workers, discovers with surprise that the establishment by conciliation boards of rules governing whole industries is, in America, not the general practice, but the exception. The British and American versions of trade unionism have often been contrasted; but it is not always remembered that the difference between British and American employers is at least equally great. The explanation of the paucity of comprehensive agreements accepted by all or most firms in an industry is one of the features of American industrial life whose explanation must be sought less on workers' than on the employers' side.

Several types of employers' associations exist in the United States. They include some, like the Store Founders National Defence Association, the American Newspaper Publishers' Association, certain organizations of mine-owners and clothing manufacturers, and a good many local associations of building contractors, which negotiate with Organized Labour in the same manner as do employers' associations in Britain. But in a large number of industries, including some of those today most important, such as the production of iron and steel, and the manufacture of machinery, including automobiles, nothing of the kind appears to exist. The majority of employers' associations, from the Associated Employers and Local Chambers of Commerce in a long list of towns to the National Association of Manufacturers, with its three thousand odd members, do not appear to include the conduct of negotiations with trade unions among their multifarious activities; and some of them might fairly be described, at any rate till recently, as union-smashing societies. To the difficulties arising from the backwardness of organization among employers must be added those due to the size of the country, and to the fact that, in a number of industries, trade unionism, on any large scale, is still a parvenu.

In such circumstances a union may look forward, as many of the younger and more active societies do, to the day when it will deal with the representatives of a whole industry, and regard anything short of that as merely a transitional arrangement. For the time being, however, it must play to the score, and, even when it can speak for the great majority of workers in an industry, must proceed on more tentative lines. It has to do its collective bargaining piece-meal, by persuading or coercing individual firms into making agreements with it one by one. The gigantic scale of some American corporations, employing, as certain of them do, fifty, a hundred thousand, or even two hundred thousand wage-earners, makes that course seem the more natural, since the sinner who repents is a large one, and the joy in the union proportionately great. A society may begin by securing recognition and an agreement at one plant, go on to secure the acceptance of the same conditions by other plants owned by the same firm in other parts of the country, and then attack, in the same succession of stages, plants belonging to other firms; or, alternatively, it may make a series of agreements with all the plants belonging to different firms in the same industry in one area, and, starting from that base, proceed to conquer new regions. In either case, it has to eat the onion leaf by leaf, and win its victories, not by negotiating an agreement which binds, once accepted, all, or most, firms in an industry, but step by step. As a consequence, a large union may find it necessary, since there is no representative body with which it can deal, to make as many as a thousand different contracts with individual corporations. The disadvantages of that procedure, in the shape of waste of time and defective standardization, are only too obvious. They are partially, but not more than partially, mitigated by the facts that, when one great firm is brought into line, the smaller fry tend to follow its example, and that the union, once it has secured certain master agreements, naturally relies on them as precedents in negotiating with other firms. Most organizations, therefore, regard it as an unwelcome necessity, forced upon them by the fact that trade unionism in America is still struggling for recognition. They look forward to the day when, as in Great Britain, agreements will be negotiated between representatives acting for the majority of employers and workers throughout whole industries.

e. The 'Closed Shop' question

The majority of provisions laid down in American collective agreements differ little, if at all, from those contained in the corresponding British documents. Standard rates, a normal working day, regulations designed to promote health and safety, to secure that union representatives have free access to the management, to provide for a prompt consideration of grievances, and to establish a procedure for the settlement of disputes, appear, in much the same form, in both. There is one range of topics, however, where American unions display a sensitiveness, and act with a pertinacity, which, as far as the particular issues in question are concerned, have no parallel in Great Britain. It is what, for lack of a better term, may be called the sphere of job control. Questions of seniority, of promotion, of pecuniary compensation for dismissal, are included in it, and some unions have succeeded in securing agreements which contain provisions on these subjects of an explicitness unknown in Great Britain; but the central issue is more far-reaching. It is that described by the phrase 'the closed shop'.

The struggle between the champions of 'the open shop' and 'the closed shop' has occupied, in recent years, a larger share of public attention than any other aspect of the Labour question. It has produced numerous disputes, has given rise to bitter controversy in the Press, has come before all the public bodies which deal with industrial matters, and has developed into a symbol of the conflict between the old régime, under which employers ignored or fought Organized Labour, and the new order which confers on the wage-earners the legal right to bargain with employers through the representatives of their own choice. The expressions themselves are not free from ambiguity. Both the open shop and the closed shop may be of several different kinds. Down, at any rate to 1937, when the Wagner Act, making the victimization of trade unionists a punishable offence, was confirmed by the Supreme Court, some employers appear to have interpreted an open shop policy as precluding the presence of any member of a union among their employees, in which case the 'open shop' meant a shop closed to trade unionists. Others understand by it an arrangement under which the preference is given to non-unionists, but trade unionists are not debarred from employment, provided that they remain in a minority and observe a discreet reticence. Others, again, regard an open shop as one in which trade unionists and non-unionists work side by side, without notice being taken of an individual's membership or non-membership of a union. The last interpretation appears to be the only logical one; but the policy suggested by it is a counsel of perfection, and it is probable that the firms consistently adhering to it have been a small minority.

The forms which 'the closed shop' can assume are equally diverse. Its mildest version involves, not only the recognition of the union, but an agreement that trade unionists shall be the first to be taken on and the last to be discharged, and that non-unionists shall be employed only when trade unionists are not available. Its most drastic interpretation requires the employer to engage only workers who are already members of a union, and, as a safeguard for the observance of that rule, to hire men only through the union office. The form of the policy most generally in force is one intermediate between these two extremes. It leaves the employer free to engage such men, whether trade unionists or non-unionists, as he pleases, but requires that men so engaged must join the union, usually after a short probationary period. This arrangement is most properly to be described, not as a closed shop, but as a union shop. It is normally accompanied by two further provisions. The first is a maintenance of membership clause, providing that all employees shall not only join the union, but continue to remain members of it during their period of employment in the shop, or sometimes, particularly in the case of war-work, till the completion of a given contract. The second is a clause providing for a 'check-off', or collection of union dues by the firm and the payment of them to the union.

A recent investigation[31] shows that practice in this matter varies widely from industry to industry and from firm to firm. At the end of 1941, either union shop or closed shop agreements were the rule in coal-mining, building, road-transport, and in the organized sections of the clothing, printing, baking, brewing, and restaurant industries, and transport services in towns, as well as in half the organized shipyards of the country, and half the machine-shops and foundries. They were fairly common in textiles, rubber, and electrical equipment; few in the manufacture of aluminium, chemicals, farm equipment, aircraft, and automobiles; and almost non-existent in the basic steel industry. In one or other of its versions, however, the policy in question is one of the dominant conceptions of American trade unionism. It is not a novel device, but has a history stretching far back into the early days of the Movement. The National Labor Relations Act gave it a new opportunity, of which full advantage has been taken; and it has recently been estimated[32] that today approximately 4,000,000 employees work under closed shop agreements. The forces which, during the war, favour the extension of organization, favour also the acquisition by unions of a strong bargaining position, in which they can successfully press their demands. It must be expected, therefore, that the union shop or closed shop will become the rule in industries where, at present, they are the exception.

To the visitor unfamiliar with the peculiar conditions of industrial life in the United States, the controversies aroused by this question seem, at first sight, surprising. To ensure that every worker in a trade or industry belongs to the union is obviously one of the objectives of all unions in all countries; and in a considerable number of industries in Great Britain as well as on the Continent of Europe and in certain of the British Dominions, something not far short of that ideal has, at different times, been achieved. In their case, however, though the 'check-off' is sometimes practised, stipulations in agreements that all workers in a given firm must be members of a union are, if they exist at all, the exception. In well-organized trades, like coal-mining, or cotton-spinning, or boiler-making, trade unionism, in normal times, is virtually compulsory, in the sense that no one not a member of the union can secure or attain employment. But it no more occurs to the powerful organizations concerned formally to bind employers to act as their agents than it does to have recourse to the legal devices by which trade unionism is in some countries made obligatory for the professions of law and medicine. Their contempt for the individual who shares advantages for which he refuses to pay is at least as strong as that of trade unionists in the United States. They deal with him, however, themselves, by refusing to work with him, by social pressure, which in districts mainly dependent on one industry, is a formidable force, and, in extreme cases, by a stoppage of work.

The reasons for the contrast in this matter between British and American trade unionism throws an instructive light on the obstacles which the latter has still to overcome. In all the major British industries, the question of recognition, which was once a burning issue, is now dead. Employers fight unions on particular issues; but they negotiate with them as a matter of course; do not attempt, except in the case of individual firms in some rural areas and country towns, to prevent or undermine trade unionism by victimizing workers who join the Movement; and, in not a few industries, would readily admit that the result of destroying labour organizations would be a state of anarchy, from which the reputable firm would be the first to suffer, since it would be undersold by its less scrupulous competitors. In the past, when trade unionism was not accepted, British Labour was too weak to enforce a union shop in the American sense, and had no legislative aid to assist it in doing so. Today, when trade unionism is generally accepted, it has no need for formal agreements compelling firms to employ only trade unionists.

In the United States the situation was, and still remains, widely different. The best comment on the attitude of many American employers is the fact that it should have been necessary to pass an Act expressly penalizing, not only the refusal of employers to bargain collectively with unions, but interference with, restraint of, or coercion of employees; domination of, and interference with, labour organizations, whether by way of financial contributions or otherwise; discrimination against trade unionists in the matter of employment; and the dismissal of workers for filing charges or giving testimony under the Act. It was only as a result of that legislation that firms which, for a generation or more, had refused work to trade unionists found themselves reluctantly obliged to deal with trade unions. Some of them still resent as an outrage the legal compulsion which has made it necessary for them to do so. Such firms, even though they comply with the Act, confine themselves, in some cases, to the bare minimum of their legal obligations, express surprise that workers should continue to pay union dues once a collective agreement has been obtained, and let it be known that they regard the power recently won by trade unions as a passing evil, which will retreat as quickly as it advanced, and will leave them once more masters of the situation.

American unions are naturally well aware of that attitude, which till recently was a common one. They know, once their vigilance is relaxed, what consequences it will produce. They are only too conscious that a post-war economic crisis or a change of Administration may result in giving anti-union animosities their opportunity. They take, therefore, their precautions. The union shop or closed shop is one of them. It is primarily a defensive device, designed to prevent the destruction or undermining of trade unionism by hostile employers. The criticisms of it as necessarily monopolistic rest on a misconception. It is perfectly true, of course, that a union which both closes its ranks by charging exorbitant admission fees and insists, at the same time, that none but its own members shall be employed is imposing on the public. What is objectionable, however, in such a procedure, is not the union shop, but the limitation of entrance into the union. Provided that a union admits new members on reasonable terms, there is nothing anti-social in its insistence that those who practise the profession shall be members of the professional association. The anti-union shop campaign is aiming, in short, at the wrong target. If its purpose is not merely to find a stick with which to beat trade unionism, but to promote a genuine reform, it ought to concentrate attention, not on the union shop, but on the removal of barriers unnecessarily obstructing the entrance of workers into unions.

IV The American Labour Movement: Interpretation and Comments

American Trade Unionism resembles American education. It conforms to no fixed standards, and combines in one movement a good not far short of the best attained in other countries with a bad below their worst. The societies composing it range from responsible and well-conducted organizations to rings of monopolists, still capable on rare occasions, of practices faintly reminiscent of those of the Ku-Klux-Klan and the Standard Oil Company. Among its leaders, statesmen, of whom any country might be proud, rub elbows with adventurers, bosses and gangsters, as well as—a commoner type—with fourth-rate businessmen tinged with a dash of all three. Indiscriminate eulogies and sweeping denunciations, whether Pegler's Penny-Dreadfuls or the pomposities of the *New York Times,* alike miss the mark. The truth is that the American Labour Movement is of a piece with the rest of American life. The realization that the wage-earners' sole safeguard against oppression is to organise a common front has been, as elsewhere, the main driving force; but the frontier mentality, agrarian populism, the lawlessness of Big Business, the religion of technological progress, the ingenious tricks of Wall Street—not to mention traditions imported by immigrants from older civilizations—have all left their mark on it. In view of its ingredients, it is not surprising that it should be a mixed grill. Attempts to interpret it which ignore its environment resemble those works on Russian Communism which have discovered everything about it except that it is Russian. Any truthful account of Organized Labour in the United States must be a speckled picture.

(i) The End of an Era

The questions which matter most are too large for a brief

answer. They are what is the real strength of the American Labour Movement, and in what direction, if it grows, will its weight be cast. Was the impressive trade union revival of the thirties a transitory episode which the war has prolonged, but will die down on the return of peace? Or does it mean that the change in the balance of social forces which has followed the Industrial Revolution in most parts of Europe is now occurring in the United States, and that, in the latter as in the former, the role of Labour in public life will be of increasing importance? The progress of Trade Unionism in the last decade has been too general and too continuous to be lightly dismissed. Judged in terms of human values, it is not a small thing that the percentage of American wage-earners belonging to unions should have more that trebled in ten years; that, in a long list of industries, collective agreements should have replaced autocracy; and that Governments should find it necessary to defer to the spokesmen of Labour as well as of Business. It is true that organization was greatly assisted by the action of the State, which, for the first time, supplied Labour with firm legal foundations on which to build. It is also true, however, that both the policy of the Goverment and the increased power of Labour were responses to strains produced by profound changes in the structure of American society, of which neither was fully conscious, but which impelled both in the same direction. It was not a case of the Administration pampering Labour, or of Labour coercing the Administration. Both had to adapt themselves to a new situation.

In a not distant past, a bad Goverment in the United States was less potent for mischief than in any great State. There was an immense margin for manoeuvre and abundant wealth to waste; while, as long as resources in relation to population still seemed almost inexhaustible, the first thought of the individual dissatisfied with his lot was to pitch his tent in some happier corner of the Promised Land, and to seek a remedy for his grievances, not in organization or legislative reforms, but in flight. That age ended in the nineties, when—after an acreage about eight times that of England and Wales had been distributed gratis in the course of half a century—free land at last gave out, and the frontier ceased to move; but its radiance lingered. The children of the pioneers were slow to realize that the vast circle had at last been closed. The lure of a west beyond the west remained a magnet to their imaginations at a time when the point where the rainbow ends was well on the way to its latest sanctuary in Hollywood.

The social movements of the thirties were a sign that the legend, as well as the reality, was dead. The legislation of the New Deal meant that, in an urban and industrial civilization, the functions of the Federal Government could not, without grave danger to the general welfare, be confined to those conferred on it, not without much shaking of heads, by the Founding Fathers. The startling emergence of Organized Labour as a force with which governments henceforward must reckon was equally a response to the challenge of a changed environment and a new era. It was a proof that common men had at last grasped the truth that, whatever the opportunities to rise, there cannot, in the nature of things, be room for everyone at the top; were discarding the optical illusion that what is possible for each is possible for all or for the great majority; and were learning to interpret democracy as incompatible, not only with political, but with economic, tyranny. The legislation will undergo, no doubt, many modifications, and the Labour Movement will have its ups and downs. But the pressure which produced them will grow in intensity. Both may be expected to grow with it.

(ii) The Contrast between American and European Trade Unionism

The position now attained by Organized Labour in the United States properly causes it to be judged by standards more exacting than those of the past. How far does it satisfy them? The American Labour Movement is at present exclusively a Trade Union Movement; and between American and European Trade Unionism there is one fundamental contrast, which is not necessarily a reflection on either, but an appreciation of which is the condition of grasping the peculiarities of both. Trade Unionism in Great Britain, which in this respect is typical, has always possessed, not one function, but two. On the one hand, it has consisted of a body of professional associations, whose members combine for mutual protection against the downward thrust of competition, and employ experts to arrange the conditions of their work and sell their labour for them, for much the same reason as a property-owner sells a home through an agent, because the latter can obtain better terms for him than he could secure for himself. On the other hand, trade unionism has been, not merely a device for the advancement of professional interests, but a social movement, focusing the aspirations of men and women outside, as well as inside, its own ranks, and providing an organ through which they can find expression. In their first capacity, unions of wage-earners display much the same characteristics as are found in other professional organizations, such as those of medicine and the law. They are practical, business-like, conservative, intent on small gains, tenaciously attached to established customs and practices, suspicious of innovations which appear to threaten the vested interests of their members. In their second aspect, they have been one of the principal channels through which the mass of the wage-earning population has absorbed new conceptions of political expediency, and formulated its own. It is primarily as bodies concerned to establish and safeguard the right of professional association that trade unions have been the object of Parliamentary legislation. It is because, in addition, they have performed the function of serving as vehicles of ideas and instruments of agitation, that all the larger movements of the last century and a half, from the conservatism of the expiring gild tradition, to Parliamentary reform, Owenite syndicalism, the struggle for Free Trade, and—more recently—the various versions of Socialism, have left their mark upon them.

The relative prominence of each of these two elements in British trade unionism has differed at different times. Both, however, are always present in it, and both have been recognized by Parliament. The peculiarity of the American Labour Movement—a peculiarity not imposed by the law, but springing from the conditions in which it developed and the character of the environment in which it has to function—is that the second aspect of the British Movement was till recently almost wholly absent from it. During the greater part of its history, it has represented, almost exclusively, not the wage-earners' discontent with the social order created by the profit-making enterprise of businessmen, but their determination to secure a larger share of its advantages by applying, for their own benefit, the methods characteristic of the world of business.

The reasons for the contrast are partly historical. When, in Europe, the Industrial Revolution was carrying all before it, many of the small masters and craftsmen whose lives it revolutionized already possessed a long tradition of organization. Their first reaction was conservative. They denounced the new order as an outrage on habits of social solidarity embodied in voluntary associations and legal codes descending from an earlier age. In America, there was no similar collision of standards, for the past supplied no criterion to which to appeal. Industrial capitalism came, in most parts of it, not as a parvenu, but as a pioneer. It had no medieval past to bury; no hoary iniquities of feudal land-law to wind up; no servile population to exploit, emancipate, and then exploit again. It did not require to reconstruct established institutions; it need only build its own, and build them on a site unencumbered by the ruined edifices of earlier architects. In most industrial regions west of the Alleghenies, the town did not precede the factory; the factory made the town. To the mobile and individualistic population which poured into both, industrial capitalism was not one type of civilization, but civilization itself. It is not surprising that their social outlook should have differed little, if at all, from that of the entrepreneurs which many of them could aspire, with good hope, to become.

Those conditions and that mentality did not only retard the development of a Labour Movement; they gave it, when it developed, a special stamp. Their influence was reinforced by the circumstances surrounding the birth of the only body representing American Trade Unionism as a whole which showed, down to 1935, a capacity to survive. The United States had been traversed in the seventies by a romantic mass-movement, preaching salvation through a vaguely formulated co-operation, of a kind somewhat similar to that which, in the eighteen-thirties, had swept over England. The sequel in both—in America immediate, in England delayed by the episode of Chartism—was a reaction to the opposite extreme. It was a revolt of the skilled craftsmen, who alone at the time possessed a firm basis for organization, into a practical, realistic and pedestrian trade unionism, bent on exploiting the opportunities offered by expanding trade, and for that purpose on creating stable and business-like societies, securing recognition for them, and elaborating the machinery of collective bargaining with employers. In both countries that phase saw the most important contributions to trade union structure and policy that had yet been made; but, while in England it was followed by the extension of organization to unskilled workers, and by the realization that collective bargaining required to be supplemented by legislative reforms, in the United States it encountered neither external shocks nor intellectual scepticism to throw doubt on its adequacy. In the former, therefore, the new Unionism of the fifties was enlarged and rejuvenated by the newer Unionism of the eighties, and that in the turn by the developments, industrial, social and political, of the next century. In the latter, the gospel of the founders of the American Federation of Labor, which enabled it to outlive the disorderly Utopianism of its rival, was confronted till the thirties by no similar challenge. Even today, in spite of the immense changes of the intervening period, it remains a sacred book, which provides the official theory of, at least, one half of the American Labour Movement, and still influences the whole of it.

The causes which gave it its long lease of life were of more than one kind. Judged by their technological triumphs, by the rapidity of the increase in output per head, and by the rise in the wage-earners' standard of life which that increase made possible, the first two generations of the Great Industry in the United States remain among the most brilliant chapters of economic history that the world has known. It was inevitable that public opinion should be intoxicated by their achievements. The legal foundations on which the structure was raised were a legacy from the heroic age of American history. It was natural that the halo surrounding the Constitution should reflect part of its lustre on the economic order which, as later interpreted by the Courts, it had helped to make possible. Business enterprise created an aristocracy of its own, whose example set a pattern of conduct to be imitated by lesser men. Business came to be regarded, therefore, as not merely a means of livelihood, or a career, but as invested with the sanctity attaching to activities which are conducive to moral edification as well as to material well-being. That temper left its mark on all American institutions, from the avocations of daily life to universities and churches. If Organized Labour had desired to stand against the current, it would have encountered even graver dangers than those which actually beset it. In reality, nothing was further from its thoughts. It swam with the stream, and bowed down in the House of Rimmon, not with reluctance, but with the alacrity of a devotee. Both prudence and conviction led American wage-earners, not to challenge the conceptions of social expediency in favour with the business world, but to emphasize their devotion to them, while asserting their right to use comparable methods for the advancement of their own interests. Thus what in Europe was one important part of the Labour Movement became in the United States the whole of it. Not only was the American Labour Movement, as has already been noted, exclusively a Trade Union Movement, but American Trade Unionism developed—to use the phrase of an American authority—as Business Trade Unionism. It emphasized that Labour was the associate, not the critic, of capital and enterprise, and confined itself to equipping it to secure a larger share in the profits of the partnership.

(iii) 'Business' Trade Unionism

This version of Trade Unionism has lost in recent years the exclusive hold which formerly it possessed, as a result of the rise of organizations less completely committed to it than the older societies, and of the increasing intervention of the State in industry. It remains, however, the standard type of over half the American Trade Union Movement, and indirectly influences the whole of it. The classical example of its effect both on Trade Union structure and on the view taken of the functions of Trade Unionism is given by the American Federation of Labor. In the field of organization it means, in so far as it continues to be consistently applied, that a position of pre-eminence is assigned to the societies of skilled workers, among whom craft traditions are strong, and who, being partially protected against competition by professional qualifications, are easiest to organize; that, while industrial

Unionism is not actually banned, different groups of workers, as they become organized, are, whenever possible, divided up among the appropriate craft unions; and that the control of the Federation rests in the hands of the representatives of the latter. The A.F. of L. guarantees its constituent Unions complete autonomy, to the point of holding that it is precluded from intervening even in the case of notorious scandals, which bring discredit on the whole Movement. The only exception to that principle which it admits is the case of 'dual Unionism', which is absolutely prohibited, and which, if persisted in, may cause the expulsion of the offending organizations, such as actually occurred in the case of the group of societies which took the initiative in preaching industrial unionism. Both the rule and the qualifications strengthen the position of the craft unions. The former means that a union which chooses to stand on its vested interests cannot be overridden; the latter that no new group of workers can organize outside the existing trade union cadre except under threat of outlawry. In practice, the composition of the Executive of the A.F. of L. is such that the control of the Federation by the representatives of craft interests is virtually complete.

The conception of trade union functions characteristic of business unionism is equally distinctive. It leads to a view of the objects of labour organizations which limits them somewhat strictly to professional activities, and which regards collective bargaining, not only as the most important of these activities, but as almost the sole purpose which they can legitimately pursue. That view, it is true, has not been consistently applied; and, here again, the last decade has seen a change. Both the great Federations, as well as the Railway Brotherhoods, have always been compelled to devote close attention to proposals for legislation affecting the right of professional association, and the latter took the initiative in securing federal legislation fixing a maximum working-day for adult men employed on railways. With the hostility to trade unionism still existing among certain groups in Congress, the need for a jealous scrutiny of trade union bills has certainly not diminished; while the new relations established between Labour and the State by the Wagner Act, the Fair Labour Standards Act, and the Social Security measures, impose a growing body of work on all Unions, and particularly, of course, on the federal organizations which together act for most of them. The fact remains, nevertheless, that American trade unionism, and especially its older forms, has inherited a tradition which causes it to concentrate almost its whole attention on the transactions of the labour market, and to dismiss as irrelevant to its objects the institutional framework and the changing currents of economic policy that determine the conditions which the market can be made to offer.

'The American Federation of Labor', writes its President, 'regards private ownership, private enterprise, and private initiative as fixtures within the democratic structure of our Government. The right of workers to organize into free, democratic Trade Unions and bargain collectively, and the right of the owners of property to operate and manage industry are fundamental rights, guaranteed by the organic law of the nation and inherent within our democratic process. We believe that industry is entitled to a fair profit, and workers are entitled to decent, fair wages'.[33] Holding such doctrines, the A.F. of L. is disposed to regard collective bargaining, not as one instrument which Labour must use for the attainment of its ends, but as the sole and all-sufficient instrument. It no longer opposes social legislation, as before the Depression it sometimes did, on the ground that it may compete with Trade Unionism.[34] But it cannot be said to be alert to take the initiative in promoting legislative reforms, or in pressing strenuously for them; and its incursions into politics, which are frequent, are designed less to secure new measures beneficial to the mass of the population than to serve as an insurance for the unimpeded continuance of trade union activities. It views industrial relations as presenting no problems which, given goodwill on both sides, will not yield to negotiations between employers and Unions; rarely looks beyond the trade agreements in which, when successful, such negotiations culminate; shares the horror of its fellow-countrymen for the spectre labelled Radicalism; and observes with a suspicious eye the disposition, not only of the political, but of the industrial, Labour Movements of Europe to stray from the narrow path of trade union orthodoxy into the perilous quicksands of social reconstruction. Thus regarded, the trade union movement represents, not the struggle of the wage-earners for a juster society, but a collection of Labour-kartells, analogous to the marketing and price associations of agriculturists, dealers, and other rings of traders. Its chief and, indeed, almost its only function, is to protect the economic interests of its members by offering them the advantages to be obtained by the orderly marketing of their labour-power.

(iv) The Shadows on the Picture

This type of Trade Unionism has played an important part in the Labour Movements of most countries. Political and economic circumstances have made it specially congenial to the United States. It has genuine successes to its credit, which cannot justly be ignored. It is never possible to determine the precise degree in which the improvement of the wage-earners' standard of life is to be ascribed to organization, as distinct from changes in the economic environment within which organization must work. Granted, however, the unusually favourable conditions created by the rapidity of American economic progress, the high capital equipment per worker, and the economies of mass production made possible by a continent forming the largest free trade market in the world, the fact that organization has enabled particular groups of wage-earners to benefit by them more promptly and extensively than would otherwise have been possible can hardly be disputed. 'Between 1880 and 1930', writes one of the spokesmen of the A.F. of L., 'the Federation enabled wage-earners to reduce the work-week from 63 to 48 hours, adding 15 hours to their leisure time, and increased their wages from 19 cents an hour to 72 cents, which, in buying power in weekly wages, meant an increase from $21·50 to $34·75 per week'. The claim thus advanced is too baldly expressed; but it states part of the truth, and an important part.

Except on the assumption, not now generally accepted by economists, that what one group of workers gains by collective bargaining another necessarily loses, the reality of the contribution which American trade unionism has made to the improvement in the wage-earners' standard of life cannot seriously be contested.

a. Union Racketeering

There are substantial achievements; but there is, unfortunately, another side of the picture. All forms of social organization are subject to perversions, which can be prevented if due precautions are taken, but which unchecked become a menace. What has been called Business Trade Unionism is not an exception to that rule. It may be noted, in the first place, that the existence of the pathological features found here and there in the American Labour Movement is not unconnected with the spirit of undiluted and anti-social commercialism which has permeated some parts of it. The prevalence of 'union-racketeering' has been greatly exaggerated—not always, it would appear, through mere ignorance—by anti-Labour propagandists. If 'racketeering' means the exploitation of a position of power, influence, or strategic advantage in such a way as to enable its practitioners to profit by intimidating, coercing, misleading, or otherwise putting under duress the victims of the transaction, then it is a procedure which exists on an immensely greater scale among corporations possessing partial or complete monopolies, owners of urban land, and not a few speculators and dealers, than in the world of Labour. As far as the Trade Union Movement is concerned, practices of the kind are rarely ascribed to the organizations established by the C.I.O. in the last decade; nor are they general in the rest of the Movement. They appear to occur, however, on a considerable scale among some transport, service, and, in particular, building unions. A union, for example, whose members are engaged in distributing milk, endeavours, with the support of firms already in the business, to put a fresh competitor out of action by using force against him, much as in the past the *Chicago Tribune* kept a rival paper off the street by hiring toughs to beat up the boys engaged in selling it; or an association is organized by a gangster to maintain 'fair' prices, and dues are collected from the firms belonging to it, under the sanction of the destruction of the goods and premises of those who refuse to pay. Certain building unions, in particular, owing to the connexion of their trade with malodorous municipal politics, and the ease with which inflated costs can be passed on to the public, use their power as unscrupulously as is done by a local Council dominated by building contractors, which awards contracts to its friends. In some towns, for example, plumbers and electricians have secured the adoption of building by-laws which make work for their members by insisting on ornamental superfluities. In other cases, a union threatens a strike at critical moments, which is held off as long as 'strike insurance' is paid. It is even alleged that some building firms add the cost of such premiums to their estimates in tendering for contracts.

The classical example of racketeering was that offered by the illicit dealing in liquor which went on—apparently with general approval—during the period of prohibition. It appears that, when that fruitful source of profits dried up, part of the talent till then engaged in the business found a new outlet in the holes and corners of trade unionism, where it became the subject of indignant denunciation by a large body of opinion which formerly had condoned, and sometimes profited by, its proceedings. The petty pilfering alleged to be practised by some union officials—inflated expense accounts, the misuse of union funds for personal purposes, and even the acceptance of bribes from employers—is, doubtless, a rare exception. In so far as it occurs, it is a further example of the misplaced business acumen, of which there is too much, not only in the American Trade Union Movement, but in American politics. An abuse which makes less noise, but which, on a long view, is equally fatal to Labour *morale,* as well as more injurious to the public, is the monopolistic practices of certain societies.

b. Excessive admission fees

An observer who compares the spirit and methods of American and British Trade Unionism can hardly fail to be struck by one general contrast. It consists in the difference between the Movements which arises from the fact that while most elements in the latter have been constantly exposed to the play of the world market, the former, as a whole has not been compelled to take that factor into account. The cotton operatives, the engineers and shipbuilders, the coal-miners, have all in turn been the leaders of British Trade Unionism, and have left their stamp upon it. All of them are engaged in exporting industries which are exposed to keen foreign competition. All of them, therefore, have been compelled to recognize that they work within the limits of a world economic system, and that, however strenuously their organizations may fight to secure for their members the best possible terms, they cannot afford to throw their aegis over methods which load industry with unnecessary charges merely because such methods are hallowed by tradition. It is only in comparatively recent years that the United States has become a great exporter of manufactured goods, and the majority of American Unions have not felt the pressure of a similar check. While, for example, the British Cotton Trade Conciliation Committee has before it, at every meeting, facts and figures showing the progress of Japanese competition in China and India, the tendency of American Unions is to think exclusively in terms of the home market. The British trade unionist is inclined to ask what the industry can afford to pay, and sometimes even takes an unduly conservative view of its possibilities. The American trade unionist is apt to consider what the trade can be made to bear.

Abuses of a monopolistic kind are, therefore, easier for American unions than they are for British. They are specially tempting, of course, in trades working for a local market, three of which,—building, transport, and the service unions—accounted in 1940 for 60 per cent of the A.F. of L. membership. The opinion is sometimes expressed that all unions are, of their very nature, monopolies; but that view is an error. The requirement that all workers in a given occupation shall be members of their appropriate professional association, and shall observe its rules, does not in itself confer on them a monopoly, provided that those rules allow of the admission to the society of new members on reasonable terms. The word 'reasonable' is, of course, ambiguous; but it has been used as a criterion by English courts for well over four centuries. In the sense of conduct which a fair-minded man would regard as equitable, it has proved to be sufficiently specific to meet the requirements of practical life.

It must be confessed that, judged by that standard, the practices of some American unions—or, more commonly, of some branches of some unions—seem, at best, somewhat questionable. Cases are alleged to have occurred of opposition being offered to new processes, such as the prefabrication of houses, and a ban on a cheap form of entertainment has recently been imposed by the powerful Federation of Musicians on the ground that the market for the services of its members will thereby be restricted; but a more important question is that of the payments required as a condition of admission to membership of the union, which in a well-organized industry is a condition of practising the trade. The new army of workers demanded by the war has aroused public interest in the subject, and allegations of exorbitant 'initiation' fees have been freely made, particularly in connexion with the building trades. Since, in the trades in question, the fees appear usually to be determined by the 'locals' (i.e. branches) of the unions concerned, subject, in some cases, to minima and maxima fixed by the central authority, they show wide variations from place to place. No comprehensive statistics appear to be available;[35] but while it is denied by the spokesmen of the unions that exorbitant fees are common, it seems to be true that they are not unknown, particularly in connexion with new works of construction for war purposes. It is pointed out, by way of defence, that some scales of fees were fixed in the last period of severe unemployment, when it was desirable to restrict the entrance to the trade, and have remained unaltered since then; while the temporary character of the war boom makes it intelligible that unions should hestitate to admit a flood of new members who, in ordinary times, will not find work in the industry. These considerations are pleas in mitigation, but they are hardly more. Demands for an initiation fee of $100, or alternatively of the payment of $1 a day till that total is paid off, from new workers taken on to build military hutments, or of $100 to $150 from persons desiring membership in certain locals of the Painters Union, are, no doubt, a rare exception; but they represent abuses which ought not to occur, and which in so far as they do, bring Trade Unionism into disrepute. The fact that the Building and Construction Trades Department of the A.F. of L., and the National authorities of certain important unions, have recently made suggestions[36] for keeping initiation fees down to a reasonable figure is an admission both that monopolistic practices are not a mere charge trumped up by the enemies of trade unionism and that they are indefensible. It ought, in fairness, to be added that in this matter, as in some others, the building trade unions are a special case. To infer from the scandals arising in connexion with some of them the prevalence of similar malpractices in the majority of societies would be highly misleading.

Morbid extravagances of the kind described receive no countenance from reputable trade union leaders, though the sanctity attached by the A.F. of L. to the right of its constituent unions to complete autonomy, as well as the fact that the building trade unions accounted, as recently as 1940, for one quarter of its membership, makes it difficult for it to put them down. If, however, the *raison d'être* of Labour Organizations is to secure for their members, by hook or by crook, the maximum of immediate economic advantages which the law allows, it is not easy to see how perversions of this order can logically be denounced. It is one of the defects of Business Trade Unionism that, in fostering an aggressively commercial spirit, it precludes an appeal to the social criteria—common decency, justice, the rights of men, the general good—in which Labour Movements less steeped in the capitalist mentality have found an ally, and thus ultimately undermines trade unionism itself. Obviously unions exist to promote the economic welfare of the wage-earners; but if economic self-interest is the only bond recognized by their members, why should any individual continue to adhere to his society at the moments, which inevitably occur, when loyalty to it ceases to be immediately profitable? Why should not every worker abandon his mates and curry favour with his employers, and every official be on the look-out to obtain a more remunerative post in the service of a business firm, which firms that have difficulties with unions are ready enough to offer? In practice, of course, since human nature is better than the theories made about it, these results occur only in rare instances. But, in that case, why weaken the case for trade unionism by emphasizing a conception of it which not only leads to occasional impositions on the public, but injures the cause of Organized Labour by opening the door to the traitor or the *arriviste,* and which the conduct of ordinary men shows that they do not accept?

c. The Trade Union Boss

Two problems which arise on a different and more important plane, though they raise larger issues, are not unconnected with this excessive emphasis on the business side of trade unionism. They relate respectively to the government of unions and to certain aspects of union policy. Trade Unionism in Great Britain, and, indeed, in most parts of Europe, with the possible exception of pre-Hitler Germany, has been a democratic movement, in practice as well as in theory. Not only are the governing bodies of unions elected, at frequent intervals, by the whole membership, often after keen contests, but the public opinion of the rank and file is a powerful force. Trade Union officials live in a blaze of publicity, and often under a continuous stream of criticism. Annual Conferences are regularly held, at which their administration of the affairs of their societies is scrutinized, and policies formulated. In some societies, for example, the Miners' Federation, no decision is taken in moments of emergency, without the consent of a specially convened delegate conference, composed of men many of whom were working the previous day in the pit or at the bench. Whatever, in short, the defects of the industrial side of the British Labour Movement, a disposition to ignore, override, or jockey with the union membership is certainly not among them. Officials may be, and are, denounced as conservative, bureaucratic, weak-kneed, and—occasionally—as demagogues; but their bitterest critics rarely attack them as autocrats.

In Great Britain these conditions are so much a matter of course as to pass virtually unnoticed. In the United States the constitutional forms are, as a rule, much the same; but they appear somewhat frequently especially in the older sections of the movement, not to work in the same way or to produce the same results. Nothing is more surprising to a visitor, accustomed to regard America as the classical land of democracy, than to encounter in some American unions, including some of the largest and most powerful, methods of government which, whatever their merits, cannot, by any stretch of imagination, be described as democratic. He is told again and again, in reply to inquiries as to this trade union policy or that, that it represents the views, not of the membership, who may not even have been consulted on the subject, but of a small group of officials, or even of a single individual. There are many unions, doubtless, to which such a statement does not apply; but the tendency of American Trade Unionism to succumb to some variety of autocracy—concealed or open, mild or ruthless—is unquestionable.

Autocracy, where it exists, begins on the lower rungs of the Movement, and extends, in ever-expanding dimensions, to the summit. As in Great Britain, branch officers are mostly unpaid, and the official hierarchy starts with the District Officers. The District Official known as a business agent or walking delegate forms the first species of a portentous genus. Appointed and paid by the local organization, he develops, when the climate is congenial, from a servant into a master, not only concentrating in his hands the whole business of the society, from the admission of new members to the supplying of firms with workers, and the negotiation of agreements with them, but using his power as a trade union leader to confer and receive such favours as the bartering, in return for a consideration, of the trade union vote to his political friends, or the allocation of public work to contractors approved by him. What these small fry do on a humble scale is done by the Leviathans on a stage embracing large areas of the United States.

Mr. Lewis, the most dramatic figure in modern American trade unionism, is one example. The absolute Master of the United Mine Workers, the officers of twenty-three out of whose thirty-one districts are appointed and paid by him, with a powerful machine at his disposal which is held together by the rewards, in the shape of jobs which he can offer and penalties he can impose, he is a political, as well as an industrial force of the first magnitude. He not only frightens politicians—a timid race—but can attempt, with some hope of success, to change the whole policy of the American Trade Union Movement, by threatening this group with his displeasure or promising the support of his legions to that. Mr Hutcheson, of the Carpenters, has not Mr Lewis's gifts as a *prima donna;* but, in his own less sensational manner, he is hardly less despotic. He contrived to conduct the affairs of his union for the nine years before 1931 without holding an Annual Convention or submitting accounts to the scrutiny of his membership. A less well-known paladin, the head of the Building Service Employees Union, is said to have cast Mr

Hutcheson altogether in the shade by dispensing with an annual Convention for close on thirty years. He has now been removed by imprisonment from the scene of his labours, but the leaders of several other organizations, though their operations are on a less grandiose scale, seem to enjoy an almost equal measure of irresponsibility, with an equally surprising acquiescence on the part of the societies of whom nominally they are the servants. Nor is the Executive of the A.F. of L. itself wholly free from symptoms of the same disease. No one would question the constitutional propriety and financial rectitude of its proceedings; but an observer imbued with a prejudice in favour of representative bodies representing something other than themselves may be pardoned if he feels a slight uneasiness when he scans its personnel. Of the thirteen Vice-Presidents, who with the President and Secretary-Treasurer, compose it, nine are presidents of national or international unions; two former presidents; one a vice-president; and one a secretary-treasurer, the majority being elderly men who are re-elected to the position year after year. It is natural that the central authority of a Federal organization should be composed of well-known leaders of its constituent bodies. In so far, however, as those leaders themselves hold their positions in their own unions by methods the reverse of democratic, the government of the Federation itself is necessarily tainted at the source. It runs the risk, in that case, of degenerating into an oligarchy of venerable notabilities, who owe their seats on it to the docility, whether natural or induced, of their respective societies.

The reasons which have made the political boss an American institution need not here be discussed. The trade union autocrat is a particular case of a general tendency, affecting, in different degrees, more than one department of American life. The factors which favour his growth vary in different unions, but the predisposing conditions are not difficult to state. The vast distances which separate the head offices of some societies from many of the members whom they serve; the difficulty of concerted action when branches in one part of the country have few opportunities of learning the views on union policy held by those in another; the racial heterogeneity of the personnel of some industries, which makes it easy to dominate;

the novelty of trade unionism itself, and the inexperience of organized action prevalent in parts of the Movement, combine with apathy, ignorance and a low standard of political education to make many American unions more malleable constituencies than are those of Western Europe. They create a situation in which a corporate consciousness does not easily develop, and democracy, as a working reality, either fails to be born or dies of inanition.

Its absence creates a vacuum. The forcible, cunning or unscrupulous adventurer, with some gifts of personality, takes advantage of it. He becomes a boss, not so much because he is the 'strong man' of romantic journalists, but because the forces which, in other countries, would defeat his ambition, are in America feeble. He reveals his capacity for his vocation by realizing the possibilities of that weakness more quickly than his more conventional neighbours, and by trading upon it. Power, once acquired, is subject to the law of increasing returns. Its possessor holds the initiative; and the conditions which made it difficult to win make it easy to retain, since they become obstacles hampering any opposition which may seek to challenge it. The trade union boss governs, like other autocrats, by rewards and penalties. He has on his side patronage, which in a large union, employing numerous paid officers, is an asset not to be sneezed at. He has trusty henchmen planted out in every district of the society, who nip criticism in the bud. He controls the union funds, with the result that districts which are known to have voted against him may be refused strike pay. He has at his disposal the whole apparatus of publicity, including the union journal, the columns of which he can close to malcontents. He can arrange the business of the Annual Convention, can influence the selection of delegates attending it, can pack committees appointed to consider resolutions, can make it difficult for opposition speakers to get a hearing, can occasionally—a last resort—have them silenced by force. Revolts against the machine periodically occur; but, in such circumstances they are difficult to organize, and unlikely to succeed.

Such considerations throw some light on the methods of the trade union autocrat. They do not explain why American trade unionists acquiesce in autocracy. One factor of some importance in a minority of cases has been the success of some unions in establishing a form of 'job-control' under which the union, not merely has a guarantee that no non-unionist will be taken on while any of its members are unemployed, but also determines the particular individuals whom an employer shall engage. Under such an arrangement, the worker depends for his chances of employment on the trade union official, and the latter, as a consequence, has a strong hold upon him. Another, and more significant, reason for the set towards autocracy is to be found in the industrial disorders of the days before the Wagner Act. The rule of the boss is a pathological phenomenon. It emerged because some of the conditions of American industrial life were themselves pathological. The government of voluntary associations, like that of States, is profoundly influenced by war. Till recently, trade unionism in the United States had to fight for its existence. Systematically persecuted by employers, and half outlawed by the Courts, it had recourse, with the consent of its members, to a high degree of centralization, because the centralization of power was the condition of survival. Thus the dictatorship of management was countered by tolerating dictatorial methods in the leaders appointed to mobilize resistance to intolerable conditions. Once adopted, that expedient has continued in existence, when the conditions which produced it are on the way to disappear.

That is part of the truth. The rise of Mr Lewis is a case in point. The Mine Workers were long terrorized by their employers, aided, in some coalfields, by armed ruffians put at the disposal of the mine-owners by public authorities. Mr Lewis led the miners out of bondage. In making them a power, he became one himself and having earned his great authority as a leader, has abused it as a despot. But there is a deeper and more constant cause for the recurrent relapse of great unions into the morass of boss government. It is to be found in the psychology of American wage-earners. The British worker expects his union to secure him economic advantages but his relation to it is not adequately expressed in terms of a cash nexus. He is not a child to open his mouth and shut his eyes, and accept such plums as his officers are good enough to offer him. At lowest, he requires to be satisfied that the affairs of his society are conducted with reasonable efficiency; that its funds, which are his, are not squandered; that the officials whom he employs do not feather their own nests; and that its policy is decided, not by some distant potentate, but by representatives whom, if he pleases, he takes part in choosing. At best, his union is to him the symbol of a cause—the emancipation of the workers—and, as such, commands, not only the formal adherence of self-interested egotism, but his loyalty, his self-sacrifice, and his pride. Trade Unionists in whom such sentiments are a dominant motive are, no doubt, a minority; but no one can have seen British trade unionism from within, without realizing that it is men of that stamp who are the backbone of the Movement. Both for practical and idealistic reasons, therefore, the government of British trade unions, though sometimes inefficient, is rarely, if ever, despotic. It does not occur to their officials to set up in business as bosses. If they made the attempt, their members, who include men not unversed in public affairs, would soon bring them to book.

It would be unjust to suggest that qualities of the kind described are not found in abundance among American trade unionists. It would probably be agreed, however, that the dominant note of the older and more conservative sections of the Movement has been of a more utilitarian kind. Nor, in the circumstances of American life, is that a matter for surprise. Trade Union cohesiveness remains weak when wage-earners believe that they can secure as individuals all that organization can give, and become strong in proportion as they acquire the conviction that they must rise as a class, or not at all. American society was for long more fluid and elastic than any to be found in Europe. The American worker in many industries has suffered cruelly from his employers; but he has not the same memories of class oppression as have given solidarity to his European brethren. He has larger opportunities of movement, both horizontal and vertical. If dissatisfied with his position he finds it easier to abandon it for one more congenial; and, even when prevented from doing so himself, he has felt a stronger assurance that a more attractive way of life will be open to his children. Most important, perhaps, of all, he lives in a society where practical success, measured in pecuniary terms, is idolized with an adoration even more naïve and less discriminating—if such a thing is possible—than that prevalent in Great Britain. His attitude to Trade Unionism takes its colour from these conditions. It not infrequently resembles the calculating prudence of a shareholder in a corporation rather than the solidarity uniting the partners in a society which commands the allegiance of its members in good times and bad. What he asks of his officers is that they should deliver the goods. If they fail, he is indignant, and, in extreme cases, secedes, when secession is possible. If they pay on the nail, in the shape of higher wages, shorter hours, and better working conditions, he is not shocked by their indifference to the constitutional formalities of conventions and adults. Business trade unionism suits him; he is himself a businessman. Being a businessman, he prefers a boss who pays dividends to the most democratic of directorates which defaults on its obligations.

d. The tendency to Petrifaction

The second problem calling for notice is one which, though not more important, has aroused more attention. No subject connected with Labour has been more constantly before the public during the last decade than that of inter-union conflicts. The elements composing the trade union movement are, in all countries, diverse; and in America that diversity is greater than elsewhere. The occurrence of friction between them is not, therefore, surprising. What has turned it in the United States into something more serious than demarcation disputes or struggles over jurisdiction is the existence, behind the particular occasions of controversy, of unsettled questions of principle. It is the connexion, actual or supposed, of these recurrent struggles with certain major issues of trade union structure and policy. One part of the Movement represents one type of mentality and organization; another part a different one. Each is apt to feel, when trouble begins, that, not only an issue of practical detail, but creeds and systems, are at stake.

The historical background of these conditions has already been indicated. In America, as in Europe, the pioneers of trade unionism were, not the new class of factory operatives created by the Industrial Revolution, but the skilled workers in the old-fashioned handicrafts. Masons, carpenters, bricklayers, shoemakers, tailors, compositors, were partially sheltered by their professional qualifications against the edge of competition. That fact, combined with their higher earnings, somewhat greater leisure, and, in some cases, a tradition of organization, made it easier for them to combine than it was for poorly-paid and sometimes casually-employed labourers and women workers. It was workers of that type, therefore, together with the rapidly growing army of mechanics and artisans produced by machine industry, who formed the first unions, and who, when a national movement developed, supplied it with its leaders. It was they who were least in sympathy with the wholesale evangelization of the Knights of Labor, and who, when a stable Federation was formed in 1886, became its backbone, imparting to it their own outlook and determining its policy. The outlook was that natural in a body of professional men, acutely conscious of their superiority to the mass of common labour, and bent on defending their vested interests as craftsmen, not only against their employers, but also from the encroachments of what seemed to them a mob. The policy, which became that of the A.F. of L., with its insistence—now much weakened—that the only, or almost the only, proper form of trade unionism was one which conformed to the divisions between crafts, and that new categories of workers must be fitted, as they became organized, into that cadre, was equally inevitable. Industry, in the meantime, was going its own way. Not only did the value of factory production approximately double between 1899 and 1903, and then increase more than threefold in the twenty years which ended in 1929, but the technique of manufacture underwent in many industries, far-reaching changes. Repetition-work, mass-production, and in some cases, the use of novel materials, though they did not supersede the craftsman, turned him from the typical mechanic into a specialist confined to certain processes and stages of the productive process; and created an army of workers on machines to whom 'skill', in the traditional sense of the word, was no longer essential. Trade Unionism, like other institutions, is a means, not an end. If it is to be a vital and popular movement, it must play to the score, and be as mobile and elastic as the practical realities which it exists to meet. The crucial question of industrial politics from 1920 to 1935—though no one, till almost the end of that period, appears to have realized it—was whether and by what means, the readjustments needed should be made.

The problem was one not confined to the United States. In Germany, where, owing to the extreme rapidity with which industry was modernized, it had been relatively unimportant, it had been solved by brigading all trade unionists, skilled and unskilled alike, into some fifty great organizations, with provision for the special representation of craft interests within them. In Great Britain, where a long-drawn-out Industrial Revolution had advanced by successive stages, the difficulty had been more serious. The able group of men who led the trade union revival of the fifties to the seventies had tended, as in the circumstances was natural, to regard the skilled workers as alone capable of organization, and to think of trade unionism in terms of societies composed of craftsmen who had served an apprenticeship, paying substantial benefits, and requiring contributions from their members on a scale beyond the means of less well paid sections of labour. When, in the eighties, the question of organizing the unskilled came to the front, the attitude of some of these older leaders, if not actually hostile, was at best, one of indifference. But British trade union organization was—as it remains—plastic. No sanction by a central authority was required before a new union could be formed; and provided that such a union did not lay claim to a field already effectively occupied by an existing organization, there was nothing to prevent it, once established, from affiliating to the Trades Union Congress, or from being represented on the General Council of that body. Among the skilled workers themselves the spirit of craft exclusiveness was less strong than it appears to be in the United States. Not only was it realized that a mass of unorganized workers is of necessity a perpetual danger to those already organized, but the Labour Movement was a cause in which all could join, irrespective of their occupations, not an association for the protection of the vested interests of a minority.

When, therefore, the dock strike of 1889 launched the first great campaign for the organization of unskilled workers, it was led by two members of the Amalgamated Society of Engineers,[37] supported by the Trades Union Congress, and financed by contributions from unions of skilled workers in every corner of the country. The question, which has caused so much trouble in the United States—how the unskilled and semi-skilled factory-workers are to be absorbed into the Trade Union Movement without prejudice to the other craft unions—has been answered in Great Britain, not in one way, but in several. There are industrial unions, such as those of the Miners, the Railwaymen, and the Transport Workers. There are societies, like the Amalgamated Engineering Union, which for long refused to admit unskilled men, but have since welcomed them, and made special provision for them in their constitutions. There are unions composed almost entirely of labourers. Finally, there are what may be called residual unions, such as the Union of General and Municipal Workers, which includes both skilled and unskilled workers of several different occupations. It is not a tidy system, and there is much needless over-lapping; but it works reasonably well. Disagreements between unions, arising from rival claims to organize some particular category of workers, from time to time occur; but they are not frequent, and are rarely serious. They are normally settled by negotiation between the officers of the societies concerned, or, failing that, by reference to the Trades Union Congress.

In the United States matters have gone a different way. In place of the gradual extension of trade unionism to the rapidly growing body of mass-production workers, there was a long period of stagnation, during which they were almost ignored; then an intensive campaign to organize them in industrial unions; and, finally, a rupture between the new societies so formed and the older sections of the Movement. The standing debate on the respective merits of craft and industrial unionism largely misses the mark. Each has its proper sphere. The choice between them in any particular case, is a matter, not for officials armed with a formula, but for the workers themselves, who have as much right to reject one type of trade unionism in favour of another as they have to decline to be coerced into a company union invented by their employer. Given no very exacting degree of tolerance, it is perfectly possible, as the example of other countries shows, for societies of both kinds to live together in one Movement.

That appears, as has already been explained, to have been the arrangement originally contemplated by the group of trade union leaders who launched in 1935 the movement to organize mass-production workers. It was not their intention either to interfere with existing craft unions or to prevent the formation of new ones, still less to secede from the A.F. of L. They proposed merely to enrol workers hitherto unorganized in unions of a type which those workers themselves were led by the nature of their occupations to desire. The reasons for the opposition of the A.F. of L. to that course have been discussed above, and it is not necessary here to reopen the controversy. It should be noted, however, that an objection to the principle of industrial unionism does not seem to have been among them. Over 30 of the 106 societies included in the A.F. of L. in 1932 were industrial unions, though some of them were extremely small ones; and the resolution passed by the A.F. of L. Convention, when the question of organizing mass-production workers was first brought before it, gave a qualified sanction to industrial unionism as the form of organizations most likely to be successful. It was only later that the Executive put its foot down, and persuaded a subsequent Convention to follow its lead. The truth appears to be that both the sentiments and the interests of powerful groups in the Federation prevented them from recognizing that a situation had arisen which could not be handled by the traditional expedients, and from employing the new methods required to deal with it.

The nemesis of all bodies which yield to the temptation of exclusiveness is a tendency to petrifaction. American trade unionism, on the eve of the depression, was not immune to that disease. It showed disquieting symptoms of arrested development. The rapid industrial expansion of the twenties might have been expected to offer an unusually favourable opportunity for a militant trade unionism. The A.F. of L., as the statistics of its membership during those critical years show, completely failed to seize it. It is always less difficult to secure advances of wages for the minority of skilled workers in a firm or industry than for the whole number; and it is all the easier where it is possible to assure the employers concerned that, if the minority are satisfied, no one will trouble them about the remainder. It was natural that a body composed predominantly of craft unions, governed by an executive consisting almost exclusively of officers of craft unions, and thinking of trade unionism in terms less of a national movement concerned to bring a fuller life to all than of the vested interests of particular societies, should be more anxious to hold the ground already won than to attempt, in face of the hostility of employers and the public, to conquer new territory. It was the more natural, because an expedient characteristic of American trade unionism surrounded those interests with barbed-wire entanglements unknown in other countries.

Reference has already been made to the system of 'chartering' unions by which the A.F. of L.[38] confers on the societies so favoured exclusive rights of jurisdiction over the workers in a given trade. Its intention was the laudable one of preventing unnecessary overlapping between unions and the dispute arising therefrom. In practice, its consequences have been more far-reaching. Since a charter confers profitable rights on its holders, it creates a powerful pecuniary interest against change and in favour of maintaining the trade union structure at any moment existing. The organization inherited from the past may have been rendered half-obsolete by industrial changes, a particular society may make no appeal to a large body of workers desiring to be organized, or may be discredited by grave abuses. Once, however, a charter has been granted, the established order becomes sacred until the charter is withdrawn. In such circumstances the weight on the side of the *status quo* is overwhelming. The official of the Union concerned can say bluntly 'these men are mine'; he has even been known to use the language of the stock market, and to remind a government official that his union possesses, in the right to organize a particular body of workers, an 'equity' which must be respected. Such pretensions sound—and are—absurd; but it is difficult to challenge them. If the workers in question join another existing union, or establish a new one, both they and the organization concerned are guilty of the crime of 'dual unionism' with the result that the latter, unless it mends its ways, may be expelled from the Federation. The

Federation itself cannot intervene to put pressure on an obstructive society, for to do so would be to infringe the principle of 'Union autonomy'.

The more mischievous consequences of a position so anomalous are often, no doubt, avoided by good feeling and common sense. It is difficult, however, to resist the conclusion that, in so far as the full logic of the charter system is applied in practice, it can, at best, hardly fail to cause an excessive rigidity in trade union organization, which makes it difficult for it to keep pace with the changing facts of industry. At worst, it appears to be a device for ensuring that the present is governed by the past, that the interests of the great mass of workers are subordinated to those of a privileged minority, and that trade unionism becomes senile before it is middle-aged. Here again, the subservience of part of the Movement to conceptions which have their origin in Business is not without its responsibility. The mentality fostered by them is at home in the world of profitable rights, lucrative franchises, and established expectations. It applies these exhilarating categories to labour with a tranquil unconsciousness of any possible incongruity.

(v) The New Unionism

The New Unionism of the thirties has already been described. In view of its origin—of the nature of the industries attacked and of the determination of the workers concerned to be organized *en bloc,* or not at all—it was inevitably in the main, of the industrial type. Room might, even so, have been found for the new organizations with the A.F. of L.; and that, as has been stated, was the first intention of the leaders of the new Movement. The attitude finally adopted, after an interval of hesitation, by the A.F. of L.—the attitude of an Established Church to heretical sects—made that course impossible. Since the workers in the mass-production plants declined to comply with the requirement that they should be divided up among a dozen or more different craft societies, the choice was between organizing them in industrial unions and not organizing them at all. The final result, after an interval of inconclusive negotiations, was the formation of a new and independent Federation. Dual unionism has always been banned by the A.F. of L. By a paradox which has analogies in the sphere both of political and ecclesiastical history, dual unionism was made inevitable by the measures taken to prevent it.

The disadvantages arising from the existence of two Federal bodies, each claiming the allegiance of the trade union movement were, and remain, grave. The extension of trade unionism to a body of workers hitherto almost wholly without protection against exploitation was, however, an immense step forward. The mere increase in the number of organized workers in the United States was in itself impressive. Since the C.I.O. includes a considerable number of unions[39] existing before it was established, not all the 5,000,000 odd members of the societies belonging to it represent a net addition to trade union strength; but well over two thirds of that figure consists of new recruits who have joined the movement since 1935, and many of whom would, but for the C.I.O., have not been associated with it. Even more significant than the rise in the number of trade unionists has been the conquest by trade unionism of departments of economic life which formerly were almost closed to it. The industries most representative of the economy of modern America are the durable-goods industries, in particular iron and steel and machinery, including the manufacture of automobiles, and of electrical apparatus. It was these industries which expanded most rapidly in the generation before the depression. It was these industries in which trade unionism was weakest down to the thirties; in which great firms, like the United States Steel Corporation and the Ford Motor Company, managed their relations with their employees in the manner rather of the rulers of a despotic empire than of mere commonplace businessmen; and in which the organization by employers of terrorist régimes to crush attempts at organization were most habitual, most ruthless and most unashamed. It is these industries[40] in which the version of trade unionism represented by the C.I.O. has won its most sensational successes. Its victories have been the most important landmark in the history of American Labour, since the foundation, nearly sixty years ago, of the A.F. of L. Their significance has extended far beyond the addition they have made to trade union membership and the improvement in wages and working conditions which they have produced. An odious régime of industrial tyranny was in process of being consolidated. In defeating that system in the main citadels of its strength, the new unionism has made, with the aid of the government, a contribution to economic freedom which cannot easily be overestimated.

The virtues and vices of institutions require time to reveal themselves. Of the 34 unions and 8 organizing Committess affiliated in August, 1940, to the Congress of Industrial Organizations,[41] only 7 had a life of as much as twenty years, while over two thirds had existed for less than a decade. It is possible that, as the first enthusiasm of youth fades, this youngest branch of the American Trade Union Movement will develop the same weaknesses as some of its predecessors. If, at present, it appears to be comparatively free from them, the reason is partly the nature of the industries in which its main strength lies; partly its own constitution; partly, also, that its more recent origin has caused it to be less influenced by conceptions inherited from an earlier stage of industrial development. Manufacturing industries catering for a wide market are not sheltered, like the building industries, against the levelling influences of competition, nor do they possess the same capacity as the latter to recoup themselves for an increase in costs at the expense of the consumer. They offer fewer opportunities, therefore, for monopolistic practices, such as the limitation of numbers and excessive initiation fees; nor are such practices easy to enforce in the case of occupations where no system of apprenticeship has ever existed, and where an intelligent recruit, with a few weeks' experience on a machine, can earn as much as the old hand. The large and representative Executive which governs the C.I.O. is favourable neither to the emergence of trade union autocracy, nor to craft exclusiveness; and it appears at present to be true to say that except in the case of the United Mine Workers, whose connexion with the Movement seems to be in process of dissolution, the rule of the boss has not yet found a foothold in any union affiliated to it. Together with the more modern organization which characterizes the C.I.O. has gone a large measure of open-mindedness, a more liberal attitude towards coloured workers, and a greater disposition to grapple with the intellectual problems which industrial policy presents. The proposals made by Mr Murray for the organization of war industries, and particularly of steel—now, it seems, only too much in need of a physician—and those of Mr Reuther relating to the conversion of the automobile industry to war production, may or may not command assent. But the older school of American trade unionists has not been fertile of constructive ideas; and the recognition that trade unionists are concerned, not only with wages and working conditions, but with industrial efficiency, ought obviously to be welcomed. It may fairly be said that the C.I.O. represents a departure, not only from the less desirable practices of business trade unionism, but from its depressing propensity to mental stagnation.

The achievements to the credit of the New Unionism are, therefore, substantial. Vitality, even if it involves internal quarrels, is preferable to organized torpor, and, if the only condition on which the mass-production workers could be organized was the formation of a separate federation, then that price was well worth paying. In view of the history and present position of the C.I.O., some opinions with regard to it held in British Trade Union circles must be dismissed as illusions. It is not true, in the first place, that the C.I.O. is an example of the bugbear of trade unionists everywhere, a 'breakaway' organization. Of the societies now affiliated to it less than one third existed before 1935, when the Committee for Industrial Organization—as the C.I.O. then was—was established; and even those societies did not 'break away' from the A.F. of L., but were—whether properly or not—suspended from membership in it. Not only have two thirds of the C.I.O. Unions been established since that unhappy episode, but well over that proportion of their membership have joined them since that date, and a large—though uncertain—percentage of it would not, in the absence of the C.I.O., have been organized at all. It is not true, in the second place, that the C.I.O. as is sometimes alleged, is 'tainted with Communism'. Some members of C.I.O. Unions are, doubtless, Communists, as also are some members—probably a higher proportion—of unions affiliated to the T.U.C.; but to describe the C.I.O. on that ground as a Communist organization is as absurd as it would be to bring a similar charge against the British Trades Union Congress. Finally, the view that the

C.I.O. is destined to a collapse is a mares' nest born in ignorance. It is accepted by no American Trade Union leader of experience, and least of all by the A.F. of L., which knows only too well the strength of its rival, and which has just given an additional proof of that fact by accepting an invitation to enter into negotiations with it, with a view to arriving, if possible, at some plan for merging the two organizations. The truth is, of course, that the C.I.O. is now a permanent and influential part of American life. It has gained in the last six years a larger accession of membership than has the A.F. of L. and, in spite of its short history, is now of approximately the same numerical strength as the latter. It is treated by the Government of the United States as of equal importance with the A.F. of L., and is accorded the same measure of representation on public bodies. On the whole, it enjoys a somewhat larger degree of public respect, since the societies connected with it have hitherto been comparatively free from the malpractices which have disgraced certain A.F. of L. Unions. It is specially important in the war industries, since the production of steel and machinery are its peculiar stronghold, and Detroit and Pittsburgh are both dominated by it. Thus the refusal of the British Trades Union Congress to enter into official relations with the C.I.O. has been due to misapprehensions, which were excusable in a foreign organization, but which all candid American observers deplore as unfounded. It has had most unfortunate repercussions not only on the C.I.O., but on opinion outside, as well as inside, the American Trade Union Movement. The British T.U.C. has, in fact, unintentionally dealt a gratuitous blow to Anglo-American relations as a whole.

As long, therefore, as the present division within the American Labour Movement exists, the C.I.O. must be recognized to be an organization as representative, as stable, and as influential as the A.F. of L. The fact remains, nevertheless that the existence of two rival Federations, whose relations in the recent past were the reverse of cordial, and, even today, leave a good deal to be desired, is a serious disadvantage to the American Labour Movement. The occasion which it offers for strikes arising from disputes over jurisdictional questions, though much is made of it by the Press, is a minor matter. In reality stoppages due to that cause accounted for less than 7 per cent of the total occurring in 1941;[42] and an uncertain, but substantial, number of those taking place were occasioned by disagreements, not between A.F. of L. and C.I.O. unions, but between rival unions within one or other of the two Federations. The more serious aspect of the rift is its effect in diminishing the moral authority of Labour, *vis-à-vis* the public and the Government. A divided Movement obviously cannot speak with the same weight as one which is known to voice the united demands of Organized Labour as a whole; and the failure of American trade unionism to be accorded adequate representation on the bodies planning the economic side of the war effort is presumably, in part, the result of its internal disharmonies. Nor should the more strictly economic consequences of the feud be overlooked. At present they are not serious, since the demand for workers is such that keenest competition for jobs is temporarily in abeyance. That situation, however, will not last for ever. Unless the quarrel is composed, it is only too likely to result, when the market turns against Labour, in a bitter struggle for work between members of the two organizations, which will profit no one but employers, and which will still further embitter the relations between them.

The case for an early settlement is, therefore, overwhelming. The impression of an observer is that the end of the conflict would certainly be welcomed by the rank and file of both organizations, who, in the provinces, live in amity side by side, and are heartily sick of the power-politics of the capital. Whether the negotiations now beginning with that object will be more successful than those attempted in 1937 and 1939 is another question. It may be doubted whether the rival claims of craft and industrial unionism were ever the real source of the conflict; but, if they were, they are now a dead issue. The A.F. of L. includes at present a considerable number of industrial unions and many of the craft unions belonging to it, which in the past prided themselves on their exclusiveness, now admit semi-unskilled and unskilled workers. The difficulties which remain are serious enough, but they do not arise on that plane. Some of the unions in the two Federations overlap, with the result that there is competition between them for members. Fusion is the obvious course; but it is not easy to merge unions with different scales of contributions, one paying benefits and the other not, or to reconcile the claims of two different sets of officers, some of whom naturally fear that they may be displaced. Such practical problems have arisen in the case of all numerous trade union amalgamations which have been effected in other countries. Experience shows that given a reasonably accommodating spirit, they are not insoluble.

(vi) American Labour and Politics

The political methods employed by Organized Labour in the United States needs no lengthy description. From the foundation of the A.F. of L. down to 1935, proposals to establish a Labour Party were brought at frequent intervals before its Conventions. They were invariably rejected, and the Federation reaffirmed its traditional 'non-partisan' attitude as recently as 1937. The C.I.O. and Railway Brotherhoods have taken no initiative in the matter; and, as far as is known, have not had the subject before them. No National Labour Party, therefore, exists. The American Labor Party of New York is confined to that State, and is largely dependent on the support of the workers in the clothing trades of New York City. A Socialist Party, founded in 1901, still survives; but it has few, if any, contacts with Organized Labour, and its influence is negligible. In addition, a variety of Labor Non-Partisan Leagues, American Labor Leagues, United Labor Committees, and—in parts of rural America—Farm-Labor Parties, have from time to time been active in particular States. Most of them have been *ad hoc* bodies, formed—as several have been in the present year[43]—to secure the return of candidates favourable to Labour at a particular election, and dissolving, or lapsing into torpor, when it is over; but some of them have had a longer life. The American Labor Party of New York, mentioned above, is an offshoot, for example, of an association founded, under the name of Labor Non-Partisan League, in 1936, by the leaders of several large unions (mostly of the C.I.O.) in order to mobilize the Labour vote in support of the re-election of President Roosevelt.

The refusal of American Labour either to establish an independent party or to enter into an alliance with an existing one does not mean, as is sometimes suggested, that Labour is non-political. On the contrary, much of the time of the officers of the A.F. of L., the C.I.O., and the Railway Brotherhoods is spent in dealing with legislative proposals brought before Congress, and in negotiating with public departments on Labour questions, while the duty of the trade unionist to use his vote is emphasized by all of them. The characteristic feature of the traditional policy of the American Labour Movement is its view of the manner in which its political weight can most effectively be used. The orthodox theory of the American Federation of Labor is expressed in the statement that 'the American Labor Movement is not partisan to a political party, it is partisan to a principle'; its traditional practice in the words, 'Stand faithfully by our friends and elect them; oppose our enemies and defeat them'.[44] The Congress of Industrial Organizations, without expressly committing itself to these pronouncements, appears hitherto to have followed the line which they suggest, though, in this year's elections, it shows signs of sitting somewhat loosely to them. It should be noted that the course which they involve is, not abstention from political action, but a procedure analogous to that followed, till recently, in Great Britain by the electorally formidable Co-operative Movement. The American version of that procedure is, however, more highly systematized. The Labour Lobby is commonly regarded as one of the most powerful in Washington, and constant pressure is maintained on Congress by the two great Federations, as well as by the Railway Brotherhoods. The mobilization of the Labour vote in elections is the business of the local Movements—the State Federations and City Centrals of the A.F. of L., the corresponding C.I.O. bodies, and the Railwaymen's Locals. To assist then in deciding which candidates are to be supported and which opposed, the Central Offices of these organizations supply them with information, material for propaganda, and, in particular, an analysis of the voting records of those candidates who have previously been members of either of the two Houses. Thus the essential characteristic of the political methods of the American Labour Movement is a refusal to discriminate between the merits of parties, combined with a discrimination, which attempts to be somewhat searching between the merits of individuals.

The attachment of American Labour to 'non-partisan' politics is an old subject of debate. A somewhat similar line was for long followed by the British Trade Union Movement; and the question is less why the policy was adopted in the United States than why its hold remains unbroken. The difficulties of organizing Labour for effective political action in a country with 49 legislative authorities, and a Congress whose Acts may be vetoed by the President and declared unconstitutional by the Courts, are obvious enough; but the decisive reasons for the traditional hostility of American Trade Unionism to proposals to engage in independent political activity lie in the character of the Movement itself. Till recently engaged in a struggle to exist, and hampered in its movements by the precariousness of its legal position, it was averse from all departures which might divide its ranks. Denounced as un-American, it was fervent in its protestations of ultra-Americanism, and indisposed to risk ventures which might compromise it with the public. Most important of all, the Labour Movement reflected the spirit of a contented and therefore conservative people. In spite of—or because of—the American press, the American working-class public is less interested in politics than the British, and appears to be below the latter in political education. In the poll-tax States, the greater part of it is, of set purpose, discouraged—to use no stronger term—from exercising the franchise; while a recent investigation in certain districts of a Northern State, where trade unionism is strong, revealed the fact that barely one third of the trade unionists had troubled to make sure that their names were on the register. The traditional procedure of the A.F. of L. is the counterpart of that attitude of popular passivity. The methods hitherto employed by it have both advantages and defects. They have been strong to prevent, and weak to compel. Well-organized pressure could make Congress think twice before enacting legislation which, by crippling collective bargaining, would alienate the trade union vote, and could even, on occasion, secure useful measures of reform, such as the Act limiting the hours of railwaymen; but no lobbying, however intensive, would induce it to support large schemes of social reconstruction. Such measures, however, Labour in the United

States has hitherto neither demanded nor desired. Thus it can reply to the critics of its policy by pointing to certain genuine successes of the kind which alone interest it. To the failure of that policy outside them—if it is a failure—it has hitherto been indifferent.

Such an account is truer of the A.F. of L., which till six years ago set the tone of the American Labour Movement, than it is of the C.I.O., which has wider horizons and is animated by a more social spirit. There are signs that the latter is likely in future to take a more positive line. Before that can be done with effect, however, a good deal of intellectual preparation will be required, which remains, as yet, at a somewhat early stage. One effect of the self-denying ordinance which requires that candidates should be judged solely by their record on matters directly affecting Labour has been to prevent it from assuming a position on matters of general policy. Since it has taken no stand on the latter, except in connexion with the present war, it has not been forced to devote attention to them; and its contributions to thought on such topics have so far been somewhat meagre. The A.F. of L. has prepared a useful list of reforms, including a federal Unemployment Insurance scheme, a draft Workmen's Compensation Act, an improved Old Age Pension system, better provision for health and housing, amendments required in the highly important National Labor Relations Act, and similar measures. The C.I.O. in addition to producing an instructive series of pamphlets on kindred topics, has gone somewhat further. Its Executive Board adopted in January 1941, a comprehensive Legislative Programme, setting out the immediate reforms demanded by the Movement; and in December of the prevous year, its President, Mr Murray, laid before the President of the United States a plan for the organization of War Production under a series of Councils for each of the major industries, composed of representatives of management and labour with chairmen appointed by the Government. All this is valuable, as far as it goes, but it falls a good deal short of the prolonged and systematic discussion of economic and political problems which is required if Labour is to make its political weight tell; nor, as far as is known, has any American Labour Organization attempted as yet to deal at length with the subject of post-war reconstruction. If it be asked what is the programme of Labour on the wide range of topics falling under that head, it can only be replied that no programme as yet exists.

The negative attitude towards politics of the American Labour Movement was crystallized in circumstances widely different from those of the present day. It remains outwardly unshaken; but some of the buttresses which supported it have undergone erosion, and it is less obviously in harmony with its environment than it was in the recent past. On the one hand, the legislation of the thirties has established a new relation between industry and the State. The Federal Government, which, even a decade ago, interfered little with economic life, now interferes much. The supersession of the individualism of the past by a constructive social policy necessarily means that the character and outlook of the government have become of vital importance to large sections of the industrial population by whom politics were formerly regarded with indifference. At present, as Labour is well aware, the buffer between it and its enemies is the President. Were that situation to change, were a Congress as hostile to Labour as that of the last two years, instead of being held in check by the Executive, to find an ally in a President of similar views, the results for Labour would be extremely serious. Not only would there be no question of further reforms, but the enforcement of the Fair Labor Standards and Social Security Acts would almost certainly suffer. Most important of all, the administration of the National Labor Relations Act of 1935, to which Trade Unionism owes much, if not most, of its recent accession of strength, would cease to offer the unions the protection which they have so far received from it. It might even, by a mere change in the personnel of the National Labor Relations Board, be turned from their principal defence into a weapon used against them. On the other hand, trade unionists are no longer the feeble folk that once they were. Forming today not much less than one in three of the industrial wage-earners, they are potentially a political, as well as an industrial, power. It is possible that, just as British trade unionists were dragged reluctantly into politics by the Taff Vale judgment, so their American colleagues might be forced to change their course by some similar menace to the survival of Trade Unionism.

The threat, if it is to move them, must be obvious and grave. American Labour is, on the whole, conservative. It is contemptuous of the lessons of foreign experience; believes, with some justice, that the American standard of life is higher than that of other countries, and shares to the full the national habit of thanking God that it is not as other men are. It may be expected, therefore, to cling to its present methods, to which the A.F. of L., in particular, is deeply committed, unless they plainly fail to yield results in connexion with some matter which touches Labour closely. It is not inconceivable that, when the moral of the last ten years has had time to sink in, the traditional 'non-partisan' policy will lose some if its charms. It does not follow, however, that its successor will be a Labour party. It is more likely, in the first instance, to be merely a decision to enlarge the tests by which candidates are tried, and to judge them by their record, not merely on Labour questions, but on matters of general policy. Under the pressure of the present crisis, some steps, whether consciously or not, have already been taken in that direction. When, as has happened in some States, the A.F. of L. and C.I.O. combine to secure the return in the next congressional elections of supporters of the Administration, or when the Illinois C.I.O. declares that the only important votes for electors to consider are those which candidates have cast on war policies; or when, as in Ohio, the C.I.O. attacks an isolationist candidate with a good Labour record on the ground that, if the war is lost, everything is lost for Labour, 'non-partisanship' is obviously wearing pretty thin.

(vii) American Labour and the War

These departures have been caused by the war; and the attitude of American Labour to the war has already been touched on in a separate memorandum.[45] It may be sufficient here, therefore, to describe it summarily by saying that, while certain important minority groups, such as Irish Trade Unionists, Catholics opposed to co-operation with Russia, Mr Lewis and his followers, and a miscellaneous, but not inconsiderable, body of Britain-haters, remain isolationist, the great mass of Labour sentiment is on the side of the Administration's policy, and favours an energetic prosecution of the war. The various strands of opinion within the Labour Movement are, in short, much the same as in the rest of the population. Like them, it did not slowly make up its mind that it was a duty to fight, but was pitched into war overnight, without any previous mental conversion, by events beyond its control. Like them, it has not been required as yet to submit to serious sacrifices; is more ignorant of the practical realities of war than a European child; is kept in the dark by the Government, which is afraid—quite unnecessarily—of frightening it; and is disposed, as a consequence, to carp and sneer when things go amiss, since it has no knowledge of the conditions which must be satisfied in order that they may go well. On the whole, however, Labour is more war-minded than most other sections of the American population. For one thing, it is tougher and less sophisticated than a good many of its countrymen. For another, it is producing munitions, and is proud of what it is doing. In the third place it knows that trade unionism has been mercilessly stamped out, not only in Germany, but in all countries occupied by German troops; and has grasped the fact that, whatever else might survive the victory of the Nazis and Japanese, the American Labour Movement certainly would not. In the fourth place, it observes that the groups most opposed to the President's foreign policy include a good many politicians and industrialists who have been among the bitterest opponents of Labour on domestic issues. Officially the A.F. of L., the C.I.O., and the Railway Brotherhoods, who between them account for well over nine tenths of the trade unionists in the country, have committed themselves to a wholehearted co-operation in the war effort. The line taken in the Congressional elections by Labour bodies in different States, as well as the resolutions passed by individual unions, and the attitude of the Labour Press, are evidence that, in this matter, the leaders have behind them the public opinion of the movement.

The support given by trade unionists to the war is not the result of any distinctive outlook on international policy. The discussions of the subject which have long gone on in Labour circles in Great Britain appear, as far as the corresponding groups in America are concerned, hardly to have begun; and the American Labour cupboard is barer of goods of that kind even than of proposals for social reconstruction. In spite of the theoretical internationalism in vogue in certain quarters, the prevalent temper of the great mass of Americans remains a bland, doctrineless, nationalism. It is still dominated by the traditions inherited from a vanished age of economic self-sufficiency; and is unable to believe that the world can have been so carelessly constructed as to be really one; is disposed to regard the United States—in the words of Mr Podsnap—as 'blessed by Providence to the direct exclusion of such other countries as there may happen to be' and is nervously apprehensive of the dangers of contamination by too close an association with less virtuous continents. Thus, while rejecting isolationism as a practical policy, it retains its isolationist premises. It reconciles its theory with its present practice by regarding the latter as a temporary concession, made by way of exception, to unpleasant necessities.

That mentality is not uncommon in the Labour Movement, though exceptional individuals and groups rise above it. The classical example of the reactions which it produces in particular cases is given by the attitude of the A.F of L. towards the Soviet Union. The A.F. of L. is officially represented on the I.L.O., and is also a member of the International Federation of Trade Unions. It ought, therefore, to possess some experience of international contacts. But the assembly of patriarchal potentates who compose the Executive of the Federation are a curious mixture of toughness and timidity. At the thought of the establishment of closer relations between Russian and American Labour, the toughness is shed like a garment, and the timidity becomes panic. The reasons for their hysteria are of more than one kind. The leaders of the Federation are terrified of publicity, and live with their eyes glued on the Press. Convinced by past experience that Russia is a compromising acquaintance, they make haste to anticipate criticism by denouncing her themselves. Their pose is Americanism; Bolshevism offers a foil by contrast with which more effectively to display the full lustre of their own unsullied purity. They have had trouble with Communists in their unions, and fear, if they appear to weaken, a revival of it. To some of them, Russian vices, which have supplied them with material for oratory for a quarter of a century, have become a vested interest that they are reluctant to surrender. Behind these utilitarian motives lies, however, something at once more absurd and more respectable. It is a genuine mysticism. Belonging themselves to a Movement which is deeply imbued with the moral and intellectual traditions of the most *bourgeois* of nations, these children of American capitalism start back in genuine horror when they encounter a spectre which appears to challenge the first principles of their faith and the very essence of their being. To one acquainted with the temperament and doctrines of the Executive of the A.F. of L., its summary rejection of the invitation of the British Trades Union Congress to be associated with it on the Anglo-Soviet Committee was not far short of a foregone conclusion.

The C.I.O. presents a different picture. Its leaders have no love for Communism, which, as usual, was for a time a disruptive force within some C.I.O. Unions. But they took the line that it was the business of the constituent societies to choose representatives whom they could trust, and declined to conduct a witch-hunt. The degree of influence on the Trade Union Movement exercised by Communists varies from time to time, and cannot be stated with precision. The present position appears to be that several of the smaller C.I.O. unions, for example the Fur and Leather Workers, whose membership is largely composed of foreign immigrants, and the Federation of Architects, Engineers, Chemists and Technicians, composed largely of intellectuals, are probably controlled by Communists, but that only two of the larger societies—the Electrical, Radio and Machine Workers and the Maritime Union of America—can be said to be in that position, and that, in Unions embracing well over four fifths of the C.I.O. membership, Communist influence, if it ever was serious, is now negligible. A more important question is the attitude of the C.I.O. to co-operation between the United States and other nations, on which the American Labour Movement is increasingly called to express an opinion. On that matter, the C.I.O. has shown a tolerance and receptivity markedly in contrast with the inhibitions that cramp the A.F. of L. As is natural in a younger organization, which has its future still before it, it is not afflicted by the intellectual arterio-sclerosis of its older rival. The men who direct its policy are internationally-minded, are fully aware of the importance of the establishment of cordial relations between the Labour Movements of the Allied Nations, and look forward to the participation of American Labour in the negotiations following the war. So far from being shocked at the thought of co-operating with Russia, the C.I.O. were only too anxious to be officially associated with the Anglo-Soviet Committee. Its National Executive Council is desirous, indeed, of going further. It recently carried a resolution authorizing its officers 'to take steps towards securing closer co-operation and unity of action between the organized workers of America, including the A.F. of L. and the Railway Brotherhoods, and the Trade Unions of the United Nations'.

Such a state of mind is not too common in any section of American society. It is all the more regrettable, therefore, that the representatives of British Trade Unionism, instead of welcoming the co-operation which the C.I.O. was eager to offer, should have gone out of their way to snub a large and influential section of American Labour, whose position as the Federation including the most powerful unions concerned with the munitions industries makes it of peculiar importance to the Allied war effort. The result of the attitude of the T.U.C. has been not only to lower the prestige, which formerly stood high, of the British Labour Movement, but to cause the relations between British and American Labour to be worse than at any time in the last decade. Nor is that all. What appears to Americans to be the uninvited assumption by the T.U.C. of the role of a partisan intervening in a domestic quarrel is resented by many of them, irrespective of their own opinions of the dispute, as a gratuitous impertinence. Thus a matter which began as a question of trade union politics threatens to end by injuring Anglo-American relations as a whole.

The issue which is the occasion of the troubles is the claim of the C.I.O. to be recognized as the Federation representing one large body of American Trade Unionists, and the refusal of the British Trades Union Congress to accord it recognition, or, indeed, to have official contacts of any kind with it. The historical ground for the British attitude is that the T.U.C. had relations with the A.F. of L. before the C.I.O. existed; the practical reason that when the matter was last raised with the

A.F. of L., on the occasion of the visit to Washington in May, 1942, of the Secretary of the British T.U.C., the A.F. of L. let it be known that it would regard any official approach by the British to the C.I.O. as an unfriendly act. Neither of these difficulties would have been insuperable, however, had not the British T.U.C. been the victim of deep-seated misconceptions as to the American Trade Union Movement of the kind already indicated, which well-informed Americans ridicule as long out of date, but which it has proved hitherto impossible to dispel. Had it adopted a more realistic attitude, it might have earned American gratitude by helping the two rivals to reach an understanding. As it is, it has alienated the C.I.O., which is not unnaturally embittered at what it regards as deliberate and repeated slights, and has not won the affection of the A.F. of L., which feels no gratitude to the British for still further complicating a delicate situation.

Unless the relations between British and American Labour are further to deterioriate, a way must be found out of the present impasse. The proper course is for the T.U.C. to attempt to repair the mischief, which, quite unintentionally, it has caused. The first step required is that it should recognize the plain fact that the C.I.O. is of equal standing and influence with the A.F. of L.; that it should refrain from inflicting needless slights upon it; that its representatives, when in the U.S.A., should show the President and other officers of the C.I.O. the same cordiality as is shown to the A.F. of L.; and that it should encourage British Trade Union leaders to accept invitations to speak, broadcast, and send friendly greetings to C.I.O. unions instead of, as recently, discouraging them from doing so. Once friendly relations have been established with the C.I.O., the obvious next step is for the T.U.C. to inform the A.F. of L. that British Labour desires to be on good terms with all sections of the American Labour Movement, and to suggest that the A.F. of L. and C.I.O. shall use the opportunity given by their approaching negotiations to discuss with each other, and with the Railway Brotherhoods, how best the American representation on the Anglo-American Trade Union Committee can be so arranged as to secure that result. If the T.U.C. makes it clear that it is not asking whether it *should* be friendly with the C.I.O., but that it is already friendly with it, and wishes that the Committee should include C.I.O. representatives, the A.F. of L. will think twice before meeting such a proposal with a blank refusal. It knows that the course suggested is in line with the wishes of the United States Government, and it will incur considerable odium if it is intransigent. Even, however, should the A.F. of L. be recalcitrant, the attempt would have been well worth while. The British T.U.C. is at present in a false position *vis-à-vis* both American Labour and the American public. By endeavouring to act as a friend of both parties, it would recover some of the influence which it has recently lost.

The nationalist temper of considerable sections of American Labour, and particularly of the A.F of L., is not unlikely to be a source of embarrassment when the war concludes. Unless previously softened by events, it may mean that, on questions of commercial policy, migration, and international economic collaboration, the influence of the American Labour Movement is exercised against the light. As far as the conduct of the war itself is concerned, both the great Federations have done their best to rise to the occasion and contribute what they can. They undertook not to countenance strikes on war work, and, though a considerable number of unauthorized stoppages have occurred in the United States, as they have in Great Britain, that agreement has been observed. Their failure to play the more constructive part performed by British Labour, however regrettable, cannot fairly be ascribed to them. In Great Britain, the Trade Union Movement does not stand outside the machine responsible for the economic side of the war effort, but has a definite status within it. Trade Unionists sit, not merely as individuals, but in a representative capacity on all the principal bodies concerned, with the result that they have a voice in matters of policy, and that statutory orders affecting industry and labour, before they are issued, are discussed, criticized and, in some cases amended, by the accredited spokesmen of those who will be required to comply with them. The A.F. of L. and C.I.O. are represented, equally with employers, on the War Labor Board, which deals with disputes, or threatened disputes, in war industries, and two representatives from each of them and from the Railway Brotherhoods, form an informal committee consulted by the

President. Labour is also represented on the advisory committee of the Man Power Board, the Labor Division of the War Production Board, and the Office of Price Administration. But the association of the Trade Union Movement with the machinery for mobilizing the economic life of the country for war has, as yet, not been carried so far in the United States as it has been in Great Britain. As far as production questions are concerned, it has hitherto been thought sufficient for some trade unionists to hold posts as government employees in the Departments concerned. In that capacity, they may do valuable work as individuals; but they obviously cannot serve the purpose of enabling Organized Labour to assume its proper share of responsibility for the direction of the war effort.

Exasperation at the manner in which Labour, as is generally believed, has been held at arm's length has long been simmering. It has been heightened by the publicity recently given to the alleged errors of the War Production Board, and led in the latter part of August to the submission to Mr Nelson of proposals for reform agreed upon by representatives of the A.F. of L. and C.I.O. The most important of them were two. It was urged (1) that a Production Planning and Co-ordination Board should be established, on which Organized Labour should be directly represented, with power to plan, co-ordinate and integrate all phases of the war production programme, (2) that joint committees, representing Labour, Management, and the Government should be attached to each of the divisions of the War Labor Board, whose functions it should be to apply the plans made to particular industries. Repeated declarations have been made by leading members of the Administration that the war is a matter of vital importance to the organized workers of America, and repeated exhortations have been addressed to them to play their part in winning it. These recommendations were advanced as representing the view taken by the leaders of the Trade Union Movement of the position which American Labour must occupy if it is to pull its full weight.

It is a matter for satisfaction that they should have been made. In the light of past experience, however, the probability of their acceptance seemed at first somewhat remote. The reason was partly the plausible excuse for rejecting them which is offered by divisions within the Labour Movement, though, as the A.F. of L. and C.I.O. work amicably together on the War Labor Board and on the President's Committee, the force of that argument was not too apparent. It was partly also the fact that the demands made on Labour in America, and the restrictions imposed on it, have hitherto been so much less exacting than those to which Labour in Great Britain has submitted as part of the price of victory that the necessity for machinery to secure consent and co-operation has not yet become so obvious in the former country as it has long been in the latter. The principal explanation, however, lay in a different region. It consisted in the reluctance of American business, supported by the Press, to agree to steps which, by establishing a partnership between the Unions and the State would admit Organized Labour to the position of one of the recognized powers of American society. It appeared probable that in this matter, as in some others, the effective prosecution of the war would be hampered by fear of the situation which might succeed it, and that different groups, in manoeuvring to secure for themselves a position of strategic advantage in the post-war world, would both prolong the conflict and jeopardize its issue, by impeding the deployment of the full strength of the nation.

If the information at present available may be trusted, that anticipation does not seem to have been fulfilled, A formal reply by Mr Nelson to the programme laid before him by the spokesmen of the two Federations has not yet been made public. Such reports of his attitude, however, as have appeared in the Press suggest that if he has not conceded their full demands, he has gone some way to meet them. The changes in contemplation appear to be five, of which three are concerned with the central organization of the War Production Board, and two with its local activities; they are (1) an increase in the number of Vice-Presidents of the Board from two to four, by the addition of two Labour nominees to the two businessmen who at present hold that position; (2) the establishment of Labor Advisory Committees within the War Production Board, to balance the present industry committees; (3) the larger use of the Labour employees at present in the service of the Board, in connexion with the preparation of programmes for the expansion, concentration and curtailment of production; (4) the appointment of a committee of five, composed of two representatives of Labour, two of Management and a chairman, to superintend the campaign for increased production, and, in particular, to direct the activities of the 1,300-odd Labour-Management Committees already established; (5) the appointment of an officer drawn from the ranks of Labour to a post in each regional office of the Committees in question.

Certain of these measures still lay what appears to British eyes an excessive emphasis on the value of appointing public officials who happen previously to have been trade unionists. Such men, on becoming public servants, inevitably and properly, give their duty to the Department employing them the first place in their thoughts, and cease accordingly, whatever their personal merits, to act in a representative capacity. The second and fourth proposals are not, however, open to that criticism. They would, if carried out, enable representatives of Organized Labour to play a responsible part in planning the industrial reorganization which the war demands. The advantage of ensuring that changes intimately affecting the lives of large numbers of men and women are approved, before being enforced, by the spokesmen of those whose co-operation is required to make them effective, should by now be a commonplace. It is a simple case of the magic of democracy. The fact that, after barely nine months of war, the United States Government would have found itself compelled to act on a principle so repugnant to powerful elements in the American business world is not without significance. It is evidence of the reality of the change in the balance of power in American society mentioned earlier in these pages.

NOTES

1. The American Federation of Labor is sometimes said to have been founded in 1881 (e.g. W. Green, *The American Federation of Labor*, p. 5), when a Federation of Trades and Labor Unions of the United States and Canada was established. The latter body, however, was without financial resources, and went out of existence with the foundation of the A.F of L. in 1886.

2. TABLE I
Total Union Membership
1910–1941

	All Unions (in thousands)	A.F. of L. (in thousands)	%	C.I.O. (in thousands)	%	Non-affiliated Unions (in thousands)	%
1910–14	2467·4	1860·8	75			607	24
1915–19	3202·4	2542·6	79			659.2	21
1920	5048	4093	81			955	19
1921	4781	3967	83			814	17
1922	4027	3273	81			754	19
1923	3622	2919	81			703	19
1924	3536	2853	81			683	19
1925	3519	2831	80			688	20
1926	3502	2715	78			787	22
1927	3547	2759	78			788	22
1928	3480	2809	81			671	19
1929	3443	2770	80			673	20
1930	3393	2745	81			648	19
1931	3358	2743	82			615	18
1932	3144	2497	79			647	21
1933	2973	2318	78			655	22
1934	3609	3030	84			579	16
1935	3928	2300	58	1050	27	578	15
1936	4575	2500	56	1500	33	575	13
1937	7159	2861	40	3718	52	580	8
1938	8240	3623	44	3788	46	835	10
1939	8311	4006	48	3700	45	605	7
1940	8642	4375	51	3624	42	643	7
+1941–2	11241	5441	48	5000	44	800	7

+ December, 1941 for Unions affiliated to C.I.O. and non-affiliated Unions, April, 1942, for Unions affiliated to the A.F. of L. The figures for 1941-2 are taken from The Labor Year-Book, 1942 (unpublished). I am indebted to the courtesy of the Bureau of Labor Statistics, United States Department of Labor, for permission to consult it.

The figures down to and including 1940 are taken from C. R. Daugherty, *Labor Problems in American Industry* (5th edn., 1941) p. 405.

3. TABLE II

Union affiliation and membership 1932-42

	Number of Unions			Membership of Unions		
	1932	1940	1941	1932	1940	1941–42+
Unions affiliated to A.F. of L.	106	108	106	2,299,500	4,374,700	5,441,600
Unions affiliated to C.I.O.	—	34	41	—	3,624,000	5,000,000
Non-affiliated Unions	49*	31	No information	782,000	643,000	800,000
Total	155	173	No information	3,081,600	8,641,700	11,241,600

+December, 1941 for Unions affiliated to C.I.O. and non-affiliated Unions, April 30, 1942 for Unions affiliated to A.F. of L.

*Including 10 Unions affiliated to the Communist Trade Union Unity League, the membership of which is not stated.

The figures for 1932 and 1940 are taken from C. R. Daugherty, *Labor Problems in American Industry* (1933 and 1941 editions); those from 1941-2 from The Labor Year Book, 1942 (unpublished).

4. *Monthly Labor Review*, May 1942, p. 1066.

5. TABLE III

Percentage which Trade Unionists formed in certain selected years of all workers in certain major industries

Industry	1910	1920	1930	1940	1940–41
All industry, including agriculture	9	18	9	25	33 (approx.)
All industry, excluding agriculture	10	19	10	27	
Mining	28	40	22	80	
Coal	37	51	33	95	
Metal	15	14	3	50	
Manufacturing (including construction & railway shops)	11	22	12	35	
Transportation	20	40	22	55	
Railroad, steam	28	53	39	60	
Street railways	24	50	58	70	
Road transportation	5	12	6	25	
Water transportation	33	81	30	80	
Communication	9	20	8	15	
Trade and Service	2	5	3	10	

The figures for 1910 to 1940 are taken from C. R. Daugherty, *op. cit.* (1941 ed.), p. 408, Table 32.

6. TABLE IV

Trends of Production, Output, and Unit Labour-cost in Manufacturing Industries[+]
Index Number 1929 = *100*

	Production	Output per wage-earner	Man-hours	Unit Labour Cost
1919	61·0	60·6	58·0	145·4
20	66·6	65·9	64·0	150·3
21	53·5	69·1	69·8	127·9
22	67·7	79·1	76·8	108·6
23	76·9	78·5	75·9	121·2
1924	72·8	80·1	80·6	119·5
25	81·9	87·1	86·0	111·8
26	86·8	90·6	89·0	108·8
27	87·1	92·9	91·7	106·4
28	90·9	96·7	95·9	103·1
1929	100·0	100·0	100·0	100·0
30	85·0	97·6	102·5	95·2
31	72·0	98·0	107·3	85·1
32	54·1	86·7	103·6	70·0
1933	62·8	90·9	109·8	72·1
34	69·6	86·2	114·5	83·8
35	82·8	96·3	120·5	80·9
36	96·7	103·6	121·2	80·2
1937	103·3	101·0	119·6	99·7
38	81·0	94·6	121·8	87·7
39	102·5	108·9	132·4	81·3
40	117·3	115·8	138·8	81·2
*41	152·1	126·4	142·7	88·4

[+]From Labor Year Book, 1942 (unpublished).
*Provisional.

7. TABLE V

Distribution of the Occupied Population among certain major industrial groups

	1910		1920		1930	
	Number	%	Number	%	Number	%
All occupations	38,167,336		41,614,248		48,829,920	
Agriculture	12,388,309	32·5	10,665,812	25·6	10,471,998	21·4
Forestry & fishing	241,806	0·6	270,214	0·6	250,469	0·5
Extraction of minerals	965,189	2·5	1,090,223	2·6	984,323	2·0
Manufacturing & Mechanical Industries	10,656,545	27·9	12,831,879	30·8	14,110,652	28·9
Transport & Communications	2,665,269	7·0	3,096,829	7·4	3,843,147	7·9
Trade	3,633,265	9·5	4,257,684	10·2	6,081,467	12·5
Public Services (not elsewhere classified)	461,442	1·1	738,525	1·2	856,205	1·8
Professional Services	1,711,275	4·5	2,171,251	5·2	3,253,884	6·7
Domestic and Personal Services	3,755,798	9·8	3,379,995	8·1	4,952,451	10·1
Clerical Occupations	1,718,458	4·5	3,111,836	7·5	4,025,324	8·2

*From *Fifteenth Census of the U.S.A. Populations,* Vol. IV, Table 2. Gainful Workers 10 years and over by general divisions of occupations and sex.

8. TABLE VI

The growth of company unions, 1919-32*

	1919	1922	1924	1926	1928	1932
Number of separate companies using employee representation	145	385	421	432	399	313
Number of separate work councils	196	725	814	913	869	767
Number of workers covered by plans	403,765	690,000	1,240,704	1,369,078	1,547,766	1,263,194

The Labour agitation of 1933 and the following years was met by an increase in company unionism. 'By 1934 there were perhaps eight hundred plans covering more than two million workers in most branches of industry'.

*C. R. Daugherty, *op. cit.* p. 643.

9. The Report of the so-called La Follette Committee of the United States Senate Committee on Education and Labor (1936-7) is a mine of information on these aspects of American industrial life. A popular version of much of it is contained in L. Huberman, *The Labor-Spy Racket,* and some information on the same subject will be found in C. R. Daugherty, *op. cit.* pp. 635 seq. So much is said in the Press about individual acts of violence by trade unionists that it is perhaps worth pointing out that large-scale violence is expensive, and that it has for that reason been an employers', not a Labour, device. The only serious cases of violence used on the Labour side arise when employers attempt to intrôduce blacklegs in disputes. In similar circumstances, such incidents occurred in England; and, if they do not occur there now, the reason is that, in well-organized industries, no factory troubles to open during a strike, as the employers know that there will be no blacklegging. Grandiose operations by American employers, on a semi-military scale, were at one time not uncommon. When the writer first visited Washington in 1920, the miners in County Logan (West Virginia) were in trenches; the owners had a corps of snipers and a captive military balloon; and he was informed that, before accepting an invitation to visit the district, he must inform the British Ambassador, in order that his relations might recover his corpse. Incidents of the kind went on down to and including 1937; the campaign of terrorism conducted from 1933 to 1937 by the sheriff, deputies, and mine guards of Harlan County (Kentucky) against the organizers and members (including their families) of the United Mine Workers is a classical example. Those happy days now seem to be over, and American industrial disputes are becoming as dull as any others. Even Ford, whose 'service-men' were beating up trade unionists as recently as 1941 has now capitulated to the Automobile Workers Union. Bennett, the tough whom he hired to organize violence, still remains, however, in his employment.

10. 'Plowshares into Swords', address by Frederick C. Crawford, President, Thompson Products, Inc., Cleveland, in *Proceedings of the Academy of Political Science,* Vol. XIX, No. 4, January 1942, pp. 34, 36-7.

11. A useful collection of documents is contained in *A.F. of L. vs. C.I.O., The Record* (Washington, D.C., 1939). The account of the controversy there given is written from the standpoint of the A.F. of L. *The C.I.O. What it is and How it Came to be* (Washington, D.C., 3rd edn., 1941) tells the story from the point of view of the C.I.O. Daugherty, *op. cit.* pp. 341-6 and 367-70, should also be consulted. A good deal of material throwing light on the quarrel is contained in the reports of the Annual Conventions of the two organizations.

12. *A.F. of L. vs. C.I.O., The Record,* pp. 5-6.

13. *ibid.* pp. 34-5.

14 *ibid.* pp. 6-7.

15. *A.F. of L. vs. C.I.O., The Record,* p. 9.

16. *ibid.* pp. 18-22, and pp. 38-9. The unions suspended were the United Mine-Workers of America, the Amalgamated Clothing Workers of America, the Oil Field, Gas Well and Refinery Workers of America, The International Union of Mine, Mill and Smelter Workers, The International Ladies' Garment Workers' Union, The United Textile Workers of America, The Federation of Flat Glass Workers, The Amalgamated Association of Iron, Steel and Tin Workers. The International Union of United Automobile Workers of America, The United Rubber Workers of America (*ibid.* p. 22).

17. *ibid.* pp. 52-8, and pp. 63-74.

18. *ibid.* pp. 11-13, letter of 2 December 1935, from Mr Chas P. Howard, secretary of the C.I.O., to Mr W. Green, President of the A.F. of L., 'During the years I have been a delegate to Conventions of the American Federation of Labor, I have observed the strongest cohesion in a controlling group for the purpose of determining every question. . . . Much to our regret, some of us have had the conclusion forced upon us that the merits of proposals are not the determining factor in rendering decisions. Proposals having to do with fundamental policies have been adopted or rejected by combination rather than by converting the delegates. It is my earnest belief that a labor organization should be the very last place on this earth where such conditions should be permitted to exist.'

19. *ibid.* p. 6. The exact words are perhaps worth quoting: 'It was principally these great international unions which had brought the American Federation of Labor into existence. When the American Federation of Labor was organized and these unions accepted charters, a contract was entered into between the American Federation of Labor and the national and international unions.

'This contract called for loyalty to the purposes and policies of the American Federation of Labor. In return, the national and international unions were guaranteed two specific things: first, jurisdiction over all workmen doing the work of the specific craft or occupation covered by the organization: secondly, guaranteeing to the national or international unions complete autonomy over all of their internal affairs.

'The American Federation of Labor could not have been organized upon any other basis of relationship between the national and international unions and the Federation. It is recognized that, where a contract is entered into between parties, it cannot be set aside or altered by one party without the consent and approval of the other'.

20. The statistical matter in this chapter is largely taken from the useful book of C. R. Daugherty, *Labor Problems in American Industry,* (1941 edn.). The figures in that work relate to August 1940; and, as already pointed out, a large increase in trade union membership has taken place since that date. It will be realized, therefore, that the figures given in the

text of the present chapter are, in most cases, considerably below those of today, and they are presented here merely because no latter figures for all Unions are available. *The Handbook of Labor Statistics*, issued by the Bureau of Labor Statistics of the United States Department of Labor, 1941 edn. (Washington, 1942), pp. 502-3, gives figures of the membership of unions with 50,000 members or more in 1941 affiliated to the A.F. of L., and of unions 'credited with more than 50,000' affiliated to the C.I.O. in the autumn of 1940. The Handbook explains that the C.I.O. has not published figures of membership since 1938, but that it published the voting strength in its 1940 Convention of its affiliated unions, and that 'this may be taken as an approximation to the membership of its constituent national and international unions'. The figures are as follows:

TABLE VII

A. F. of L. and C.I.O. membership, 1940, 1941

A.F. of L. Affiliated Unions with 50,000 members or more in 1941		*C.I.O. Unions credited with more than 50,000 votes in November, 1940*	
Teamsters, chauffeurs, etc.	408,300	United mine-workers	600,000
Carpenters & joiners	300,000	Steel workers Organizing Committee	535,100
Ladies garment workers	225,000	United automobile workers	412,000
Machinists	221,800	Textile workers union	314,100
Hotel & restaurant employees	214,000	Amalgamated clothing workers	259,831
Electrical workers	201,000	Electrical radio & machine workers	206,824
Hod carriers & common labourers	183,700	Cannery, agricultural, packing & allied workers	123,250
Railway clerks	110,000	Packinghouse workers Organizing Committee	90,000
Painters	104,900	Transport workers union	90,000
Musicians	100,000	Retail, wholesale employees	80,000
Retail clerks	85,400	Mine, mill & smelter workers	70,000
Meat-cutters & butchers' workmen	84,900	Fur & leather workers union	60,563
Bakery & confectionery workers	84,400	Rubber workers of America	55,406
Street-railway employees	80,700	United shoe workers	53,627
Operating engineers	80,000	Construction workers Organizing Committee	52,940
Building service employees	70,000	State, county & municipal workers	52,904
Maintenance of Way employees	65,700	National Maritime Union	52,000
Bricklayers, masons & plasterers	65,000		
Railway carmen	65,000		
Longshoremen	61,500		
Letter-carriers	60,000		
Bridge & structural ironworkers	52,000		

21. For two of these, the Industrial Workers of the World and the Workers Alliance of America, no figures are available.

22. The membership of the A.F. of L. in August 1940, is put by Daugherty at 4,374,700 *(op. cit.,* p. 351). The figure for January 1942, is given as 4,800,000 for dues-paying members, plus 500,000 for members not on a dues-paying basis (*Monthly Labor Review,* May 1942, p. 1066).

23. The A.F of L. is represented on the I.F.T.U. and I.L.O. It also supplies the American members of the recently established Anglo-American Trade Union Committee. Owing to its youth, the C.I.O., which is probably more international in outlook than the A.F. of L., has not yet secured representation on these international bodies.

24. The corresponding figures for August 1941, given by The Labor Year-Book (unpublished) were 106 National and International Unions, 1,440 Local Trade and Federal Labour Unions; 49 State Federations, and 800 City Central Bodies.

25. The membership of the C.I.O. in August 1940, is put at 3,624,000 (Daugherty, *op. cit.* p. 355), and in October 1941 at 5,000,000 *(Monthly Labor Review,* May 1942, p. 1066.)

26. The corresponding figures given by The Labor Year Book, 1942, (unpublished) for October 1941, are 41 National or International Unions and 9 Organizing Committees, and 236 Local Industrial Union Councils.

27. Report of Executive Council of A.F. of L., October 1941, pp. 143-52.

28. Sumner H. Slichter, *Union Policies and Industrial Management,* 1941, p. 29.

29. Loew *v.* Landlor, 1908.

30. *Monthly Labor Review,* May 1942, pp. 1066-1070. A more recent work, *How Collective Bargaining Works* (Twentieth Century Fund, 1942) puts the figure at approximately 25 per cent of all American wage and salary workers.

31. *Monthly Labor Review,* May 1942, pp. 1069-70.

32. *ibid.*

33. *Labor and National Defence,* by William Green, President, A.F. of L., April 1941.

34. The A.F. of L. for long opposed both old age pensions and unemployment insurance. It was only in 1927 that it became converted to the former, and only in 1932 that it began to support a State unemployment insurance act.

35. *We Work for the Future,* by William Green, President of the A.F. of L. (Pub. A.F. of L., 1941), gives the following figures of initiation fees charged by certain A.F. of L. unions:

TABLE VIII
Initiation fees charged by certain A.F. of L. Unions

	Rules of National Body as to Fees		Fees fixed by Locals	
	Minimum	Maximum	Minimum	Maximum
	$	$	$	$
Hod carriers, building & common labourers	*5	*50	No information	
Painters	5	not fixed	5 to	50
Brick & clay workers	1·50	not fixed	2 to	5
Teamsters	2	not fixed	No information	
Photo-engravers		None stated	25 to	200
Electrical workers				
(1) Construction locals		None stated	class A Locals	10-200
			class B Locals	1·50-150
(2) Electrical utility locals		None stated		10-75
(3) Railroad locals		None stated		10-25
(4) Manufacturing locals		None stated		2-60
(5) Radio locals		None stated		10-100
(6) Telephone & telegraph locals		None stated		50

*See note 36.

It is impossible to say where, within the limits given, the majority of fees fall. It will be observed, however, (1) that only one of the above societies is stated to fix a maximum initiation fee by its national rules, (2) that the fees charged by locals run, in some cases, up to a somewhat high figure.

36. W. Green, *op. cit.* pp. 26-46, and App. B. The following letter (*ibid.* pp. 28-9) of 5 December 1940, from the President of the International Hod Carriers, Building and Common Laborers Union of America to the officers and members of its local unions shows the attitude of a particular society and the action taken by it: 'Numerous stories have appeared in the press charging that unions affiliated with this International Union have levied exorbitant initiation fees and excessive down payments against workers seeking membership in the union in order to qualify for jobs on defense projects. I believe these reports have been greatly exaggerated, but, in any case, we regard such action by local unions as an abuse. We will not tolerate it. . . . Because of varied local conditions and differences in pay rates, it is impossible . . . to set a fixed initiation fee on a national basis. The ceiling will be based on local wage rates and conditions. In all instances it is my intention to issue orders that no man desiring to join the union where jobs are available should be required to pay an initiation fee higher than twenty-five dollars ($25.00) and then only when his earnings are at a rate of

more than eighty cents (80¢) an hour. The fee will scale down to as low as two dollars ($2.00) in some instances where pay rates are lower. In this connection, I wish to point out that the minimum initiation fee hitherto provided for in the laws of the International Union was five dollars ($5.00) and the maximum fifty dollars ($50.00). Furthermore, I will provide that a man joining the union will be permitted to pay his initiation fee out of earnings, so that no hardship will be imposed on workers taken off relief work, who may not be in a position to produce the money in advance'.

37. Now the Amalgamated Engineering Union.

38. The C.I.O. also charters Unions. The criticisms here made on the affect of A.F. of L. charters are quite likely, after the lapse of the necessary number of years, to be equally true of charters granted by the C.I.O.

39. The figures of the dates of the foundation of C.I.O. unions existing August 1940, are given by Daugherty, *op. cit.* pp. 355-6. They show that out of 34 Unions then existing, 11 were formed before 1934, 5 in 1934, and 18 later than 1934.

40. TABLE IX
The growth of Trade Unionism, particularly represented by the C.I.O., in the mining, oil, natural gas, and manufacturing industries.

	1932 A.F. of L.	1940 A.F. of L.	1940 C.I.O.	1940 A.F of L. and C.I.O. combined
1. Mining, quarries, oil & natural gas	155,000	35,000	721,000	756,000
2. All manufacturing industries	726,900	1,352,070	1,127,000	2,479,700
Total	881,900	1,387,700	1,848,000	3,235,700
a) Clay, glass & stone products	35,700	76,800	23,000	99,800
b) Lumber and its products	1,700	19,900	98,000	117,900
c) Iron and steel, metals and machinery	148,400	393,300	1,030,000	1,423,300
d) Rubber	—	—	55,000	55,000
e) Textiles	51,000	4,000	314,000	318,000
f) Garment industries	220,800	317,600	260,000	577,600

41. The corresponding figures in October 1941, were 41 unions and 9 organizing committees.

42. *The Monthly Labor Review*, May 1942.

43. Missouri, Connecticut, Maryland and New Jersey.

44. *Non-Partisan Declarations*, pub. by American Federation of Labor, pp. 3-4.

45. *Labor and the Congressional Elections, 1942.*

POVERTY AS AN INDUSTRIAL PROBLEM (1913)*

Since the deliverer of an inaugural lecture spends the rest of his official life in endeavouring to explain the object of his existence by his work, he may perhaps be excused if his initial address is more dogmatic than argumentative; and I do not on this occasion propose to do more than state shortly my own conception of the spirit in which our benefactor's gift may be most usefully applied, without pausing to discuss the controversial issues which the exposition of any plan of social study must necessarily evoke. Nor, perhaps, is it necessary for me to explain that I do not ascribe any excessive potentialities of practical service to such detailed inquiries as this Foundation exists to promote. Social research has in the last ten years become an industry. Whilst progress was undoubtedly retarded in the nineteenth century through the contempt of our grandfathers for economic investigation, there seems some danger that it may be paralysed in the twentieth through a superstitious reverence for accumulated facts; and I should be very sorry to be thought to suppose that the future welfare of mankind depended principally upon the multiplication of sociologists. There are, it is true, a considerable number of matters where practical action is delayed by the absence of sufficient knowledge. There are more, perhaps, where our knowledge is sufficient to occupy us for the next twenty years, and where the continuance of social evils is not due to the fact that we do not know what is right, but to the fact that we prefer to continue doing what is wrong. Those who have the power to remove them have not the will, and those who have the will have not, as yet, the power. To realize that the establishment by law of minimum rates in the chainmaking industry was proposed in 1889 and legalized in 1909, that for at least thirty years it has been a commonplace that most of the evils of East London, 'sweating,' married women's labour, the employment of children, were due to the disorganization

*Inaugural Lecture as Director of the Ratan Tata Foundation.

of labour at the Docks, that since 1890 a scheme by which casual employment could be made less casual has been before the public, that the Act establishing the Port of London Authority in 1908 expressly directed it to take steps to regularize employment, and that employment at the Docks during the last two years has been as irregular as, if not more irregular than, at any recent time, is to have a tragic lesson in the impotence of knowledge to alter conduct. All that, at the best, economic enquiry can do, is to deprive society of its excuse either for inaction or for unwise action—in England, of course, the former—by supplying it with materials upon which to base a reasonable judgment.

Within these limits the student of problems connected with poverty can hope to do work which may not be altogether useless. In planning his line of approach he naturally reflects on the principal achievements of his predecessors in the last twenty years, and if he examines these he can hardly fail to notice a well defined movement in the direction of certain principles and methods of study which is the more significant because it is common to the most different schools of thought, and is quite independent of the conclusions of particular writers. I do not refer merely to the obvious canons which every student constructs for himself in the course of his work. That, though the object of his study may be practical, he will be wise to start much higher up the stream than the point which he wishes to reach; that what thoughtful rich people call the problem of poverty, thoughtful poor people call with equal justice the problem of riches, and that to concentrate attention on the phenomena of destitution is to beg the questions which most need investigation; that the cases of distress which come before public or private relief authorities are usually for that very reason abnormal, and that personal experience in dealing with them will no more enable one to reach conclusions of any value as to the causes and prevention of poverty than walking the hospitals will by itself make a Medical Officer of Health; that each district creates its own optical illusion, and London, which (thank heaven) is not England, a more potent one than any other; that, since half the thought and money spent on relieving existing evils would probably have prevented many of them from coming into existence at all, it is, on a long view, more important to lay bare causes than to plan immediate remedies; that schemes for imposing on one class the habits thought desirable by another are usually futile and always impertinent, and that those of us who spend time in considering 'what we can do for the poor', would be better occupied in reflecting what the poor ought to do with us; that it is easier to prevent economic oppression than it is to prevent poverty, and that if men are free, in the sense of controlling, within the limits set by nature, the material conditions of their own lives, they may be poor, but they are not a problem: quite apart from these and similar commonplaces there have been some noticeable changes in the standpoint from which social studies are approached, which are encouraging to the student because they suggest that social theories displace each other less through the influence of individual talent than through that of general currents of thought.

The departments of economic thought in which the greatest advances have recently been made in England are the study of the origins of modern industrial society, and the realistic investigation of special problems of contemporary life. The former has emphasized the importance in social studies of attending to economic institutions, the legal framework of society, the main outlines set by the distribution of property, the methods of industry and the division of classes which economists immersed in detailed work are apt to take for granted and forget. It has shown the impossibility of enquiring into poverty without enquiring also into riches, that nearly all economic generalizations apply only within the limits drawn by a particular set of juristic arrangements, that such arrangements have been transformed repeatedly in the past by a process which may be described either as revolution or as evolution, and that there is no reason to suppose those at present existing will be any more permanent than those which have disappeared. Economic history does not profess to supply conclusions capable of practical application. But by changing the presuppositions by which such conclusions are tried, it has caused a silent evacuation of many fortresses which long resisted a direct attack. The latter has led us to approach problems of poverty, as, in the first place at any rate, problems of industry, to emphasize the fundamental economic contrasts common to numbers of men, rather than individual peculiarities of earning and spending, to take the trade, the town, the school as the unit of inquiry rather than the isolated individual or family. Both together have had two results. In the first place, they have led to attention being concentrated on the normal rather than the abnormal, on the rule not the exception, on poverty rather than on destitution, on the causes which raise the standard of life among masses rather than those which cause individuals to rise much above it or fall much below it. Whatever may be true of more primitive communities, the characteristic note of modern poverty is its association, not with personal misfortunes peculiar to individuals, but with the economic status of particular classes and occupations. The problem of poverty, as our generation understands it, is not primarily why certain persons fall into distress. It is why the product of industry is distributed in such a way that, whether people fall into distress or not, large groups among them derive a meagre, laborious, and highly precarious living from industries from which smaller groups appear to derive considerable affluence. The problem of preventing poverty is not primarily to assist individuals who are exceptionally unfortunate. It is to make the normal conditions under which masses of men work and live such that they may lead a healthy, independent and self-respecting life when they are *not* exceptionally unfortunate; so that, when they *are* exceptionally unfortunate, misfortune may not descend upon them with the crushing weight with which it falls today upon large sections of the working classes, for many of whom an accident or an error, which for most of my audience would be trifling, means economic ruin. The question, I repeat, is the condition of the normal man in normal circumstances, neither better nor worse off than his neighbours, not of those whose failings qualify them to be a text for the moralist, and who are no more common in the manual working classes than in other sections of society. It is in short the question of the economic status and opportunities of those who make up seven eighths of the community, not of a submerged residuum. I can best put what I mean by a concrete example. In a certain small town of my acquaintance, there is a works employing about 2,500 men, on which, therefore, about 8,000-9,000 persons depend. During the three years prior to the present boom most departments in that works were on short time, which meant that wages were reduced by roughly one third; that the man who was previously getting 30s. got 20s., and the man who was getting 24s. got 16s. During each of those years the dividend paid by the firm was 22 per cent, while considerable sums were transferred to reserves. Of the men employed a certain number were thriftless and a certain number spent too much on drink. This was very regrettable. But the primary question for the student of poverty is not, I suggest, why some score individuals incurred more distress than others, but why some thousands of persons were pinched and why some hundreds were half starved while employed by a business which was to its shareholders a gold mine. Improve the character of individuals by all means—if you feel competent to do so, especially of those whose excessive incomes expose them to peculiar temptations. This is a good in itself which needs no justification. But unemployment, short time, and low wages fall upon just and unjust alike; indeed the first is apt to fall especially on the just because they have a way of making themselves unpopular by asking awkward questions. And assuming—an absurd assumption—that you have eliminated all those whose personal characteristics cause them to fall below the average in energy and foresight, there still remains the fact that the normal conditions of the normal worker are precarious, that the barrier which separates him from actual distress is thin, and that his economic prospects are to a great extent, except in a very few well organized industries, beyond the control of himself or of persons like himself. Nor in reality will you be able to deal with exceptional distress till you have improved the normal conditions of those who are not in distress. For, on the one hand, as long as the status of large classes of persons is as precarious as it is today, you cannot discriminate between those who are personally incompetent and those who are not. And, on the other hand, the capacity of an individual to resist exceptional misfortune depends mainly on the habits of life and economic resources which he has acquired before exceptional misfortune occurs. A man who is paid 18s. a week and pays 4s. 6d. in rent has no margin either of money or of energy with which to meet an emergency. If I am told that individuals here and there do in fact succeed by exceptional effort or good fortune in doing what is called 'rising', I answer that this is no doubt, so far as it goes, a matter for congratulation, but that it leaves almost unaltered the general problems arising from the existence of economic inequality. 'Sweating' does not disappear from our towns because a certain number of those who are sweated become, as they do, sweaters in their turn, any more than tadpoles disappear from our ponds because a large number of them are annually converted into frogs; and the vision of an Elysium to be attained by continuing to play with marked cards and simply shuffling the pack, by everyone who is squeezed now watching for his opportunity of squeezing in the future is, happily, as impracticable as it is sordid.

In the second place, the problem of poverty with which the student is concerned is primarily an industrial one. It is to be studied first at its sources, and only secondly in its manifestations, in the mill, in the mine or at the docks, not in casual wards or on the Embankment. The most conspicuous result of the general restatement of problems which has taken place within recent years has been the diversion to questions of social organization of much of the attention which, a generation ago, was spent on relief. During the first three quarters of the nineteenth century the great English superstition as to the supreme importance of methods of relief was all-powerful. Not only did Poor Law administration monopolize the attention of social writers of the earlier period to the neglect of other and more important topics, but it is perhaps not too presumptuous to say that most of the studies of Poor Law problems themselves down to the last decade seem to suffer from a self-imposed limitation of subject which prevented even the statement of the very questions which most require solution. The Poor Law histories of that period, such as the well-known books of Sir George Nicholl and Mr. Mackay, by failing to realize that distress stands to the general economic conditions of a community in the relation of reverse to obverse, effect to cause, disease to environment, failed to make intelligible even the account of Poor Law legislation and administration with which they were avowedly concerned.

The popular theories of pauperism spoke much about the danger of making provision for the unemployed, but next to nothing about the nature of unemployment; much about the evils of casual charity, and next to nothing about those of casual labour; much about the danger of supplementing wages out of the rates, and nothing whatever about the method by which wages may be made more adequate without being supplemented by the labour of children and married women; much about the duty of the wage-earner to provide for sickness and old age, scarcely anything as to how the causes which make sickness and premature old age the lot of thousands of men as industrious as their neighbours might be removed. It precluded, in fact, any comprehensive inquiry into the prevention of poverty by its placid assumption of the immutability of the economic conditions with which poverty is proved by experience to be associated; as though economic classes and institutions had stepped out of a kind of political Noah's Ark, sharply defined, highly coloured, with an unalterable destiny graven upon each wooden feature, and, once the English upper classes had, like Shem, Ham, and Japhet, divided the world between them, their inferiors were to accept the misfortunes of subordination as the dispensation of Providence itself.

It is not any reflection upon the value of the work done by this school of thought within the narrow limits of its own peculiar self-denying ordinance, to say that the greatest advances made in economic knowledge and practice in our own day have been achieved precisely through that study of the environment, physical, industrial, and sanitary, which its exponents neglected, in deference partly to its supposed unalterableness, partly to the presumed ability of the individual to be master of his fate. The Poor Law Report of 1834 may be taken as marking the formulation of one attitude; the Poor Law Reports of 1909 not, indeed, the formulation of another, but at least a realization that another is needed. Between the two the centre of interest in social studies shifted from pauperism to poverty, from poverty to the distribution of wealth, from the distribution of wealth to the control of industry. Historical investigation has undermined the doctrines contained in that brilliant, influential and wildly unhistorical piece of special pleading, the Report of Senior and Chadwick. Recent research, based on a far more extensive study of documents than its authors pretended to make, so far from confirming the famous theory which ascribed the distress of the first three decades of the nineteenth century to 'improvidence and vice' wrought upon by a bad administrative system, have shown that administrative abuses were themselves the outcome of an attempt to cope with distress created by large economic causes. Held, Mantoux, Cunningham, Mr and Mrs Webb, Mr and Mrs Hammond, and a host of humbler historians, by placing in their proper light the change in the land system, the decay of rural industries, the immigration into towns, the effects of an unregulated factory system, the instability of trade, the rise in food prices, facts which the Poor Law Commissioners, with a magnificent disregard for contemporary State papers, thought unworthy of mention, have not discredited in their own sphere the destructive value of the principles of 1834, but have shown that their sphere was far less extensive than was at one time supposed. And exactly the same readjustment of emphasis is visible if one examines the achievements of the last century in dealing with sickness, and of our own, such as they are, in dealing with unemployment and wages. Progress in the prevention of disease began when the reports of Arnott, Kay, Southwood Smith and the other doctors employed by the permanent Poor Law Commission, convinced Chadwick that no methods of relief, however ineligible, will deter into independence persons suffering from fever caused by insanitary conditions, and thus led the way to the Report on the Sanitary Conditions of the Labouring Classes of Great Britain, which produced the first Public Health Act of 1848. Since unemployment is not as infectious as disease, and Whitehall and Kensington are not fluttered by casual labour at the London Docks as easily as by cholera in Whitechapel, it was not till two generations later that these questions were investigated with anything like the same care as the prevention of sickness. When, however, the subject of unemployment was taken up, the methods which led to the most important of recent advances in our knowledge were similar in principle to those which produced the removal of some of the principal causes of disease by sanitation. Thanks to modern studies of the question the public is gradually ceasing to visualize unemployment as tramps walking. Look at any recent work on the subject and you will see that it treats it principally from the standpoint of industrial organization. Whereas, for example, the Report of 1834 denied by implication that there were any economic causes of distress whatever, the Majority Report of the last Poor Law Commission gives the whole of Part VI, no less than 136 out of 670 pages, to analyzing the industrial aspects of the question, trade cycles, casual labour, the displacement of men by machinery, the exploitation of juvenile and adolescent labour. The best and most authoritative books on the subject are, I suppose, that of Mr Beveridge and that of Mr Rowntree and Mr Lasker. The most remarkable things in the former are, on the one hand, the correlation of cyclical movements in the unemployment percentage with other tests of industrial activity and stagnation; and, on the other hand, the demonstration that casual employment is a normal feature of all industries in which there is no organization for centralizing the demand for labour. The latter, by showing the connexion between certain types of juvenile labour and subsequent distress, confirms for one locality the conclusion that some methods of employing boys manufacture unemployment among adults, which had already been stated in a more extensive manner in Mr Jackson's Report of the Poor Law Commission. The emphasis laid in each of these works upon the industrial factors in the problem is paralleled by the change which has overtaken our conception of the manner in which questions as to wages should be approached. The attitude of mind which regarded the sempstress or shirtmaker as a tragic but not altogether unedifying spectacle of uncomplaining industry has been replaced by one which looks beyond the sufferings and merits of the individual to the economic environment which determines her position. Instead of accounts of the lives of those who used to be classed vaguely as the 'poor', the Board of Trade is now giving us a wage census embracing all workers from the best paid to the worst paid, by which, for the first time, the word 'poverty' can be given a meaning of some precision. When Mr Rowntree's book on *Poverty* showed that in York 15½ per cent, between one-sixth and one-seventh, of *all* the wage-earners in that city were living in a state of 'Primary Poverty', defined as the condition of the families whose 'total earnings are insufficient to obtain the minimum necessaries for the maintenance of merely physical existence', he deprived the word 'sweating' of much of its sensationalism, while adding to its significance, by suggesting that if wages inadequate to support physical existence are the criterion of sweating, then a very large proportion of all unorganized workers must be sweated. And Mr Rowntree's inquiries in York have since been reinforced by even more remarkable inquiries in Reading. Dr Bowley has shown that something between 25 per cent and 30 per cent of the working-class population of Reading in 1912 were, in so far as they were dependent upon their earnings, pensions, or possessions, living below Mr Rowntree's standard, that in the case of 49 per cent of these the immediate cause was the fact that they were 'in regular work but at low wages'—which means, I suppose, in most cases, making biscuits for Messrs Huntley & Palmer—and that 47 per cent of all the children in the elementary schools were at the time of the inquiry living in households where the standard of life in question was not attained. Nor is it without significance that the best realistic study of the problem of wages should have been made in the course of a work upon Trade Unionism. For Trade Unions are concerned with the normal worker, not with exceptions; and by explaining some of the conditions under which the cotton-workers of the thirties of last century, then notoriously a degraded class, have become the relatively prosperous workers of today, Mr and Mrs Webb have taught us that, however much individuals may differ, the sources of the large movements which improve and deteriorate the status of masses must be sought primarily through the study of industrial relationships. I mention these writers, not to endorse their opinions, but to illustrate a movement. To admit the fruitfulness of their method is not to endorse all their conclusions.

All this emphasis upon the necessity of studying the conditions in which disease and poverty arise does not, of course, iHply that the personal factor is unimportant. On the contrary, except on the supposition that the majority of persons will respond to favourable conditions, it would be meaningless. The reason for holding that the main problem with which the student of social conditions is concerned, is not so much that of the man below the margin as that of the low normal standard must be justified by an appeal to experience. It is that if any group of people have what may be called, for want of a better phrase, adequate economic resisting power, they may usually be relied upon themselves to protect the weaker members of the group against the principal accidents of life; whereas, if they have not, merely to supplement their immediate needs, though it may often be necessary, is often to pour sand through a sieve, a process at once tantalizing and degrading to the performer, and positively maddening to the subjects of his operations, who want not to be given their living by someone else but to earn it under fair conditions for themselves. To a man who is in difficulties, the rivers of his own country are better than all the waters of Damascus, and the cry of 'curse your charity' will be as heartily reciprocated by nearly all those who have any experience of charitable administration as it is by working people themselves. It is in proportion to its possession of such resisting power that a class is able, when some larger protective apparatus than the family is needed, to build up its own institutions with its own habits and ideals, to interpose a whole network of personal relationship between the individual and either the offensive intrusion of sympathetic outsiders or the bare machinery of bureaucracy, to make him superior to exceptional misfortunes by establishing the routine of life upon a rock, to maintain its self-respect by making other people respect it. It is in Lancashire, where labour is protected by factory acts and trade unions, not in East London, where it is not, that family life, co-operation, friendly societies, education, social institutions for a hundred different purposes, find their fullest development.

Is it beyond the power of society to increase this capacity for resistance in those of its members who are in a weak position? Certainly not—provided it really desires to do so. It is done in one sphere by public health legislation, in another by factory legislation, in a third by education. It is done by action which substitutes regular for casual employment, for example by employing a permanent staff on a weekly wage, which is the practice at some docks on the continent, instead of engaging men by the half-day, which is the practice, as far as I know, at all docks in England. It is done by taxation which transfers economic surpluses from private individuals to the public. It is done by direct intervention to raise wages, and could and should be done far more vigorously and persistently. Let me illustrate the latter point by a single example. As most of my audience will be aware, the Trade Boards Act of 1909 set up Trade Boards to fix minimum rates of payment in certain industries. The first industry dealt with was Hand-hammered and Dollied and Tommied Chain-making at Cradley Heath, which, as readers of official reports will know, has been the protagonist of half-a-dozen inquiries, and where all the evils associated with the absence of any standard wage, the beating down of rates by employers, unendurably long hours of labour, the constant indebtedness of the workers to the middlemen, have in the past been rampant. The Trade Board fixed minimum rates for hand-hammered chain on 22 August 1910, and the rates were made obligatory by the Board of Trade in February 1911. What has been the effect? In the first place, the piece prices paid for the poorest qualities of chain were raised from 40 to 80 per cent and the workers' hourly earnings were increased in proportion. In the second place, the hours worked are shorter, for it is no longer necessary to work 70-80 hours in order to make a living. In the third place, the quality of the chain made has improved, for the speed of working, though extraordinary, need no longer be so frantic as it was. In the fourth place, the whole standard of life in the district has been raised. The workers are better nourished and better dressed; shopkeepers state that their sale of provisions has increased, employers that 'the workers take more pride in themselves and show more care in their work', insurance agents that arrears are less, school teachers that the school children are 'better fed, better clothed and better shod'. Trade unionism, once almost hopeless, has grown apace, and the workers' representatives on the Board have now asked for, and are likely to obtain, another 10 per cent. And this has been accomplished without, as yet, creating unemployment, and at the cost of a rise in the price of chain which is far less than the rise in the price paid the worker, and is only in part due to the advance in the latter.

That example illustrates what I mean by the development of economic resisting power through public intervention. For it is a mistake to think that, if it develops at all, it must always develop spontaneously. The possession of it depends on a combination of factors which none but the most fortunate individual can determine for himself, the distribution of property, the organization of industry, the regularity of employment, the level of wages, the healthiness of the environment; and when it is absent it is little use urging individuals to display the characteristics which develop spontaneously when it is present. To expect an English agricultural labourer to exercise the thrift of a small landed proprietor, or a bricklayer's labourer the independence and professional pride of a cotton-spinner, or a dock labourer, whose life is a weekly gamble between £2 and nothing, the foresight of an official with a quarterly salary, is like asking people to be clean in Manchester, free from sickness on the West Coast of Africa, or cheerful at an inaugural lecture. There is something at once pathetic and amusing in the ingenuous assumption of a great part of the modern world that if it seeks first and with sufficient assiduity material riches, the spiritual qualities which it professes to approve will be added thereto. To the sociological version of the eternal desire of mankind to have their cake and eat it, which is embodied in the hypocrisy of suggesting that it is possible to combine the moral advantage of a certain type of character with the economic advantage of industrial arrangements in which that type is shown by experience to deteriorate, neither commonsense nor social science lend any support whatever. What experience suggests is that there is always going on a process which—if one must comply with the current fashion in phraseology—may be called psychological selection. Certain qualities are more indispensable than others in a certain environment, and those which are less indispensable tend to disappear, not through the actual elimination of the individuals who possess them, but through the suppression of the qualities themselves. When it is only by the severest struggle that the most elementary needs for food, clothing, or shelter can be satisfied, secondary needs, such as those for security in old age, health, and education, tend to be eliminated almost before they develop, because, however important in themselves, they are in such a struggle less important as a means to immediate success, or rather as a safeguard against immediate failure. Conversely, the satisfaction of these primary desires leaves room for the growth of those others, the presence of which makes the difference between living and merely existing. We must not fall into the fallacy of the Royal Commissioners who investigated the conditions of the Handloom Weavers in 1835, and who expressed much naïve distress that the weavers, once a grave and godly class, had ceased to go to church, till a witness explained that their wages had fallen to such a point that they could not buy clothes, and that they had to work all Sunday in order to earn them. If, for example, it is really necessary to the transport of goods by rail that able-bodied adults should be paid in towns less than 20s. a week, it is not practicable to expect them to save, because to-morrow's dinner is more indispensable than a minute income twenty years hence. They are most thrifty when they spend the whole of their income, when they are what their critics call thriftless. If it is really necessary to the unloading of ships that employers should give dock labourers not more that three days' work a week, we must not expect the habits of dockers to be other than speculative, for the man with speculative habits has the best chance of holding his own. If it is really necessary that a man's normal income should be insufficient to support a family of the normal size, one must not reproach him for sending the eldest girl half time, for it is less important that she should prolong her education than that her brothers and sisters should not be underfed. Nemesis, of course, comes sooner or later. It comes when people find that they have succeeded in obtaining the type of character for which they asked; when shipowners, for example, who desire at last to regularize employment, find that dock-workers cannot change the habits of a lifetime in three months; when employers of cheap juvenile labour lament that there is a scarcity of skilled workers; when Health Visitors discover that the impossibility of securing cleanliness in a house between two mill-chimneys has created a class of persons who have forgotten even how to try to be clean, and housing reformers that there are some tenants who will use the fittings of a decent house for firewood. Since one cannot skip a generation, the administrator concerned with the alleviation of existing destitution, will always have his hands full, and it is part of the business of this Foundation to accumulate knowledge which may be of service to him. But on a long view social science, like medical science, is most practical when it least considers what is immediately practicable. No one would suggest that it would have been better to spend the money devoted to discovering the bacillus which produces sleeping sickness to alleviating more of the individuals suffering from that disease; and no one should suggest that work on industrial or sanitary or administrative organization is wasted because it does not immediately alleviate poverty. It is less urgent, I would suggest, for the student of poverty to devote himself to the consideration of the palliatives with which the administrator, who lives in the present, is necessarily concerned, than it is to endeavour to discover whether these things are really necessary or not. On the view that environment is, compared with heredity, a relatively unimportant factor in determining social characteristics, such a method of approaching this subject would seem to be indispensable. For the more unreservedly onc grants the existence of a class of persons whose personal defects disqualify them from regular employment or a living wage, the more essential it is that the environment should be such as to discriminate between those who can respond to improved conditions and those who cannot. Discrimination is only possible when there is a standard. In the social strata where large properties are inherited the fool and the genius have an equal chance of 'survival'. Where sanitary conditions are such as to produce cholera, good stock and bad stock perish together. It is when it is raised that selection takes place. In an unorganized industry there is little incentive to the selection of the most efficient worker; for when men are so helpless as to accept any kind of conditions, employers will usually accept any kind of men. It is when there is a standard wage and a fixed working day that discrimination is exercised. Almost anyone has a gambler's chance of employment at some docks. In the spinning-room of a cotton-mill a man must get so much yarn off the mules or he goes. The school of thought which holds that progress takes place mainly through the elimination of inferior stocks is, therefore, one to whose argument the advocacy of improvements in environment appears to be logically essential.

The first task, therefore, of such a Foundation as this should be, I suggest, to assist the study of the causes which make the livelihood of large groups of people meagre and precarious; and of the action by which these effects may be averted or diminished. Of the numerous questions which arise in this connexion we have selected three, low wages, casual employment, and juvenile labour. We hope to aid an understanding of the actual volume of crushing poverty in certain areas by promoting in other towns inquiries similar to those which Dr Bowley has carried out in Reading; and we propose to publish studies of the effect of the legal minimum wage set up by the Trade Boards for those industries in which they have been established long enough for their effect to be ascertainable. We hope to publish a study of the organization of labour at certain ports and of plans which have been made for regularizing it, together with investigations made into different aspects of the questions surrounding the employment of youths in industry which will throw some light on one small side—though only one—of the question of unemployment. Further, in connexion with such investigations it is essential that a prominent place should be given to the historical study of changes in social conditions in the past hundred years and of the causes which have improved and degraded them. To regard such historical work as a luxury or a bypath is a profound mistake. The history of social theory is strewn with the wrecks of proposals which took account of everything except the obvious. Before one can estimate the value of proposals for practical action, it is necessary to have at least an opinion of the principal agencies which have modified social life for better or for worse in conditions sufficiently similar to our own for the comparison to be of value. On this subject the accumulation of materials has far outrun research. Even the mines of information contained in offical inquiries are still largely unworked; and it should be the aim of a Foundation such as this to do something, in a small way, by lectures if not by publications, to contribute to the social history of the 19th century.

It does not, however, follow that because social study starts with the framework of industrial organization it should necessarily end there. A second principal task is an examination of the results of different types of administrative intervention which at present are aiming at the relief of poverty. In this field there is much room for comparative study. Take for example such matters as the Feeding of School Children, the Medical Treatment of School Children, the Juvenile Departments of Labour Exchanges, Old Age Pensions, Poor Law Administration or Unemployment Insurance. The methods employed in administering the first three of these in different parts of the country vary very largely, and they are certainly not all equally satisfactory. It is desirable that the experience of different localities should be pooled, that we should know how far differences in method are due to differences in the problem faced by different districts and how far to differences in the quality of administration, that the practice of London, Manchester, Bradford, and Birmingham should be set side by side, and the results appraised. What we are doing in this connexion is to take two recent forms of social legislation, the Education (Administrative Provisions) Act of 1907, and the Education (Provision of Meals) Act of 1906, and to try to discover the main results of the experience derived from them. The former, as my audience will know, has thrown much light upon the prevalence of disease among school children, and we have just published a monograph[1] on the subject by Mr Arthur Greenwood, which should be of considerable value to the School Medical Officer, the educationalist, and the citizen. The latter raises far-reaching questions of the proper relation between private and public provisions and between different types of the latter. My colleague, Miss Bulkley, has carried out what I consider to be the most exhaustive study yet made of the subject, which we hope will appear in the course of a few months.[2] Such work should, we think, be of some assistance in providing materials for the guidance of practical persons. Whether it leads itself to any practical results depends on causes which it is beyond the power of the student to create.

NOTES

1. *The Health and Physique of School Children,* (1913).
2. [*The Feeding of School Children* (1914)—Ed.]

THE ASSESSMENT OF WAGES IN ENGLAND BY THE JUSTICES OF THE PEACE[1]

I Introductory

The Authoritative Assessment of Wages in England is a subject which extends from the first Statute of Labourers passed in 1349 to the repeal of the wage clauses of the Statute of Artificers in 1813. In the present essay I shall deal with a strictly limited portion of this wide field. I shall consider only the assessment of wages as it was carried out under the Statute of Artificers of 1563, which superseded the earlier legislation and reorganized on a wider basis and in a more elastic shape the system which it had introduced, and I shall confine myself mainly to the operation of that Statute in the century and a half after it was passed. I shall therefore leave on one side both the regulation of wages by the State in the fourteenth, fifteenth, and early sixteenth centuries and the rules with regard to the remuneration of labour made independently of Statute Law by gilds and municipal authorities, except in so far as it may be necessary to consider these in order to interpret the Elizabethan legislation. Nor shall I deal with the attempts to revive that legislation as a means of protecting the wage-earner against exploitation which were made both by philanthropists and by bodies of organized workers at the end of the eighteenth and at the beginning of the nineteenth centuries. The latter topic is an extremely interesting one, but it involves considerations peculiar to the rise of modern industrial conditions and quite foreign to the circumstances in which the assessment of wages was administered as a working system. A discussion of the earlier Statutes of Labourers prior to 1563 would take us into fields which, except for Miss Putnam's admirable work, have been scarcely explored, and the political conditions of which are so remote from those of the Tudor age as to require a separate dissertation.

The industrial code of Elizabeth is a topic which has received considerable attention from English economic historians, and with regard to which there has been in the last few years both an increase of material and a change of standpoint. On the one hand a good deal of new evidence has come to light. When Thorold Rogers called attention to the subject in his history of Agriculture and Prices, he could print only twelve assessments of wages made by the Justices. This number of assessments has been increased by subsequent historians, notably Dr Cunningham[2], Miss McArthur[3] and Professor Hewins[4]. But even the latter, whose list of assessments was more complete than that of any other writer, tells us that he knows only of 47. Since these authors made their contributions the anticipation that other assessments were only waiting to be discovered has been substantiated both by the explorations of private investigators among Quarter Sessions records and by the work of the Historical Manuscripts Commission and of the Victoria County History. As will be seen from the tables given below, I calculate that the number of distinct and complete assessments at present available for analysis is 73, and that when their reissues and references to other assessments are included the total number known with certainty to have been made is not less than 112. Moreover the assessments are only part of the new material which calls for treatment. Mere tables of wages by themselves tell us little except that the Justices were administering the law. They require to be related to the general social conditions of the age, and to be viewed as a piece of regulation as characteristic of the economic environment of the sixteenth and seventeenth centuries as, in a widely different sphere, factory legislation is of modern industry. The view, which we take of them must clearly depend upon our view of the part which the wage-worker played in the economy of the period when the Statute of Artificers was passed; and the work of recent investigators of industrial and agrarian conditions has done something to supply us with the background which is essential to the interpretation of economic legislation, and which, in the days of Thorold Rogers, was almost entirely lacking.

On the other hand not only have materials been increased, but standpoints and canons of criticism have been considerably modified since attention first began to be paid to the subject. The change of opinion among historians as to the objects and merits of the economic legislation of the old régime is a curious illustration of the influence of contemporary problems upon historical judgments. The naïve and self-confident Philistinism of the Committees of the House of Commons which pronounced judgment in the early nineteenth century both upon the authoritative regulation of wages and the statutory system of apprenticeship, 'The age of Elizabeth', reported one of them, 'was indeed glorious, but it was one in which the true principles of commerce were not rightly understood', may perhaps be regarded as so obviously the outcome of immediate and pressing material considerations as to fall below the horizon of serious history. It is, however, instructive to compare the views of Thorold Rogers with those of subsequent writers. The greater part of Rogers's work was done during a period when, though the Combination Laws had long been repealed, the legal status of trade unions was still precarious, and when the distrust of the interference of the state with questions of work and wages which (in spite of occasional agitations for factory legislation) characterized their leaders down to about 1889, was still extremely strong. That distrust Rogers, himself a mid-nineteenth century radical, shared to the full, and it is no injustice to his services as a pioneer among English economic historians to say that it coloured his estimate of Elizabethan legislation. He condemned the apprenticeship clauses in the Statute of Artificers for the reasons long ago advanced by Adam Smith, that they were a bar to the mobility of labour from one occupation to another, and created a monopoly of skilled workers at the expense of an unprivileged residuum. He condemned with far greater vehemence the wage clauses in the same Act, dismissed the allusion in its opening words to the need of making wages keep pace with advancing prices as 'the hypocrisy which the Preamble of an Act of Parliament habitually contains' and described the whole system as 'a conspiracy concocted by the law and carried out by parties interested in its success . . . to cheat the English workman of his wages'.[5] Clearly there lies behind these full-blooded denunciations the assumption that the intervention of the State in matters of wages was an object of detestation to the workers concerned that it invariably operated to prevent wages from being as high as they would have been under a régime of free competition, and that, in short, the prescribing of rates of payment in the sixteenth century was open to the same objections as would fairly be adduced against a similar policy in the nineteenth century.

Rogers's criticism of the Statute of Artificers, though it has passed into the textbooks and has been repeated in some works of a more serious order,[6] has been considerably modified both by subsequent research, and by the different point of view from which more recent writers have approached the subject. The latest study[7] of apprenticeship in England by no means endorses the verdict of the early nineteenth century as to the inutility or harmfulness of a compulsory system. The exploration of town records shows the assessment of wages to have been a policy to which the word 'conspiracy' is peculiarly inappropriate, since it was carried out independently of any national enactment by a large number of town authorities. A comparison of the Act of 1563 with the legislation of earlier periods, which Rogers did not bring into relation with it, shows that his view that it was the grand beginning of the English workman's troubles, is quite unjustified, and that there is some evidence to suggest that on occasion it was used not to lower but to raise wages. Moreover a fuller appreciation of the objects and conceptions of the statesmen of the sixteenth and early seventeenth centuries has modified the standpoint from which their economic policy is regarded. The age of 'Tudor despotism' is no longer contrasted with that of constitutional government as darkness with light. Its tendencies are seen to have been in some respects popular, and its attention to the administrative supervision of economic conditions is congenial to modern historians, who are constantly confronted in their own age with the task of securing what Tudor statesmen called 'good order' in industrial matters. In particular it is realized that the assessment of wages cannot be treated, in the manner of Rogers, as though it were something unique, instead of being, what it really was, one part of the absolute monarchy's general system of economic regulation. It requires to be related to the Poor Laws, to the attempts made to check enclosures and to prevent evictions, to the fixing of prices and the limitation of the rate of interest, the three last of which measures might, if Rogers's canons of criticism were adopted, be described as a conspiracy to cheat the English landlord, employer, and money-lender of their profits. Miss Leonard's description of the personal government of Charles I from 1629-1640 (a period in which several attempts were made by the central government to enforce the assessment of wages), as 'remarkable for more continuous efforts to enforce socialistic measures than have been made by the central government of any other Great European Country', is an exaggeration which errs almost as much in one direction as Thorold Rogers did in another. The policy of 'Thorough' was at best, as its two advocates are constantly reminding us, a sadly slipshod affair. But she does well to emphasize the fact that the assessment of wages was part of a general system of Government intervention in economic matters, which was on the whole endorsed by the public opinion of the age, and that it must be judged in relation to that system, not as an isolated freak of arbitrary despotism.

II The Act of 1563 and its Antecedents

The Statute[9] of Artificers was passed in January 1563. After reciting in the preamble that the existing statutes affecting apprentices, servants, and labourers are both mutually contradictory and unsatisfactory on the ground that the rise in money prices has made the rates of wages paid to them out of date, so that 'the said laws cannot conveniently, without the greatest grief and burden of the poor labourer and hired man, be put in due execution', it proceeds to repeal such legislation as concerns 'the hiring, keeping, departing, working, wages or order of servants, workmen, artificers, apprentices, and labourers', and to lay down a large number of provisions which may be grouped under five heads. First, there are a series of clauses designed to secure stable and regular employment. A list of 30 occupations is set out in which contracts of services are to stand for not less than one year at a time, and in which a quarter's notice is to be given before either party can terminate the contract. All persons who are unmarried or under the age of thirty years, who have been engaged three years in either of the above occupations, and who neither have a certain minimum of real or personal property, nor are employed by any gentleman or nobleman, nor are working on a farm of their own, may be compelled by the Justices to work for any employer in any of these industries who desires their services. Second, an attempt is made to secure a sufficient supply of labour for agriculture. All persons between the ages of 12 and 60 who are not otherwise employed, and who have not a certain minimum of real or personal property laid down in the Act, may be compelled to serve as labourers in husbandry in times of hay or corn harvest. Justices and constables may require 'all such artificers and persons as be meet to labour' to serve by the day for the mowing or inning of corn, grain and hay; and youths between the age of 10 and 18 may be bound as apprentices to husbandry. Thirdly, there are certain provisions as to apprenticeship, the object of which is partly to secure that youths are adequately trained, partly to prevent the overstocking of industries with juvenile workers, partly to secure an adequate supply of labour for employers, partly to preserve social distinctions by preventing free movement from one grade into another. After the first of May following the passage of the Act, no one may practise 'any art, mistery or manual occupation' without first serving a seven years' apprenticeship. In certain industries there must be at least one journeyman to the first three apprentices employed and an extra journeyman for every apprentice beyond that number. In cities, towns corporate, and market towns, merchants engaged in the export trade, mercers, drapers, goldsmiths, ironmongers, embroiderers, or clothiers may take as apprentices only either their own children or else the children of parents with a certain minimum property qualification. Fourth, provision is made for the assessment of wages. Justices of the Peace in counties, and Mayors, Bailiffs, or other head officers in cities, are, at their first general sessions after Easter in every year, after taking the advice of 'discrete and grave persons', and 'conferring together respecting the plenty or scarcity of the time or other circumstances necessary to be considered' to 'rate and appoint the wages as well of such of the said artificers . . . or any other labourers, servants or workmen whose wages in time past hath been by any law rated and appointed, as also the wages of all other labourers, artificers . . . which have not been rated'. They are to make a return of their assessments into Chancery; whereupon the Lord Chancellor or Lord Keeper, after submitting them to the Privy Council, may cause them to be printed and despatched to the respective counties concerned before the following 1 September, in the form of a proclamation. Masters giving more than the rates fixed are liable to a fine of £5 and 10 days' imprisonment, servants taking more to 21 days' imprisonment. The hours of labour are to be as follows: In summer not less than from 5 am to between 7 and 8 pm with 2½ hours' interval for meals; in winter from dawn to night with the same break. Finally an attempt is made to facilitate the working of the whole system of regulation by restricting the mobility of labour. No one who is employed in agriculture or in any other of the occupations mentioned in the Statute may leave the city, town, parish, hundred, or county where he was last employed, unless he obtains a 'testimonial with the seal of the said City or of the Constable or other head Officer and of two other honest householders of the City, Town, or parish where he last served, declaring his lawful departure . . ., which testimonial shall be delivered unto the said servant and also registered by the parson of the parish'. Anyone having a servant who has not got such a testimonial is to be fined £5, and the servant who migrates without one is to be imprisoned and whipped.

In the following pages we shall be concerned only with the wage clauses of this famous Act. But they cannot be treated in isolation from the general system of which they were a part. To understand their significance it is necessary to give a short account of the type of intervention which preceded the Statute of Artificers, and which to some extent it replaced. It was closely related on the one hand to the economic activity of town authorities, and on the other hand to the attempts which had been made to regulate wages by statute. A characteristic common to all Tudor legislation upon economic matters, and accounting for the readiness with which its very drastic provisions were accepted by the classes concerned, was that so far from being an original departure, it almost invariably proceeded by erecting into a national system regulations which had long been the common property of minor authorities. Thus the statutes against depopulation, which forbade the conversion of arable land to pasture and limited the number of sheep which a man might keep, did little more than aim at constructing a universal customary out of the local customs of thousands of manors all over England. The famous Elizabethan Poor Law was based on the experiments made for nearly a century by the most enterprising, or the most unfortunate, localities. The statute of 1563 was no exception to the rule. In drawing up its great industrial code, the state only applied on a national scale what had long been the practice of a large number of towns.

That this was so in the matter of apprenticeship, of the restrictions imposed on the mobility of labour, of the compulsion to work which was to be brought to bear upon the unemployed requires no proof. The municipal records of the fifteenth and sixteenth centuries are full of regulations limiting the entry into occupations, providing for the expulsion of 'foreign' immigrants, requiring the workless man to stand every morning with his tools in the market-place and hire himself to the first person demanding his services. And the clauses in the Act relating to the assessment of wages were to almost an equal extent grounded in the industrial practice of the towns. True, rules on the latter subject are not so common in municipal records as are rules on the former. Outside the larger towns the number of permanent wage workers was small; the typical 'workman' even in the sixteenth century was still a master craftsman; and the public was sufficiently protected against exploitation by the regulations fixing the price of goods. Nevertheless, as far as the more important boroughs are concerned, there is ample evidence to show that from very early times it was the practice for corporations to fix, quite independently of any national legislation on the subject, the wages of journeymen, and to punish those by whom their ruling was broken. The records of London, Leicester, Norwich, Beverley, Coventry, Gloucester, Chester, Bury St. Edmunds, Southampton, Reading, and Nottingham all offer examples to the practice. The crafts which are most commonly the object of regulation are those connected with building (carpenters, tilers, sawyers, masons, etc) but the wages of porters, bowyers, bakers, and several different classes of workers in the woollen industry are often fixed as well. The mention of the latter industry raises the interesting point that the wages of the person engaged in it are frequently treated in a quite special manner, the town authorities, when they deal with spinners, walkers, and weavers being frequently concerned with establishing not a maximum but a minimum wage. I shall return to this matter later in speaking of the assessment of the wages of woollen workers under the Act of 1563. I mention it now in order to enter a caveat against the conclusion that gilds and town authorities, as a rule, fixed a minimum, while the state fixed a maximum, wage, which one writer[10] has drawn from the instances of minimum wage regulations which undoubtedly are to be found in municipal records. The distinction which should be based upon them is not a distinction between the action of the State and the action of local bodies, but between the policy of both types of authority towards workers in the woollen industry and their policy to all other classes of wage-earners; for the state itself treated wages in the woollen industry in a special way. Apart from this particular industry there is no doubt that towns, like the national government, were concerned with establishing maximum rates of payment and minimum hours of labour. In a few—a very few—cases, gilds direct that workers are not to accept less than a certain price. But in almost every instance which I have examined gilds and town authorities act together to fix the terms of the contract between employer and employed, and it is hardly to be doubted that the masters who governed the gilds were frequently the rulers of the town. When journeymen's associations are mentioned they are either denounced, and threatened with proceedings under 3 & 4 Ed vi c. 3, or are bound over not to inconvenience masters by raising wages. Two documents will illustrate with sufficient clearness the type of municipal regulations of which I am speaking. The first comes from Coventry[11] in 1553: Enacted

> That no master carpenter or sawyer shall take for his wages from Candelmas to Allhallentyd above viiid a day, and for a journeyman or a sufficient servant above 6d a day, and also that no master Tyler or rough mason

during the said time shall take above 7d a day, and for their sufficient servant not above 5d a day, and no dauber during the said time shall take above vi d a day, nor his servant above v d; nor no common labourer during the said term above v d a day.

The second comes from Chester[12] in 1576. It will be noticed in the first place, that though at this time the Statute of Artificers has been passed for 13 years a town goes on regulating wages quite independently of it; and in the second place, that though the woollen industry is the object of regulation, the wage fixed is a maximum, not a minimum.

It was then and there ordered by the said Mayor, Alderman Sheriffs and Common Council that the rate, price, and weight, of spinning, carding and weaving, walking, fulling and dyeing of wool hereafter following shall be from henceforth observed and kept, and that no manner of persons or person within the city shall take or receive for spinning and handcarding of one weight of wool above 6d, nor for stock carding of every stone of wool above 6d, nor for weaving any piece of woollen cloth containing XXII yards in length above 12d, nor for walking any such piece of cloth above 8d, nor the shearman for dressing any such piece of cloth above 10d, nor for the dyeing of any stone of wool above 16d.

Rules of this kind, entering sometimes into greater, sometimes into less, detail, are typical. The establishment of a maximum wage was in fact a settled part of municipal policy from the thirteenth to at least the seventeenth century. Since the earliest example comes from the year 1264[13], nearly a century before the first Statute of Labourers, and the latest which I have noticed from 1634, a period when the personal government of Charles I was making exceptional efforts to get the Statute of Artificers successfully administered, municipal action must be regarded as having anticipated that of the state, and having run parallel to and continued independently of, the intervention of the Justices. To the small oligarchies of master craftsmen and traders who governed most sixteenth century towns the wage clauses of the Statute of Artificers must have come as an extremely welcome enforcement of their traditional policy.

If the assessment of wages was in accordance with the ideas of the town bourgeoisie, it was equally in line with those of all the rural classes, great and small, who were interested in the employment of labour. Of the labour problem in the rural districts I shall have something to say later, when I come to speak of the economic aspects of the assessment of wages. The establishment of a maximum wage by the state had been in origin an attempt to help those classes out of the difficulty created by the Great Plague of 1348-9. The Act which set the precedent, however, for subsequent legislation was not the first Statute of Labourers, but an act of 1389[14], which placed the assessment of wages in the hands of the Justices of the Peace subject to a Statutory maximum imposed by Parliament. It was this Act, re-enacted in 1445[15], 1496[16], and 1514[17], which Elizabethan statesmen found ready to hand as the embodiment of traditional wisdom on the subject of state interference with wages; which they examined, partially preserved, and partially improved upon.

They improved upon both it and the experiments of the towns in two ways. In the first place, though the main ideas of the Statute of Artificers had been applied for centuries to particular trades, particular localities, or particular problems, the statute of 1563 made a new departure by dealing in one comprehensive measure with all the principle relationships surrounding the contract between employer and employed. In the second place, it abolished the statutory maximum which had hitherto limited the Justices's discretion in the assessment of wages, and thus made it possible for them, in the not very probable contingency of their thinking wages too low, to make the scales which they drew up slide freely in both directions. The former innovation was one which was peculiarly congenial to the ideas of the age. Both political reasons—a worship of the state amounting to idolatry—and economic reasons—the destruction of customary relationships by the swift changes of the preceding half-century—caused the establishment of a great industrial code to be an expedient foreshadowed by several writers in the first half of the sixteenth century. To many of the better minds of the generation which grew up between 1530 and 1540 the world seemed to have experienced within their memory a complete collapse of the forces making for stability in economic life. Whether politicians who noted the absence of 'good order' in industry, or moralists denouncing the exploitation of the weak by the powerful, or municipal authorities lementing that 'the wretched life of ociosite or idleness is the rote of all vice and engendreth slothe, poverty, miserie and other inconveniences as voluptuositie and all other vayne things', what struck them most was the fact that the dislocation of traditional standards seemed to be general, all-pervading, and increasing. It was this universal disorganization which explains why it is that scientific economic thought really begins in England about the middle of the sixteenth century. What supplied the stimulus to it then was what gave it its impetus both in the eighteenth century and in our own day, namely the existence of grave practical evils. People had been accustomed from time immemorial to ascribe a rise in prices to the covetousness of brewers and bakers and the uncharitableness of artificers and merchants. Now they saw all prices rising together, and to attribute price movements to the exorbitant demands of some particular monopolist was no longer a satisfactory explanation. They had seen groups of peasants evicted by a tyrannous landlord. Now there was a complete alteration in the balance between the life of the country and the life of the towns. They had grumbled often enough that the justices did not do their duty in fixing wages. Now the disturbance of customary levels of remuneration had brought with it an upward movement in wages, which, though it did not correspond with the upward movement in prices, carried them well beyond the statutory maximum by which the Justices' discretion had been limited. The bewilderment which the collapse of traditional standards produced is expressed very clearly by one of the few contemporary writers who understood it, in the dialogue composed probably about 1549, and called *The Commonweal of this Realm of England* where husbandman blames landlord, and landlord artificer, and artificer merchant, and merchant foreign exporter, for a movement for which neither of them is primarily responsible, but which occurs, in the words of the writer, 'as in a press where the foremost is driven by him that is next him, and the next by him that follows him, and the third by some violent and strong thing which drives him forward'[18]. The demand for a measure of economic reorganization as comprehensive as these changes themselves was expressed in several works, of which the *Dialogue*[19] *between Cardinal Pole and Thomas Lupset,* composed by Starkey, Henry VIII's chaplain, about 1536, may be taken as typical. Starkey's programme, though in some respects more drastic than the Statute of Artificers, is in others a most remarkable anticipation of its main provisions, and shows that the sort of regulation which it contained was such as political thought found congenial. He proposed to compel parents either to apprentice their children, when they reached the age of seven, to a craft, or to send them to school; to empower the authorities of cities and the curate in every village, together with 'the gentleman chefe lord of the same' to inquire into the characters of all persons who have no settled occupation, and to appoint officers 'to see that there be no idle persons without craft or means to get a living', suggestions which anticipate both the compulsory apprenticeship of the Act of 1563, and the clauses which authorized the Justices of the Peace to compel persons who had practised certain occupations for three years to work in them for any master requiring their services. Equally illuminating as a comment upon the Statute of Artificers is his lamentation over the growth in the number of beggars, over the tendency of one craft to encroach upon the province of another, and over the emigration from the country districts. These were precisely the evils which the act tried to meet by giving Justices power to compel unemployed persons to labour in husbandry, and by stratifying social classes by means of the clauses providing that no parent who had not a certain property qualification should apprentice his child to certain occupations. The belief in the necessity of an all-comprehensive system of regulation was, in fact, a commonplace. When the act of 1563 was passed, it was welcomed as meeting an urgent need. 'In times passed', ran a memorial[20] addressed to the government in 1573, and urging the better administration of the Act, 'while order was observed among artificers, they found their trades and occupations such a stay of living that by means thereof they might maintain themselves in all things necessary for their calling . . . But since disorder hath entered among them and increase of offences grown, they have found their trades and occupations so uncertain and their earnings and gettings so abated that they want to maintain themselves with things necessary . . . Wherefore to stay the further increase of such offences, they do become suitors and earnestly desire to have the said Statute executed and observed.'

But what of the other new departure in the Act of 1563, the removal of the statutory maximum of wages? This was a policy which was not so readily accepted. It is a curious illustration of the tyranny of an established idea that the proposals first made by the Government should have apparently aimed simply at re-enacting a maximum wage by act of Parliament, and that the decision to leave the assessment of actual rates to the Justices for their yearly revision, which was the only original[21] feature in the Elizabethan wage policy, should have been adopted as an afterthought, probably as the result of debate in Parliament. That this was so is suggested by a document which a fortunate chance has preserved, and which appears to be an outline of the Bill[22] before its introduction, and of certain other measures as well, drafted by Cecil, in accordance with his usual practice, for preliminary consideration, It throws such an extremely interesting light upon the ideas of the statesman who was principally responsible both for the Act of 1563 and for the other economic legislation of Elizabeth's reign, that I may be pardoned for quoting it at some length:

Considerations delivered to the Parliament 1559

1. Vagabonds—That the Statute 1 Ed. VI cap 3, concerning idle persons and vagabonds being made slaves, now repealed, be revived with additions.
2. Labourers and servants—That the statutes Richard II cap 3 that no servant or labourer at the end of his term depart out of the hundred where he dwells, etc and 13 Richard II cap 8, ordering the Justices to appoint by proclamation the wages of artificers, be confirmed, with the addition that no man hereafter receive into service any servant without a testimonial from the master he last dwelt with, sealed with a Parish seal kept by the Constable or Churchwarden witnessing he left with the free license of his master, penalty £10. So, by

the need of the masters servants may be reduced to obedience, which shall reduce obedience to the prince and to God also; by the looseness of the time, no other remedy is left but by awe of the law to acquaint men with virtue again; whereby the Reformation of religion may be brought in credit, with the amendement of manners, the want whereof has been as a thing grown by the liberty of the Gospel.

3. Husbandry—That the statutes of 4 Henry VII cap 9 for reedifying house of husbandry to avoid the decay of towns and villages, and 5 Ed. V cap 5 for maintenance of husbandry and tillage be put in execution.
4. Purchase of lands—No husbandman, yeoman, or artificer to purchase above £5 by the year of inheritance, save in cities and boroughs, for their better repair; one mansion house only to be purchased over and above the said yearly value. The common purchasing thereof is the ground of dearth of victuals, raising of rents etc.
5. Merchants—No Merchant to purchase above £50 a year of inheritance, except aldermen and Sheriffs of London, who because they approach to the degree of knighthood, may purchase to the value of £200.
6. Apprentices—None to be received apprentice except his father may spend 40s a year of freehold, none to be apprenticed to a Merchant except his father spend £10 a year of freehold, or be descended from a gentleman or merchant. Through the idleness of these professions so many embrace them that they are only a cloak for vagabonds and thieves, and there is such a decay of husbandry that masters cannot get skilful servants to till the ground without unreasonable wages.

The document then goes on to matters into which we need not follow it, such as the education of the nobility, the necessity of securing a supply of bullion and the erection of tariffs against imported articles. The important point for us is to compare Cecil's draft with the shape which legislation finally took in the hands of Parliament. It will be seen that while a considerable part of it was actually embodied either in the Statute of Artificers or in other acts, its general tendency is at once more conservative and more repressive than the statutes which actually became law. It proposes for example to re-enact an extremely brutal Act of 1547 providing that a vagrant should after the third conviction become the slave of anyone arresting him, which had been repealed only two years after it was passed. The suggestion was quite in accordance with the legislation of the first half of the sixteenth century, when the economic causes of unemployment were not understood. But, as a matter of fact, the Elizabethan Poor Law legislation proceeded upon the quite different principle of distinguishing between the man unemployed for personal reasons, who was to be punished, and the man unemployed for economic reasons, who was to be 'set on work'; and forty years later Cecil's own son, then Secretary of State in his father's place, penned a memorandum[23] preliminary to the introduction of the Poor Relief measure of 1597, which altogether threw overboard his father's earlier ideas. The impracticable rigour of Cecil's views with regard to the suppression of vagrancy should be remembered in considering his proposals for the regulation of wages. It will be noticed that while he makes the object of the enforcement of maximum wages perfectly clear by his allusion to the 'unreasonable wages' demanded by servants in husbandry, what he actually recommends is simply the re-enactment of the second Statute of Labourers passed 170 years before. What can only be called the unreasoning conservatism of this suggestion is doubly noteworthy in view of the extreme improbability that the Act which Cecil wished to see re-enacted was ever successfully enforced. Our information about the assessment of wages in the fifteenth century is, it is true, very meagre. The Justices were not required, as under the act of 1563, to make returns to Chancery of the rates fixed, and it is not until the organization of the Tudor bureaucracy that a close supervision of local authorities by the Council begins to supply us with masses of material in the shape of letters of justices, orders, and proclamations. We have only two assessments made under the Act of 1389, one from Coventry[24] in 1420, and one from Norfolk[25] in 1431, a proclamation[26] issued in 1452 directing that labourers and artificers should take such wages as were fixed by the statutes, one or two cases of men being brought before the Courts for taking excessive wages[27] and a few records of attempts on the part of town authorities to insist that labourers should 'offer themselves to be hired to labour for their living according to the King's laws and Statutes provided for labourers.'[28] While, however, researches into the administration of the act in the fifteenth century similar to those which Miss Putnam has made for the years 1349-59, may possibly show the Justices to have been more active than our scanty evidence suggests, they are not likely substantially to modify the picture of the general inefficiency of the Acts in the fifteenth century, and still more in the sixteenth century, which we get from other sources. The Rolls of Parliament[29] are full of complaints that the Justices are not doing their duty, that masters who refuse to pay more than the legal maximum find themselves without workmen, that men escape service by pretending to be living upon their own holdings. The passage of subsequent Acts raising the maximum suggests that economic forces were too strong for the law. And of course the depreciation of money which took place with increasing rapidity from the accession of Henry VIII intensified all difficulties. In the very year after the last Act of the old model was passed, in 1515, it was found necessary to allow workers connected with the building trades in London to take the higher rates[30] which had been customary before it. The fearful hardships which spasmodic attempts to enforce the legal maximum involved were described in burning words by More[31]. Ten years before Cecil drafted his Bill, Hales pointed out that in a time of rising prices servicing-men could not possibly live on 'their old stinted wages'. That sad, precocious child, Edward VI, in a catalogue of the signs of the evil days in which his lot was cast, had set down that 'labourers have enhanced their wages and artificers the price of their workmanship'.[32] It is not surprising, therefore, that Cecil's proposal to re-establish a fixed statutory maximum, a maximum which, if his proposals are to be taken literally, was to stand at the figures settled when the purchasing power of money had been at least from three to four times what it was in the middle of the sixteenth century, should have roused bitter resentment. 'The business,' writes one of Cecil's agents to him, 'touching what wages workmen should take, was much cried out upon.'[33] The remarkable thing is that the re-enactment of the old maximum rates should ever have been thought possible for a moment. The episode is a comment upon the views of those writers who speak as though the Tudor régime were that of an enlightened bureaucracy using the resources of scientific administration to pursue a farsighted and clearly conceived economic policy. The whole economic environment had been revolutionized by the fall in the value of money, and here is the ablest statesman of the Elizabethan age on his knees before medieval precedents, till (apparently) the country gentlemen in the House of Commons bring him up to date! Clearly in the early years of Elizabeth economic rationalism was not a mighty force.

III Was the Act carried out?

The first question to be considered in relation to the wage clauses of the Statute of Artificers concerns their administration. To what extent did the Justices of the Peace fulfil the obligations to 'rate and appoint wages' once a year, which was imposed upon them by the Act of 1563? An answer to this question must be based, in the first instance, on a statistical survey of the evidence at our disposal, and such a survey I attempt to give in the two tables set out below. The second table groups assessments according to their dates, the first according to the districts—counties or boroughs—for which they were made. It will be seen from the first two columns of Table X that the total number of complete and different assessments which are at present known to exist is 73, and that, in addition to these, we have 24 assessments which appear to be mere reissues or repetitions of assessments already made. The total number of wage lists, therefore, which are at present known to be extant is 97.

Seventy-three original and independent assessments, 24 re-issues of assessments already made, though representing a considerable increase over the documents known to exist when Professor Hewins and Dr. Cunningham treated the subject, is not a large number to be produced by an Act which applied to the whole of England and Wales, and which was nominally in force for a period of exactly 250 years. It is not surprising, therefore, that most economic historians, with

TABLE X
Assessment of Wages, by district.

	Number of complete assessments exclusive of re-issues	Number of re-issues	Orders continuing assessments already made	Assessments referred to, but not included in first three columns	Action ordered by Privy Council
Buckinghamshire	4	—	—	—	—
Cambridge	—	—	—	—	1
Cheshire	—	—	—	1	—
Devonshire	3	—	—	—	—
Derbyshire	2	—	—	1	—
Essex	2	—	—	1	1
Gloucestershire	3	—	—	1	—
Hertfordshire	1	—	—	—	—
Kent	1	—	—	—	—
Lancashire	1	—	—	—	—
Lincolnshire	5	—	—	1	—
Middlesex	1	—	—	1	—
Norfolk	1	—	—	—	1
Northamptonshire	2	—	—	—	—
Nottinghamshire	1	—	—	1	—
Rutland	2	—	—	—	—
Shropshire	1	5	—	1	—
Somerset	9	—	—	1	—
Suffolk	2	—	—	—	1
Warwickshire	5	4	1	—	—
Wiltshire	6	—	82	—	—
Worcestershire	1	—	—	—	—
Yorkshire, E.R.	1	—	—	—	—
Yorkshire N.R.	2	—	—	1	—
Yorkshire W.R.	1	6	—	—	—
Cardigan	1	—	—	—	—
Chester	5	1	—	—	—
Kingston-upon-Hull	1	—	—	—	—
Lancaster	1	—	—	—	—
Leicester	—	—	—	1	—
Lincoln	1	—	—	—	—
London	3	8	4	—	—
New Sarum	1	—	—	1	1
Norwich	—	—	—	—	—
Reading	—	—	—	1	—
St. Albans	1	—	—	—	—
Sandwich	1	—	—	—	—
Southampton	—	—	—	1	—
Warwick	1	—	—	—	—
Colchester	—	—	—	1	—
Total	73	24	87	15	5

the exception of Thorold Rogers (who expressed the opinion that the actual course of wages did follow the Justices' assessments down to 1813, but who did not produce any satisfactory evidence for his statement, and, indeed, could not do so, owing to the extremely small number of assessments which he had before him) should have held that the wage clauses of the Act of 1563 were largely inoperative; inoperative not merely in the sense that assessments, when made, were not enforced, but in the sense that it was only on quite exceptional occasions that they were made at all, except, perhaps, during a limited period after the passage of Cecil's bill into law. Professor Hewins[34] and Dr. Cunningham[35] agree in thinking that, though the Act may possibly have been administered fairly frequently during the first eighty years or so after its enactment, the fall of the Stuart monarchy, which involved the weakening, and later almost the complete cessation, of interference by the central government in local economic conditions, brought anything like the regular assessment of wages to an end. Such opinions seem to me, however, to be considerably overstated. The view that the

TABLE XI Assessments By Date (Decades)
Number of assessments, including reissues which can be dated

1560-69	5	1670-79	3
1570-79	2	1680-89	7
1580-89	1	1690-99	1
1590-99	11	1700-09	6
1600-09	3	1710-19	5
1610-19	3	1720-29	3
1620-29	1	1730-39	10
1630-39	6	1740-49	—
1640-49	4	1750-59	1
1650-59	12	1760-69	3
1660-69	3	1770-79	—

Total: 90

constitutional changes brought about by the destruction of the old régime were such as to make it improbable that the Act was ever carried out subsequently with the same regularity as during the reign of Elizabeth and of the first two Stuarts appears to be based on reasoning of an *a priori* character which requires several qualifications. It is not easily reconciled with the actual records of assessments which we possess. A glance at Table XI will show that, as a matter of fact, the reigns of James I and Charles I are not a period for which we possess many assessments, and that assessments do not by any means cease with the years 1640 or 1642. On the contrary there are 25 assessments for the 40 years from 1650 to 1689, as against 13 for the years 1600 to 1639. After 1660 the century-long rise in prices came to an end. Prices began to fall, and the downward movement in prices was naturally an opportunity for trying to force a similar movement in wages. This was avowedly the reason for the assessment of wages by the authorities of the City of London[36] in 1655, and it is probable that the operation of the same motive elsewhere is the explanation of the comparatively numerous assessments of the Restoration period. Moreover the analogies which may be adduced—and the argument is admittedly one from analogy—to suggest that with the decline in the administrative activity of the Privy Council the assessment of wages declined also will not bear examination. It is, of course, perfectly true that the victory of parliamentary government, which carried with it as a corollary the abolition of 'administrative law' did involve a laxity in the control of local affairs which, in the course of time, and in certain departments of administration, produced something like complete anarchy. The attempts, for example, which had been fitfully made under James and Charles, to protect the peasantry by checking enclosures involving depopulation, came to an end with the restoration of parliamentary government in 1640, and Laud lived to be reminded in the day of his ruin of the sharp words with which he had barbed the fine imposed by the Commission for Depopulation upon an enclosing landlord[37]. The effective enforcement upon parochial authorities of their statutory obligations to relieve the aged and infirm and to set unemployed persons to work, was replaced, when the pressure of the Council upon the Justices was removed, by a neglect which resulted in each Board becoming a law to itself, so that, by the middle of the eighteenth century, there were in England almost as many Poor Law systems as there were counties. But the analogy between these types of intervention and the assessment of wages is an extremely superficial one. Interference in disputes between landlord and tenants over commons and copyholds, insistence on the efficient administration of the Elizabethan Poor Law, these things came to an end in 1640, not because there was any general prejudice in favour of *laisser faire*—of any general economic policy Parliament was quite innocent—but because these were just the matters to which the interests of the triumphant landed gentry, who wanted to be free to increase their rent rolls and to escape the Poor Rates, were opposed. The fixing of maximum wages by the action of the Justices stood upon a quite different footing. The system had been originally introduced, and had been re-enacted in 1563, in order to protect not the wage-earners but the wage-payers, and though this object was not incompatible with occasional attempts by the Privy Council to use the Act to fix in certain industries a minimum, there is no reason whatever to suppose that the policy of fixing a maximum wage was other than highly popular with the employers of agricultural labour, whose complaints of the 'unreasonableness' of the workers' demands are quite common in the latter part of the seventeenth century. The Commonwealth[38] Government in April 1649 directed Justices to assess wages, and Petty[39], one of the few writers who suggests that assessments were regarded as a grievance by the poor, writes in 1662 as though they were not uncommon practice. Hence, while the use of the wage clauses of the Statute of Artificers to fix a *minimum* certainly was bound up with the administrative intervention of the Privy Council, and thus terminated in 1640, the use of them to enforce a *maximum*—the normal object of assessing wages—certainly was not; and to suggest that the latter policy must have disappeared with the former when the period of absolutism came to an end, is to confuse the general purpose of the Act with an occasional deviation from it. The probabilities of the case are at one, in fact, with the direct evidence of documents, in suggesting that the assessment of wages was carried out as regularly in the forty years after the outbreak of the Civil War as in the forty years before it.

To say this, it may be answered, is not to say much. The question remains whether the 97 assessments, which are all that have as yet been unearthed, can be taken as in any way representing the full activity of the Justices, or whether there is reason to suppose that the Act was more regularly administered than this small number of detailed tables would indicate. To this question the answer must be given that the scantiness of the specimens available for analysis must certainly not be taken as implying that for the years and places for which no assessments exist, no action was taken by the Justices in pursuance of the law. It is not merely that new assessments are constantly being discovered, though this, indeed, is striking enough; I estimate that since the third edition of Dr. Cunningham's volume appeared in 1903, evidence showing the existence of at least 32 assessments not mentioned by him has come to light. Nor can much weight be allowed to the utterances of contemporary writers, which imply that assessments were habitually made. Smith[40] and Lambard[41] in the sixteenth century, Shepperd[42] in the seventeenth, certainly speak of the assessment of wages as being one of the ordinary duties of a Justice of the Peace. But then so does FitzHerbert[43] at an earlier date, when there is little doubt that the Acts fixing wages were not administered; and, in any case, little reliance can be placed on the general statements of authors of legal textbooks. What suggests that the assessments in our possession must not be taken as representing anything like the full activity of the Justices is, first, the existence of references in official documents which show that numerous assessments were made that have not come down to us, and secondly the fact, which is apparent from the Quarter Session records, that in some counties and cities it was the custom to continue existing assessments by order from year to year, so that the administration of the law was receiving attention from the Justices, even when no new assessments were made.

The first point may be illustrated by the examples of Derbyshire, Essex, the North Riding of Yorkshire, Reading, and Leicester. The earliest assessment which we possess from the first county is one of 1634, and, in default of further information, the absence of others might be taken as evidence that the administration of the Act of 1563 was neglected in Derbyshire till that date. That this would be an error is proved by the fact that a document[44] of the year 1618 mentions the delivery to the Clerk of the Peace (probably by a servant of one of the Justices) of 'three several rolls of parchments containing the rates of servants wages'. The only full assessment known to exist for Essex was made in 1651. But there remains the preamble[45] of an assessment drawn up in 1612. There is no complete assessment for the North Riding of Yorkshire before the year 1658. But presentments[46] of offenders for breaches of the wage clauses of the Statute of Artificers, made at intervals between the years 1608 and 1647, showed that at least one assessment, and probably more than one, had been issued by the Justices before that date. The Quarter Sessions records of the same county show no assessment under the year 1691. But since an order made in 1692[47] directs 'the same rates of wages . . . to stand this year as they were appointed and settled by order of this Court last year', an assessment must have been made in the preceding year. For Reading and Leicester no assessments at all have survived. But in 1598 offenders against the Act were being tried in the Court of the Mayor of Reading[48], while from Leicester there is conclusive evidence that the Act received attention regularly from 1564 down to at least 1603 and possibly longer. The records[49] of that borough show that in every year of that period a certificate was forwarded by the borough authorities to Chancery, setting out the wages of servants, labourers, and artificers. Similar evidence of the enforcement of the Act at a time for which few assessments are known to exist is supplied by the registers[50] of the Privy Council, which prove that assessments were issued by the authorities in London on at least eleven occasions between 1563 and 1596. This source of information is, it is true, disappointing. It comes to an end with the passage of the Act of 1598[51] relieving Justices of the duty of making returns of their assessments to Chancery. Further, there is no reason to suppose that a formal letter was always or usually written by the Council to the Lord Keeper directing him to print the assessments which had been made, and it would, therefore, be quite erroneous to regard the small number of entries in the Privy Council registers as implying that no assessments were made upon other occasions. What these entries, and other references of the kind mentioned above, do prove, is that wages were assessed in many years and places for which no assessments have yet been discovered, and that it would, therefore, be quite erroneous to use the absence of assessments as proof that the Act was administered with laxity. They show that the assessments in our possession are a mere residuum of a much larger number which have perished. In each of the instances mentioned above the absence of assessments might have led us to argue that the Act was a dead letter, and in each instance the inference would be wrong. From these and similar miscellaneous references I estimate that we know that at least 15 assessments were made of which we have no particulars. That is a minimum figure; but it brings up the number of assessments of whose existence we have proof from 97 to 112. More important, it suggests that a very large number of assessments must have perished, without leaving any trace whatever behind them.

In the second place, when the regularity of the administration of the Act is being considered, due weight must be given to the practice of containing existing assessments by order of Quarter Sessions in years in which no full assessment was made. Such orders are, of course, evidence for the practice of assessment as complete as the issue of actual rates, and prove conclusively that an omission on the part of the Justices to publish fresh rates did not necessarily imply a failure upon their part to comply with the law. Miss McArthur[52] has shown, for example, that during twenty-one out of the twenty-eight years immediately following the passage of the Act of 1563 the authorities of the City of London either issued assessments or issued orders continuing existing assessments. My own investigations have led me to believe that this continuous activity was by no means exceptional. The practice of the Wiltshire[53] Justices supplies a case in point. In that county new assessments were made at various dates in the seventeenth century, 1602, 1603, 1605, 1635, 1655, 1685. But the fact that assessments were made in this county only at long intervals does not prove that the administration of the Act was at a standstill in the intervening years. As far as the letter of the law went the Justices were discharging their statutory duties if they renewed the old rates without a change. This they did in Wiltshire every year from 1603 to 1696, with the exception of an interval of eleven out of the whole ninety-three years, four out of the eleven being those from 1642-3 to 1645-6, when country gentlemen had sterner work in hand than the routine business of Quarter Sessions. The question whether the regular confirmation of rates fixed many years before was due to mere carelessness, or was justified by the fact that conditions had not altered, is of course, quite another matter. When the Clerk of the Peace read out a schedule containing, like that drawn up for Wiltshire in 1603, some 200 separate items, and asked whether it was to be continued or revised, somnolent Justices meeting in a bar parlour were probably disposed to have a high opinion of the wisdom of their predecessors. On the other hand it would certainly be wrong to assume that the frequent reissue of old assessments necessarily implied negligence. On the economic objects and effects of the policy something will be said later. But one may point out here that the assessment of wages in the sixteenth and seventeenth centuries did not involve the problem of readjusting them in accordance with constantly fluctuating economic conditions, which confronts any authority interfering with wages at the present day. The practice with regard not only to wages but to prices and the rate of interest was based on the idea that values were objective realities, which could, as it were, be held in position, irrespective of the higgling of the market. In the slowly-moving life of the time, with its almost stationary population, and its absence of rapidly growing industries, there was, in general, not the same reason for changes in the rates of remuneration as exist today. One such reason there was. Food prices fluctuated violently, far more violently than they do in modern industrial communities. If movements in wages had been adjusted with any accuracy to movement in prices, it would have been necessary for them to take place not only from year to year, but from month to month, and, indeed, almost from day to day. The machinery for dealing with such temporary oscillations was not so much, however, the Statute of Artificers, as the regulation of markets and the fixing of the prices of food supplies. It cannot therefore be assumed that the admitted omission of the Justices to make wages correspond with the short period fluctuations necessarily implies that they failed to carry out the intentions of the Act.

To sum up this part of my discussion: the view taken by

most economic historians that the wage assessment clauses of the Act of 1563 were, except on special occasions, a dead letter, and that whatever vitality they had under Elizabeth and the first two Stuarts disappeared after the Civil War, must be regarded as, to say the least, not proven. In the first place, neither was there any reason why the rise of parliamentary government should have had the effect of making the Justices of the Peace less disposed to fix maximum wages, nor does the actual distribution of assessments over different periods bear out the conclusion that it had. In the second place, the discoveries recently made of new assessments and the considerable number of references proving that assessments were made which have not come down to us, show that those which we possess are a remnant of a much larger number. In the third place, the fact that in years when no new assessments were made, the Justices nevertheless attended to the duties imposed upon them by the law, suggests that the mere absence of assessments cannot in itself be taken as an indication of laxity of administration.

IV The Motives for the Assessment of Wages in Non-Textile Trades

In what light are we to regard the system of regulating wages which was set up by the Statute of Artificers? Are its opening words, with their declaration that 'wages are in divers places too small . . . respecting the advancement of prices' to be taken as indicating a paternal solicitude on the part of the government for the well-being of the wage-earning classes? Or should we follow Thorold Rogers in discounting this pious preamble as mere hypocrisy, and see in the assessment of wages simply one outcome of the enduring instinct of the governing classes in favour of using the law to buttress their economic privileges?

Between the hypotheses of philanthropy and class tyranny it is not, perhaps, necessary to make a definite choice. The medieval ideal of equity in bargaining, of which the fixing of wages was one expression, was based on the assumption that it was possible to do substantial justice to the interest of all parties to a contract; and though there are some indications that in the seventeenth century Puritanism, with its insistence on the duty of labour, and its severe condemnation of luxury, led to a harsh view being taken of the moral evils supposed to result from high wages, the establishment of a maximum wage did not in itself necessarily involve any more injustice to the wage-worker than the establishment of a maximum price did to the dealer. That, as far at least as all trades except the textile industries were concerned, the prinicipal object of the assessment of wages was to prevent them rising above the level thought 'reasonable' by the Justices, there is no doubt whatever. Quite apart from the connexion between the Act of 1563 and the earlier Statutes of Labourers, both the wording and the administration of the law leave no room for uncertainty as to its purpose. It imposes penalties on those who pay or accept more, not on those who pay or accept less, than the legal rates. A form commonly employed in the assessments is that 'wages shall be such and no more than are hereafter set down'. When punishment is incurred by masters and workmen, it is invariably for exceeding the figure fixed by the Justices. The writers of legal textbooks all state that the wage was a maximum. The cases to be considered later, in which a minimum was established, are of a special and peculiar character, and in no way invalidate the conclusion that, as a general rule, the object and effect of assessments were to prevent the worker demanding more than a certain sum for his labour.

To say this, however, is neither to substantiate Rogers's charge of hypocrisy, nor to imply that, in the circumstances of the age, the establishment of maximum rates was a piece of intolerable tyranny. In the first place, there is the minor point that the view sometimes expressed as to the discrepancy between the preamble of the Act and its substance appears to have been formed in forgetfulness of the fact that it was one, and the least harsh, of a series. As a matter of fact the wage clauses did exactly what the preamble indicated that they should do. They substituted a sliding scale for the fixed maximum imposed by previous statutes. The effect of this is seen in the words with which assessments frequently begin, stating that they are made 'in respect and consideration had of the great dearth and scarcity of things at this present', or 'having a special regard . . . to the prices at this time of all kinds of victual and apparel, and all other necessary charges, wherewith artificers, labourers and servants are more grieviously charged than in time past'. Whether the movement of wages did in fact correspond to the movement of prices is, of course, another question. As will be shown later, there is good reason for believing that in most districts it did not. But that should not be allowed to obscure the fact that the Statute of 1563 made possible a movement of legal rates, which, under the earlier Acts, had been out of the question. By directing yearly assessments it certainly fulfilled the declaration of its preamble, that it was enacted in order to 'yield unto the hired person both in the time of scarcity and in the time of plenty a convenient proportion of wages'.

In the second place, the policy of fixing a maximum wage must be interpreted with reference to the general economic circumstances of the Tudor age. The two fundamental facts in the social structure of the sixteenth century were the wide distribution of property and the scarcity of wage-labour. It is, of course, quite true that the process of commutation which, in spite of the existence of backwaters where the remnants of labour services still lingered on, was virtually complete by the reign of Elizabeth, can be explained only by the existence of a considerable number of persons who were available for employment as hired labourers. It is true also that the agrarian revolution which was taking place with growing rapidity from 1450 onwards resulted in the increase of a landless proletariat dependent upon wages for its livelihood. But though forces were at work to replace the medieval wage problem, which consisted in the scarcity of labour, by the modern wage problem, which consists in its abundance, they certainly had not by the middle of the sixteenth century proceeded so far as to effect any substantial alteration in the balance between the relatively large number of property-holders and the relatively small number of wage-workers. Statistical evidence on this subject is naturally not very easy to obtain, but such as it is, it confirms the view that except in those parts of the country, like East Anglia, where a large population was employed in the textile industries, the family entirely dependent for its livelihood upon wage-labour was in rural districts the exception.

That this was the case is suggested, in the first place, by such incidental evidences of economic status as are supplied by the descriptions of offenders presented for justice. In the Quarter Sessions records[54] of the North Riding, for example, at the beginning of the seventeenth century, the large number of yeomen and husbandmen presented is very striking. Out of 3,780 persons mentioned in recognizancies in the records[55] of the Worcestershire Quarter Sessions between 1591 and 1643, 667 are described as labourers, 1,303 as husbandmen, 1,810 as yoemen, the latter always, and the second usually, implying a holder of land. The more detailed evidence of manorial surveys points in the same direction. Taking 52[56] manors in the sixteenth century, I find that, of the 1,664 Customary tenants upon them, rather less than one third, 562, has less than 5 acres of land, while of these 255 had more than 2½ acres, and only 167 are entered as holding no land other than gardens. In Norfolk or Suffolk, the proportion of landless cottagers, is, as one would expect, considerably larger, and, of course, though the head of a family held land, he had usually a family of sons who would be employed for a time, at any rate, by the large farmers of the district. But such figures suggest that the proportion of persons holding land in sixteenth century England was still large; while if we approach the matter from the other end, and examine the staffs employed both on demesne farms and by small land-holders, we shall be inclined, I think, to say, that the number of employees, even when there is no reason to suspect any sweeping change in the direction of pasture farming, was singularly small. On the demesne farms of twenty-two religious[57] houses in Leicester, Warwick, and Sussex there were on the eve of the Dissolution 255 hinds, and 76 women servants, an average of about 11 hinds and about 3 women to each farm. Best[58] narrates how he worked a considerable farm in Yorkshire with 4 men, 2 boys and 2 maidservants; and we read of a village[59] where in the latter part of the seventeenth century, 13 freeholders farmed 580 acres with the aid of only 10 men-servants before enclosure, and of 7 afterwards. The smallness of the permanent staff of wage-workers suggests that at times of unusual pressure, labour must generally have been drawn from men who normally were occupied on their own holdings, and quite explains why the Statute of Artificers empowered the Justices to press artisans for work on the land during the corn and hay harvest.

A recollection of the large part which was played in sixteenth century England by the small property-holders should warn us that to estimate the wage policy of Tudor and Stuart governments by presuppositions drawn from the experience of modern industrial communities is an error in the very foundations of the subject. In countries where the 'Great Industry' has developed, the vast majority of the population are workers for wages; the principal social problem is the problem of wages; to fix a maximum wage by law would be to depress the price of something, which is already, often, a drug in the market. In the England of the Tudors and Stuarts, though the proportion of the people employed as wage-labourers was growing, the typical 'workman' was not a wage-labourer, but a small master craftsman of a land-holding peasant. The economic problem which received most attention both from writers and statesmen was not the problem of wages, but that of usury and prices, matters which were felt acutely by the man who had to stock his farm or his shop with borrowed capital, and who was easily exploited by a large dealer who cornered the supplies of raw materials or foodstuffs. The wage-labourers scattered between the interstices of a society based on property were often in a strong position relatively to their employers. To check by law the demands which they might make was often no doubt a grievance analogous to that of the speculator in grain, who found his profits swept away when prices were lowered by a proclamation from the Privy Council, or when an energetic Justice inspected his barns and exposed to compulsory sale below the market rates the corn which he had hoarded against a time of scarcity. The object, however, of assessing wages was not to benefit a privileged oligarchy of employers at the expense of the vast majority of workers, but to protect one class of workers against another. The system is evidence not so much of the defencelessness of the wage-worker against oppression as of the fact that he was often able to drive a hard bargain with a master who was not much better off than himself.

Such an account of the economic environment which produced the system of assessing wages will not seem fanciful to anyone who studies contemporary complaints of the difficulties caused by the scarcity of labour. One must of course enter a caveat against taking the arguments of employers or of those who write from the employers' standpoint *au pied de la lettre.* But their statements, even when discounted, harmonize too well with what we know from other sources, to be other than reliable. To give an extreme example of the situation which sometimes arose, one may cite in the first place the difficulties of the English colony of Massachusetts. The experience of the colonists is worth attention, because the scarcity of labour which is to be expected in a new country naturally causes the problem to be seen there in its simplest form. The journal of Winthrop[60] the governor of the colony, gives us an insight into the situation produced by the high prices of labour. 'The scarcity of workmen had caused them to raise their wages to an excessive height, so as a carpenter would have three shillings a day, a labourer two shillings and sixpence etc and accordingly those who had commodities to sell advanced their prices sometimes double that they cost in England . . . which the Court taking knowledge of, made an order that carpenters, masons, etc. should take but two shillings a day, and labourers eighteen pence, and that no commodities should be sold at above fourpence in the shilling more than it cost for ready money in England'. 'I may upon this occasion report a passage between one Rowley and his servant. The master being forced to sell a pair of his oxen to pay his servant his wages, told his servant he could keep him no longer, not knowing how to pay him next year. The servant answered he would serve him for more of his cattle. "But how shall I do?" saith the master, "when all my cattle are gone?" The servant replied, "You shall serve me, and so you may have your cattle again".' The answer scandalized the decorous Winthrop, and if the servant had made it in England, the neighbouring Justices would probably have made him rue his impudence. But though the economic conditions of a colony were peculiar, there were times, even in England, when the wage-earner could make his own terms. Side by side with the remarks of a statesman like Cecil as to difficulties caused by the high price of agricultural labour, one may set a complaint from a rural community which is all the more remarkable, in that it comes from the latter part of the seventeenth century. 'We desire' say the Grand Jury of Worcestershire in 1661, 'that servants' wages may be rated according to the Statute, for we find the unreasonableness of servants' wages a great grievance, so that servants are grown so proud and idle that the master cannot be known from the servant, except it be because the servant wears better clothes than the master'.[61] It would, at any rate, be a grave error to think of agricultural labourers in the sixteenth and seventeenth centuries as the helpless victims of economic oppression. Combination to raise wages was, of course, forbidden by statute, nor need we place much reliance on the statements of writers like Roger Coke[62] and the author of *Britannia Languens*[63], who find a stick with which to beat the Elizabethan Poor Laws in the alleged fact, that by making the worker independent of his master, they are 'the principal, if not the only, reason of the excessive wages of servants as well as of labourers, who will neither serve nor labour.' Quite apart, however, both from trade unionism and parochial relief, there were two methods of raising wages to which the workers could have recourse. In the first place they could practise passive resistance by refusing to enter the labour market, and, instead of working for an employer, employing themselves at home. This alternative, which in modern England, at any rate, is beyond the reach of the worker whose wages are reduced, was made possible by the predominance of small-scale production both in agriculture and in many, though not all, branches of manufacturing industry. The peasant could work on his own holding, the village weaver for customers who dealt with him direct, the village joiner in doing odd jobs for his neighbours. That it was used as a lever for raising wages is proved by the orders which Justices found themselves obliged from time to time to issue, directing that since 'young people both men and maids . . . will not go abroad to service, without they may have excessive wages, but will rather work at home at their own hands, whereby the rating of wages will take little effect, therefore no young men or maids fitting to go abroad to service . . . shall remain at home . . . but shall with all convenient speed betake themselves to service for the wages aforesaid'.[64]

In the second place, there was nearly always the possibility of turning from employment with a master to some sort of rough subsistence-farming. In the sparsely populated England of the Tudors the land under cultivation was everywhere an island set in an ocean of unreclaimed barrenness, and well into the eighteenth century the wastes available for occupation by settlers were enormous. As a consequence, the worker who was discontented with the terms offered for his labour could often make an independent, though precarious, living, by squatting upon unoccupied land, and working for himself. It was, indeed, in this process of spontaneous colonization that many of the peasants displaced by the spread of pasture-farming found an alternative to wage-labour, and in the seventeenth century the issuing of licences for the erection of cottages on waste lands by able-bodied men who had come with their families from a distance became a regular part of the business of Quarter Sessions. The economic effect of the existence of these reservoirs of unoccupied territory is indicated by the lamentations of contemporary economists over the high wages which they enabled workers to demand. 'In all or most towns, where the fields lie open', writes a pamphleteer, 'there is a new brood of upstart intruders or inmates . . . loiterers who will not work unless they may have such excessive wages as they themselves desire'.[65] 'There is with us now,' states another, whose words offer a striking parallel both to the story told by Winthrop and to the complaint of the Worcestershire Grand Jury, 'rather a scarcity than a superfluity of servants, their wages being advanced to such an extraordinary height, that they are likely ere long to be masters and their masters servants, many poor husbandmen being forced to pay near as much to their servants for wages as to their landlords for rent'.[66]

That such complaints were exaggerated, that the workers would have given a very different account of their conditions, is highly probable. But the fact that it should have been possible to make these statements with any show of verisimilitude shows how radically different was the situation of the wage worker at the time when the fixing of maximum rates was enforced from that with which the modern world is acquainted. Remembering the multitude of small property-holders and the comparative fewness of the families who had no holdings of land at all, we shall be in a position to understand the extreme suspicion with which petty farmers and craftsmen regarded any attempt at independence on the part of their employees, and to realize that the assessment of wages may have been a policy popular not only with the governing classes who sat on the County Bench, but with large bodies of humble people; for humble people were property-holders and employers themselves. Readers of *John Bull's Other Island* will remember the horror with which the Irish peasant, who had just acquired land under the Land Purchase Acts, greeted the proposal to pay the labourer, Patsy Farrell, 20s. a week. The attitude of the yeomen and small masters in the England of the sixteenth and seventeenth centuries towards the Patsy Farrells of their day was much the same. In the 'Distributive State' to which some modern admirers of small-scale agriculture and small-scale industry look as an ideal, the laws regard with an eye that is anything but favourable the claim of the wage-earner to make the best bargain for himself that he can. Happily for him, the economic conditions which produced a demand for the assessment of his wages were such as to facilitate his escape from a life of continuous wage-labour. If the establishment of maximum rates had been widely regarded as oppressive we should almost certainly have heard of some petitions, some riots, against it, such as were made so frequently by peasants who resisted enclosures. That nothing of the kind has come down to us from any bodies of agricultural labourers is evidence of some weight for the belief that the interference of the state with wages was not regarded as an intolerable grievance.

V The Economic Motive for the Assessment of Wages in the Textile Trades

There was, however, another side to the wage-policy of the Tudors and Stuarts than that which we have hitherto considered. If the labour problem in agriculture arose in the sixteenth and seventeenth centuries, as in the middle ages, from the scarcity of wage-workers, the labour problem in the textile industries was nevertheless of a quite modern character, and consisted in the inability of large bodies of artisans to resist the reductions forced upon them by their employers. It was the attempts spasmodically made by the government and some boards of Justices to use the Statute of Artificers to maintain a standard wage in the textile trades, which has led to the suggestion that its general effect was to protect the worker against exploitation. In reality the policy pursued towards workers in the woollen industry was a special departure arising from the peculiar circumstances of that trade. The production of woollen cloth was the branch of manufacture in which, in the sixteenth century, capitalism had proceeded furthest. There were, of course, a certain number of independent weavers who worked to the order of purchasers in their own immediate neighbourhood. There were also, especially in the northern counties, a large number of small masters, of a type that survived in the West Riding of Yorkshire well into the nineteenth century, who bought their own raw materials, marketed the finished product themselves, and were not far removed in economic status from the two or three journeymen whom they employed. But these were the irregular forces of the industry, not the main army. In the principal 'clothing counties', Norfolk and Suffolk, Wiltshire, Gloucestershire, Somerset, and Devonshire, several causes had combined to supersede the simple organization under which the same individual was at once merchant, master, and artisan, to specialize in separate lands the commercial and industrial sides of the industry, and thus to run the greater part of it into a capitalistic mould. For one thing, a large part of the cloth manufactured in the south and east of England was exported to Continental markets. For another thing, the collecting, sorting, and distributing of raw materials was a business in itself. Different kinds of wool were produced in different parts of the country. Different kinds of cloth required different kinds of wool, and it was therefore common for wool produced in one county to be distributed for manufacture over half a dozen different counties far removed from each other and from its place of origin. 'The places of growing and the places of converting are as far distant as the scope of this kingdom will give leave. The wools growing in the counties of Worcester, Salop, and Stafford, are spent partly in Worcester, and a great part of them in the counties of Gloucester, Devon, and Kent, and much of them in Southampton. The wool of the counties of Lincoln, Northampton, Rutland, Leicester, Warwick, Oxford, and Bucks are thus dispersed: one sort of it is carried into the North parts, to Leeds, Wakefield, Rochdale, etc., and another sort is carried into part of it into the East parts, to Norwich . . . and part of it into the West parts into Exeter . . . some wools growing in Norfolk are brought three score miles or more to London and from thence carried eight score miles or more into North Wales, then draped into cloth and so sent back again and sold in London'[67]. The result was that the commercial side of the industry passed into the hands of a special body of capitalist entrepreneurs, who bought and sold on a large scale and could afford to take risks and wait for their returns. The actual operatives were no longer independent craftsmen, but entirely dependent on these great 'clothiers' for their employment. One outcome of the overshadowing of the artisan by the entrepreneur was the tentative growth of a rudimentary factory system. A large number of towns in the sixteenth and seventeenth centuries, when confronted with the difficulty of finding work for the unemployed, used to lend money to capitalist clothiers to establish what were factories[68] in all but name. The most general consequence, however, of the spread of capitalism in the textile industries was not the appearance of a factory system, which was hampered both by the laws forbidding the engrossing of looms, and by the fact that most of the families engaged in the production of cloth could not easily be massed together, since they practised agriculture as a by-employment. It was the so-called 'Commission-System', under which a single great clothier provided the raw materials worked up in hundreds of cottages, paid the artisans their wages, and collected the finished product for the home or foreign market when the process of manufacture was over. It was calculated that in Suffolk in the reign of James I one large merchant would keep 500 workers employed.

The natural outcome of the organization of the industry on a capitalistic basis was the appearance of complaints as to low wages and payment in kind. In 1539 the weavers of Suffolk were complaining exactly in the manner of the handloom weavers in the early nineteenth century. 'The rich men the clothiers be concluded and agreed among themselves to hold and pay one price for weaving, which price is too little to sustain householders upon, working night and day, holiday and weekday, and many weavers are thereby reduced to the position of servants[69]'. 'The rich clothier,' said an observer, 'that buyeth his wool of the grower in the wool counties in the winter time hath it spun by his own spinsters, and woven by his own weavers and fulled by his own tuckers, and all at the lowest rate of wages[70]'. A draft bill[71] of 1593 states that spinners are driven to embezzle yarn, and weavers to weave faulty cloth, because 'necessity doth many times enforce them thereunto for lack of sufficient wages and allowance for the workmanship at the hands of the clothiers'. The fixing of maximum wages directed by the Statute of Artificers was obviously not a remedy for such conditions. On the other hand, in view of the interference with wages being a traditional part of the policy both of town authorities and of the government, the step involved in fixing a minimum wage was not a long one. It was taken first by the former. At intervals from the middle of the fifteenth century onwards the Court Leet of Coventry, where the journeymen weavers and the masters had already (in 1429) made a collective bargain[72] binding the latter to pay the journeyman a third of the value of every cloth woven, was busy with the issue of ordinances regulating wages in the woollen industry. In 1452 any spinner who was given more than two-and-a-half pounds of wool to spin was directed to bring his or her complaint before the Sheriffs, who were to pay the spinner for his labour, and to confiscate the spindles provided by the employer[73]. In 1460 it was enacted that all weavers, fullers, spinners, and carders should be paid in ready money. In 1514 clothiers who gave out wool to spinners were ordered not to put more to each weight than two-and-a-half pounds, and to pay in ready money 5d per pound for the best quality, and 4d for inferior qualities[74]. In 1524 a price list was drawn up for weaving. The usual rule was made as to payment in ready money, and payments were fixed for standard patterns of cloth, ranging from 5s for the heaviest, to 4s 6d for medium weights, and 3s 4d for the lightest. This was followed by a similar list for walkers, 'for a low-priced cloth 3s 6d, and for a middle cloth 4s and for a fine cloth 5s, and for a very fine cloth as the owners and he can agree'.[75] What was done at Coventry in the way of protecting the journeymen against exploitation seems to have been a fairly common practice on the part of town authorities, though not so general as the attempts to protect the consumer by fixing maximum wages in the building industries. At Norwich in 1502 a body of woollen-weavers requested the authorities to enact a rule fixing XXd as the minimum price for cloth of a certain quality[76]. At Reading in the early seventeenth century the Court of the Borough fixed the rates of spinners at '13d a padd for spinning ordinary work, and so ratably for better work', and when the workmen in a local woollen factory partly financed by the town complained that their wages were too low, appointed three arbitrators to report upon the dispute.[77] In 1648 the Common Council of Nottingham, who had followed the common practice of lending capital to a clothier provided he would start work in the town, fixed a fairly elaborate scale of prices for spinning and carding different kinds of wool[78].

These examples, though not sufficient to prove that the fixing of minimum rates was a common practice, do at any rate point to the conclusion that there was a disposition to treat workers in the textile industry in a different way from the great mass of labour, and that in fixing minimum rates for workers in that industry, the State would have some experience which it could follow. It was not, however, till the latter part of the reign of Elizabeth that this aspect of the wage problem began to receive attention from the Government. In 1593, a year in which, owing to the failure of the harvest, distress was unusually severe, four bills[79] were drafted which can still be examined in the Record Office. One of them need not detain us long. It is headed 'The rate of the wages for clothiers to give unto their spinsters and weavers'; it is simply a list of piece-prices for spinning and weaving, with certain provisions as to the pattern of tools to be used, containing six rates for the former and eleven rates for the latter; there is no preamble and no enacting words, and it was intended perhaps to appear as a schedule to any Acts which might be passed upon the subject. The other three drafts are more elaborate. They deal not only with wages, but with frauds practised on clothiers by spinners and weavers—of which they complain in terms almost identical with those used by the Commission on Handloom Weavers in 1835—with the length of cloth to be woven and with that bugbear of sixteenth-century statesmen, the speculator, 'yarn choppers or jobbers' who 'for their own private gains, without having any regard to the maintenance of the Commonwealth, using no trade either of making woollen cloth or any other thing made of woollen yarn . . . do . . . buy up and get into their hands so great quantities of woollen yarn'. There is some difference between the bills in the matter of wages. One of them does not set out any 'list' in detail, but enacts that the wages of spinners of warps shall be advanced 30 per cent, that those of spinners of wefts and those of weavers shall be advanced 25 per cent, and that the clauses in certain Acts allowing clothiers to make cloth of a length greater than that fixed by law shall be repealed, on the ground that the effect of them has been that 'divers poor artificers, as spinners, weavers, tuckers, carders, clothworkers, and divers others have been secretly and most unconscionably deceived, oppressed and wronged in their labours, for that the masters and owners of the said long clothes neither have given nor do give wages answerable to the great length of the said clothes'. The other two bills set out of a list of piece-prices for spinning and weaving, fix a fine of 12d for every penny that a 'clothier shall withold or detaine . . . contrary to the charitable intent of this Statute', but provide that where higher rates have hitherto been paid than those contained in the bills, they shall continue to be paid in the future. Neither of these measures became law. But their existence proves that the idea of fixing a minimum wage for workers in the woollen industry was one to which the government was prepared to give consideration. Ten years later Parliament returned to the subject, this time with some result. By an Act of 1603 (1 James. cap VI) the Statute of Artificers was re-enacted with the addition of three significant clauses. The first stated that there had been some ambiguity in the Act of 1563, which had resulted in its being uncertain whether the Justices had power to rate the wages of workers other than those engaged in husbandry and other than those whose wages had been assessed under previous Acts. It accordingly enacted that it was to be interpreted as giving authority to assess the wages of any 'Labourers, Weavers, Spinners, and Workmen whatsoever'. The second clause definitely laid down that as far as workers in the woollen industry were concerned the rates fixed were to be a *minimum*, and that clothiers were to be fined for paying less, not for paying more, than that rate. It is so important that I quote it in full:

> 'And furthermore, be it enacted by the authority aforesaid, that if any clothier or other shall refuse to obey the said order, rate, and assessments of wages, as aforesaid, *and shall not pay so much or so great wages to their weavers, spinsters, workmen or workwomen, as shall set down, rated, and appointed,* according to the true meaning of this Act, that then every clothier and other person or persons so offending shall forfeit and lose . . . for every such offence to the party grieved ten shillings'.

The third clause took the important step, without which that just quoted would have been of little value, of forbidding clothiers who were also Justices of the Peace to take part in assessing wages 'for any weaver, tucker, spinster, or any other artisan that dependeth on the making of cloth.'

If the Statute of 1603 is strictly construed, it would appear to have directed the Justices to fix a minimum, not a maximum, rate for workers in *all* occupations, not only for those engaged in the manufacture of cloth. If this was its intention, it does not appear to have been carried out. Subsequent assessments allude to 5 Elizabeth c. 4, but scarcely ever contain any reference to 1 James I c. 6 and, as has been explained, above, they usually say that wages are not to be *more* than a certain amount. It is plain, however, from the references in the Statute to clothiers, that its main object was to empower the Justices to fix a minimum for the woollen industry, and though evidence as to the effect of this part of it is not so abundant as could be desired, there is no doubt that both local authorities and the central government did from time to time administer it in this sense. To see the line taken by the former we may examine the dealings of the Justices of Wiltshire, one of the most important of the cloth-manufacturing counties, with the wages of spinners and weavers. My first example[80] comes from the year 1602. The drafting of piece-rates for the woollen industry was an extremely technical matter, involving expert knowledge as to qualities of wool and yarns, breadth of looms, etc. What the Justices did, therefore, was to ask the clothiers who gave out the materials and the weavers who worked them up in their cottages to submit a statement of the prices which they thought reasonable. In 1602 a piece-list—'the just proportions of the severall works usually put forth by the clothiers of the County of Wiltshire both to the weavers and spinners with the valuation of the wages according as every sorts of work do deserve by reason of the fineness of the wool and spinning of every sort of work'—was signed by seven clothiers and six weavers, and was submitted to the Justices. The Justices confirmed it as it stood, and reissued it in 1605[81] with certain trifling variations. It would be too much to say that the Justices ratified a collective bargain which had already been made by the representatives of the employers and the workmen, for one does not in these documents find traces of a permanent organization among either party, nor would it have been lawful for them to combine to alter working conditions prescribed by the state. It is evident, however, that the Justices did not simply settle matters over their heads, and that some attempt was made to ascertain the opinion of the industry before thrusting the rough hands of Quarter Sessions into its delicate mechanism, Moreover, the fixing of rates was certainly regarded as an advantage by the workmen concerned. This is proved not only by the part which the journeymen weavers took in preparing the price-list, but by the fact that they later petitioned the Justices to enforce the assessment of wages as a means of protecting them against their employers. In 1623 the artisans engaged in the Wiltshire cloth-making industry were in deep distress. 'May it please you', they write to the Justices, 'to be informed of the distressed state of most of the weavers, spinners, and others that work on the making of woollen cloths, that are not able by their diligent labours to get their livings, by reason that the clothiers at their wish have made their work extremely hard, and abated wages what they please. And some of them make such their workfolk to do their household businesses, to trudge in their errands, spool their chains, twist their list, do every command, without giving them bread, drink, or money for many days labours. May it please you, therefore, for the redressing of these enormities done by Clothiers, to appoint certain grave and discreet persons to view the straitness of work, to assess rates for wages according to the desert of their works, now especially in this great dearth of corn, that the poor artificers of these works of woollen cloths may not perish for want of food, while they are painfull in their callings'.[82] The Justices responded to this appeal. They issued an order summoning the clothiers and workmen to meet them at Devizes; directed the observance of the piece-list, which was already nominally in force, though broken by the clothiers; and ordered its publication on market-day at Devizes 'in order that workmasters and workmen alike may take notice thereof, and that the workmen who desire that the same rates may stand, may be the better satisfied'.

The fixing of minimum rates for artisans in the woollen industry had not the same reasons for commending itself to the Justices as had the fixing of maximum rates for other classes of workers. It is, therefore, not surprising that the interference of the Privy Council should often have been required in order to induce them to do their duty. To see its economic activities at their height one must, of course, turn to the period between March 1629 and April 1640, when 'that noise', as Laud called parliamentary debate, was silent. The government's intervention to control economic conditions was one side of the attitude which found its more famous expressions in arbitrary taxation and the enforcement of conformity in religion, a natural outcome of the authoritarian conception of the state held by Charles and his advisers. It did not imply any popular sympathies, but simply a desire to prevent agitation by removing the material causes of discontent, and incidentally to put pressure on the middle and upper classes who were the stronghold of religious and constitutional opposition. To levy fines upon an enclosing landlord was a convenient financial expedient. The Bishops who punished the usurer, or the dealer who charged extortionate prices, before the Courts[83] of Star Chamber and High Commission had an excellent opportunity of expounding the duty of obedience to the established authorities, and scolded the offender with all the more gusto when he was suspected of being a Puritan as well. In the matter of wages there was no general change of policy. From a letter[84] which the Derbyshire Justices wrote to the government in 1631 stating, in reply to a circular from the Council, that 'we find none presented to us that. . . . refuse to work for reasonable wages', it is plain that in the case of agricultural labourers the fixing of maximum wages still went on. But attempts to get the Justices to carry out their obligation of fixing minimum rates for workers in the cloth-manufacturing industry were made more regularly than either before or since. In 1629[85] the Council wrote to the Earl of Warwick and the Justices of Essex directing them to take steps to raise the wages of the weavers of baize who worked in the neighbourhood of Braintree and Bocking. In September[86] 1630 they circularized the Justices of Norfolk, Suffolk, Essex, Cambridge, all cloth-manufacturing counties, and the Mayor of Norwich, stating that 'the Statutes of 5 Eliz & 1 Jac have so carefully provided against these inconveniences it were a great shame if, for want of due care in such as are specially entrusted with the execution of these lawes, the poore should be punished in these times of scarcity and dearth', and requiring them to see to the assessment of wages. To these instances, which I take from Miss Leonard's *Early History of English Poor Relief,* one may add the example offered by the proceedings of the government in the matter of the cloth trade of Sudbury and the neighbouring parts of Suffolk and Essex. They illustrate excellently the grievances of the workers, the attitude of the Privy Council, and the difficulties of the Justices.

The question was first raised by a petition addressed to the Council in February 1630 on behalf of the workers in the trade by one Sylva Harbert[87]. It stated that the clothiers of Sudbury had reduced the wages of combers, spinners and weavers to such an extent that 'they (who in times past maintained their families in good sort) . . . are constrained to sell their beds, wheels, and working tools', and asked the government to interfere. The Council directed that the petition should be forwarded to a committee composed of the Justices of Suffolk and Essex together with two aldermen of Sudbury, who were instructed to call before them representatives of both parties, to insist on wages being raised to the level hitherto customary, and to bind over any refractory person to appear before the Council. The clothiers began[88] by attempting to show that Sylva Harbert had no real grievance, but had acted at the malicious instigation of a third party who had a grudge against one of them. The committee, after examining the complaints of the workpeople, decided that they were justified, and drew up a price-list for spinners and weavers which forbade deductions ('fines'), and stated the length of reels to be used for the yarns. They informed the Council, however, that the reason alleged by the manufacturers for reducing wages was the competition of the trade in other parts of the country, and that 'if the like order be not more general than to Sudbury, and to towns adjacent, it must necessarily be their ruin and utter undoing'.[89] This eminently reasonable request does not appear to have received any attention from the government. But it continued to lend an ear to the complaints of the Sudbury wage-earners. In 1637 three weavers again approached the Star Chamber with the complaint that, not content with reducing their wages, a manufacturer named Thomas Reynolds insisted on their accepting payment in truck 'dead commodities, such as they cannot put off, and at a far undervalue, he himself refusing to take them again without great abatement, making merchandize of the petitioner's labours'.[90] The Star Chamber found on inquiry that Reynolds was a bad character who had already been punished for a similar offence—'this way of oppressing and abusing poor weavers hath been ordinary with him'—and committed him to the Fleet till he should have repaid the wages due, together with the plaintiff's costs. Having complied with the order of the Court, he was released a week later.[91]

What had been said above of the objects of the assessment of wages may now be summarized. The principal aim of the wage clauses of the Statute of Artificers was to prevent the scarcity of agricultural labour driving wages above the point thought 'reasonable', and at the same time to allow that point to be shifted upwards by the Justices as prices rose. In the textile industries, however, where owing to the development of a capitalistic organization, the wage problem was of a different character, the policy of fixing a minimum wage had been pursued by town authorities from an early date. It was given statutory sanction by the Act of 1603 and was enforced at intervals both by the Justices of the Peace and by the Privy Council. After the constitutional revolution of the seventeenth century the assessment of maximum wages continued; but the fixing of a minimum for artisans in the cloth-manufacturing industry, which was opposed to the interests of the wealthier classes, fell into desuetude. The clause in the Act of 1604 stating that doubt had been expressed as to whether the wage clauses of the Act of 1563 applied to other than labourers in husbandry shows that even in the generation immediately following the passage of the Statute of Artificers there was a tendency to limit its application; and in the reign of Anne (if not before) it was definitely decided by the Judges that only the wages of agricultural workers fell within the jurisdiction of the Justices;—'the statute extends only to service in husbandry, not to gentlemen's servants, nor to journeymen with their masters'.[92] Memories of the earlier practice survived, however, into the latter part of the eighteenth century, and prompted the demands for the establishment of a minimum wage advanced both by the Gloucestershire weavers in 1756, and by many other bodies of textile operatives at the time of the rise of the factory system.

VI The Effects of the Assessment of Wages

It remains to ask what was the economic effect of the system of assessing wages. On this question I can throw little light. I will begin by describing the procedure in making assessments, and examining the movements in wages as set out in some of them, and then go on to say what I can of the actual administration of the law.

By the Act of 1563 the Justices were directed to consult 'grave and discrete persons', and to confer together 'concerning the plenty and scarcity of the time, and other circumstances necessary to be considered'. The view taken of the administration of the act must depend to some extent upon the degree to which the Justices are thought to have complied with these instructions. Did they take the trouble to obtain the necessary economic information before issuing their rules? or did they act entirely upon their own discretion? That some attention was paid by the Justices to the movements of prices is suggested by the allusions to them which are frequent in the preambles of assessments. That they went further, and made any regular attempt to secure advice from persons qualified to judge as to the economic conditions of the wage-earners is, as far at any rate as agricultural labour is concerned, extremely improbable. In one case, indeed, we do get a hint of inquiries preceding the issue of rates. In 1648 the inhabitants of the Eastern division of the Hundred of Portbury in Somerset[93] called the attention of the Justices to the fact that twenty-three years before the wages in their district had been fixed by the 'two next Justices', and stated that the assessment was now disobeyed. Accordingly, Quarter Sessions referred the matter to a committee of three 'to examine the said proportion or rate, and to certify the true state thereof at the next General Sessions'. But in no instance is there any evidence that the views of the wage-workers themselves were in any way consulted. The agricultural labourers were then, as now, entirely unorganized. The Justices, who were mainly country gentlemen, were naturally biased in favour of keeping down their wages. The course which they seem to have followed when it was thought desirable to take the opinion of persons other than those of the county bench was to refer the matter to the Grand Jury. As judicial charges show, the presentment of 'labourers or servants' who 'take any more wages than the rate of wages allowed by the Justices'[94] was part of its ordinary duties. What more natural than that it should be consulted when rates were being fixed? The records of Wiltshire, Worcestershire, and Somerset supply examples of what was probably a common practice. In the former county[95] an assessment of 1625 which considerably raised the wages of workers in husbandry was embodied in the Grand Jury's presentment. In Worcestershire[96] the Grand Jury addressed the Justices with some vigour in 1661, remonstrated with them for failing to administer the Statute of Artificers, and, among other demands, requested that servants' wages might be assessed according to law. In Somerset[97] eight assessments were issued between 1647 to 1655. The formula most commonly used is, first, 'This Court desired the Grand Jury to present their opinions what wages they thought fit to be set and assessed';

second, 'the presentment of the grand inquest' containing the rates proposed; third 'This Court doth approve thereof'. It is scarcely necessary to point out that the intervention of the Grand Jury, consisting as it generally did of gentry and yeomen, was anything but a protection to the wage-earner. If the exhortation addressed by George Fox to the Nottingham Justices, 'not to oppress the servants in their wages, but to do that which was right and just to them' was not always necessary, the cause was not the goodwill of the 'grave and discrete' persons, but the comparatively strong position of the agricultural labourer.

In the case of workers other than those employed in agriculture it was easier for the Justices to take expert advice. We have already seen that in fixing the wages of spinners and weavers in Wiltshire they consulted both the employers and the journeymen. In the towns, gilds and companies supplied an obvious source of information. In Chester in 1588 wages were fixed by the Mayor with 'the advise and consultation of divers others of the city',[98] and in 1607 the London Justices specially directed the wardens of the London companies to attend the meeting at which wages were to be assessed[99]. Whether the intervention of a gild was a safeguard to the wage-earners or to their employers depended entirely upon its constitution. In the smaller towns, where capitalist industry was little developed, and where, therefore, the gap between master and man was still only a narrow one, gilds seem occasionally, as at Bristol, Norwich, Coventry, and Carlisle, to have prevented the reduction of wages below a certain minimum[100]. In most cases, however, the gild was only too ready to be used by the Justices as a means of preventing a rise in wages inconvenient to the masters by whom it was governed, and to assist them in seeing, in the words of the authorities of Bury St Edmunds, that 'every journeyman do serve according to the Queen's Majesty's Statutes'.[101] In Chester, where there was much complaint of the great exactions of 'the artisans and servants belonging to the corporation of Wrights and Slaters', the Mayor fixed their wages and compelled the governors of the society to enter into bonds to see that the rates settled by him were observed[102]. In London many of the companies had, by the middle of the seventeenth century, developed into extremely aristocratic and exclusive bodies. It is not surprising, therefore, to find the wardens of the Company of Carpenters making recommendations to the Lord Mayor 'in pursuance of your lordship's desire of our opinion for the reducing of the excessive wages of labourers and workmen'[103].

According to the preamble of the Act of 1563 the Justices should have made wages move in correspondence with prices. The question how far they did this is not easily answered, partly because there was no common form in which assessments were issued, so that it is often impossible to compare different assessments made for the same county, even when there is only a few years between them; partly because, though we know the general course of prices, we do not know their local variations. By way of testing whether there was any close correspondence between wages and prices, I set out below an index number of wheat prices[104], and of the rates assessed at different dates in one borough and four counties. They are as follows:

Chester		*1570*	*1597*	
Wages		100	141·7	
		1571–81	*1593–1602*	
Wheat prices		100	209	
Rutland		*1563*	*1610*	
Day wages		100	104·16	
Yearly wages		100	101·2	
Wheat prices		100	274·6	
Devonshire		*1594*	*1654*	
Day wages		100	107·04	
Yearly wages		100	132·4	
Wheat prices		100	135·4	
Wiltshire	*1603*	*1635*	*1665*	*1685*
Wages	100	125	137	150
	1603–12	*1633–42*	*1653–62*	*1680–92*
Wheat prices	100	117	134	97
Gloucestershire		*1632*	*1655*	
Day wages		100	131·3	
Yearly wages		100	108·1	
		1623–32	*1653–62*	
Wheat prices		100	108·1	

It will be seen that there is a rough parallelism between the rise of wheat prices and the rise of wages in Wiltshire up to

1655, and of yearly wages in Devonshire up to 1654. For the rest, there seems to be no correspondence at all. At Chester, wages rise by over 40 per cent when prices rise by 109 per cent; in Rutland wages rise by under 5 per cent, when prices rise by 174 per cent. In Wiltshire, where prices and wages move with the same correspondence up to 1655, wages rise after that date and prices fall. Even if the means for making a comparison were more satisfactory than they are, I doubt very much whether any close correspondence would be established. It was hardly to be expected that the Justices who saw prices doubled would meet the situation by doubling wages. They themselves belonged to a class which felt the rise severely, for the rents of their copyhold and freehold tenants were fixed, while they were buying everything dearer. An advance in wages as great as the advance in prices would have benefited the worker while aggravating their own difficulties. Moreover, all sorts of factors influenced wages besides the movement in prices. Custom was very powerful, and one board appeals to the fact that wages have always been lower in the northern part of the country than elsewhere as a justification for refusing to raise them[105]. After the Civil War the scarcity of labour forced wages up, and the assessments, as the Gloucestershire Justices pointed out, had to follow the market rate[106]. A motive which tended to raise the price of agricultural labour while lowering that of artisans was the interest of the country gentlemen in preventing a shortage of the former. This is probably the reason why the wages of workers in husbandry were advanced in Wiltshire, on the recommendation of the Grand Jury, in 1635, while those of other classes of wage-earners were unaltered; and why in Warwickshire the wages of certain classes of agricultural workers were fixed at a much higher rate in 1672 than in 1657, while those of masons, tilers, plasterers, and bricklayers were reduced by from 75 to 100 per cent[107]. Such a double movement was a simple method of ensuring that the supply of agricultural labour would be sufficient. It is not surprising, therefore, that wages and prices should not have risen and fallen together.

When assessments were made, were they operative in practice, or did the market rate of wages move quite independently of them? The methods employed to secure the observation by employer and workman of the legal rates were very various. Under the Act of 1563 the Justices were bound to forward their assessments to the Court of Chancery. The Privy Council was to examine them, to have them printed if they were approved, and to send them, in the form of a proclamation, to their respective counties before 1 September, where Sheriffs and Justices were to cause them to be proclaimed on market-days and to be posted up in some conspicuous place. When the act of 1598 relieved the Justices of the necessity of forwarding their assessments to London for confirmation, the ordinary practice was to send them to the Sheriff of the county with the request that they should be published in every city and market-town. Sometimes, however, the Justices sent them to the constables direct, and on one occasion they ordered that, with a view to giving them publicity the rate should 'be read every Quarter in their Parish Church or some other convenient place upon Sunday or festival day after morning prayers'[108]. Occasionally, special expedients were adopted for discovering breaches of the assessments. In Buckinghamshire,[109] for example, a special 'governor of labourers' was appointed in every township in the Chiltern Hundreds in 1562 to supervise the movements and hiring of labourers, and to present masters who gave too high a rate of wages. In Devonshire[110] in 1601 the Justices divided themselves into sub-committees to deal specially with offenders in different parts of the county. In the North Riding of Yorkshire[111] in 1610 on account of 'much complaint, as well by masters as servants, of sundry abuses committed against the Statute of Labourers and Apprentices' the Justices decided that in the future they would hold an additional summer session every year for the purpose of hearing cases under the Act. It was, however, the parish constables who supplied the hinge upon which the whole system turned. For the Justices to supervise the actual hiring and discharge of labour, was of course, out of the question. But when the machinery of the law was working properly no man could get a master, and no master could get a man, without the constable knowing the terms of the bargain. It was the duty of the workman to show the constables (or the curate or churchwarden) a testimonial from his last master. It was the duty of the employer to register with the constables the names of his labourers and the wages at which they were engaged, and to notify to him anyone who left his service without giving the statutory notice of one quarter. The whole system depended in fact, on the presence of a third party at every contract made between master and man; it was only workable in so far as publicity was given to the engagement of labour, and it was for this reason that rules are so frequently made requiring young people to go into service, unemployed workmen to stand in some conspicuous place until they find an employer, employers to hire publicly and not in secret, masterless men to take masters. The man who had labour to sell was in fact treated exactly like the corn-dealer. Neither was to be allowed to forestall the market or to take advantage of an exceptionally good offer to force up the price. Neither could pick his purchaser or refuse to sell except upon his own terms. Hence, when the machinery was working properly, the constables had in their possession a register of persons hired and of the wages offered to them, which they could compare with the assessments issued by the Justices, and by means of which they could check any alteration in wages which might subsequently be made or demanded.

That in some districts and at some periods the constables succeeded in keeping in close touch with their duties is proved by the appeals which the Justices made to them for information, and by the presentment of offenders who break the law. The punishment of offenders at Reading has already been mentioned. In the court of the manor of Ingoldmells[112] in Lincolnshire, fourteen persons were summoned in 1567 'before the steward appointed to execute the Statute of Labourers'. In the North Riding of Yorkshire, there were numerous presentments of both masters and journeymen for paying and taking more than the statutory rate of wages, or otherwise evading the Act: 'John Bulmer of West Cottam, husbandman, for hiring servants without recording their names and salaries before the chief constable', 'The inhabitants of Thirkleby . . . for refusing to give the names of their servants and their wages to the constables of the said Town and to the head constables', 'the inhabitants of Kilbourne for giving their servants more wages than the Statute doth allow', 'Thomas Gibson of Easingwold for retaining and accepting into his service one Will Thompson without showing to the Head Officer, Curate, or Churchwarden, any lawful testimonial', 'Thomas Wawne yeoman for giving wages . . . Rymer his servant to exceeding the rate set down by the Justices'[113], such examples show that in parts of the country the administration of the statute was a reality. Occasionally we find particulars of wages which show that the market rate and the legal rate coincided. In Rutland[114], for example, where an assessment was made in 1610, the High Constable's list of persons hired between 1624 and 1626 proves that the rates then fixed were closely followed. In Derbyshire[115] the masons and labourers who worked at Chatsworth in 1693 obtained the rates per day, 1s 4d and 10d, which had been fixed by the assessment of 1648. Usually, however, the evidence which could enable us to determine whether assessments when made were effectively carried out is lacking. There are no presentments of offenders for exceeding the legal rates in the manuscript proceedings of the Warwickshire Quarter Sessions which I have examined from 1610 to 1680. Nor have I found any in the records of other counties which have been printed, with the exception of those contained in the proceedings of the North Riding Quarter Sessions. As far as my evidence goes at present, which is not very far, the legal rate often differed considerably from the market rate, and usually fell short of it. In Buckinghamshire[116] for example, some workmen in the building trades were being paid in the latter part of the sixteenth century a wage more than double that fixed by the assessment of 1562, and though the legal scale was considerably raised in the latter part of the following century it was still exceeded by the actual rates paid by masters. In the eighteenth century at any rate, the courts seem to have countenanced the evasion of the Act by ruling that a master might 'reward a deserving servant, over and above his wages, according as he shall decide; so it be not by way of promise or agreement upon his retainer'[117]. While, therefore, it is probable that the practice of assessing wages tended to keep them down by setting up a standard to which the master could appeal, it is also probable that it was evaded by the exceptionally competent journeymen, or by the master who was in difficulties through a shortage of labour.

NOTES

1. I desire to acknowledge the assistance of Mr J. G. Newlove of Ruskin College and of Miss Drucker, who have kindly helped me to collect materials for this article. *Vierteljahrshrift für Sozial-und Wirtschaftsgeschichte* (1913-14) pp. 307-37, 533-64.

2. *Cunningham, Growth of English Industry and Commerce. Modern Times,* Part I, pp. 37-44, and Part II, appendix A.

3. McArthur, *English Historical Review,* vol. xiii and vol. xv.

4. Hewins, *Economic Journal,* vol. viii.

5. Rogers, *Six Centuries of Work and Wages,* pp. 398-9.

6. G. Steffen, *Studien zur Geschichte der englischen Lohnarbeit,* Band I, p. 339.

7. Dunlop and Denman, *English Apprenticeship and Child Labour.*

8. Leonard, *The Early History of English Poor Relief,* p. 164.

9. 5 Eliz e 4.

10. Hutchins, *Economic Journal,* vol. x.

11. Harris, *Coventry Leet Book,* vol. iii (under the year 1553).

12. Morris, *Records of Chester,* p. 409.

13. Bateson, *Records of Leicester,* III, 105; see also III, 186.

14. 13 Richard II, c. 8.

15. 23 Henry, VI, c. 13.

16. 11 Henry VII, c. 22

17. 6 Henry VIII, c. 3.

18. *The Commonweal of this Realm of England,* ed. Lamond, p. 100.

19. E. E. T. S., *England in the reign of King Henry VIII.*

20. S. P. D. Eliz., vol. 93, No. 27 'The causes whie bothe lawfull artificers and unlawefull artificers do desyer to have the statute towchinge them to be put in execution and obs'vid.'

21. I am aware that Miss McArthur, *English Historical Review,* vol. ix infers (a) from Fitzherbert's book, *The Boke for a Justyce of the Peace,* and (b) from the Rot. Part. III, 268b and 269, that the sliding scale was not first introduced in 1563. This is correct. But before 1563 its movement was limited by a statutory maximum.

22. Hist M. S. S. Com. Mss of Marquis of Salisbury, Part I, pp. 162—5. I have to thank Professor G. Unwin for referring me to this document.

23. *ibid.* Part. VII under Nov. 1597, 'Notes for the present Parliament.'

24. Harris, *Coventry Leet Book,* I, 21.

25. McArthur, *English Historical Review,* vol. xiii, 'A fifteenth Century assessment of wages'.

26. Hist M. S. S. Com. Cd 3218, p. 201.

27. Morris, *Records of Chester,* p. 366.

28. *ibid,* p. 356. See also McArthur, *English Historical Review,* vol. xv, for rules made in the city of London in 1514, 1521, and 1538 in pursuance of the act of 1514 assessing wages, and *Coventry Leet Book,* III, p. 653, where rough masons and daubers are directed 'to take such wages as is limited them by the statutes hereupon made'.

29. Rot. part. III, 269 330, 352; Iv, 330-1, 352; V, 110.

30. McArthur, *English Historical Review,* vol. xx.
31. More's *Utopia,* 'They invent and devise all meanes and crafts . . . how to hire and abuse the worke and labour of the poor for as little money as may be'. The context shows that the reference is to legislation.
32. *King Edward's Remains; 'a discourse about the Reformation of many abuses'.*
33. Hewins, *Economic Journal,* vol. viii.
34. Hewins, *Economic Journal,* vol. viii.
35. Cunningham, *op. cit.* Part. I, pp. 43-4.
36. Hutchins, *Economic Journal,* vol. x. 'Wee, the Mr and Wardens of the Company of Carpenters, in pursuance of your lordships desire for the reducing of the excessive wages of Labourers and Workmen in these times of great plenty, we humbly conceive to be sufficient that Labourers take for wages but 16d a day only etc'.
37. S. P. D. Charles I, vol. I, p. 499, No. 10.
38. Gardiner, *History of the Commonwealth and Protectorate,* vol. I, pp. 39-40.
39. Petty, *A Treatise of Taxes and Contributions,* Chapter I. 'Besides, it is unjust to let any starve, when we think it just to limit the wages of the poor, so as they can lay up nothing against the time of their impotency and want of work'.
40. Smith, *De Republica anglorum,* Lib. III, Chap. 19. 'The Justices of the Peace doe meete also . . . sometimes to take order for the excessive wages of servants and labourers'.
41. Lambard, *Eirenarcha.*
42. Sheppard, *Whole Office of the Country Justice of the Peace.*
43. Fitzherbert, *The Boke Longyng to a Justice of the Peace:* see also McArthur, *English Historical Review,* vol. ix.
44. *Victoria County History of Derbyshire,* vol. ii, pp. 182-3.
45. Hist M. S. S. Com. M. S. S. of Custos Rot. and J.P.s' of the County of Essex, p. 491. '23 April 1612. Roll and schedule of the Particulars of Wages for all manner of artificers and servants; set forth by the Justices of the Peace for the Co. Essex; under the seals and signatures of the same Justices'.
46. Atkinson, Quarter Sessions of the North Riding of Yorkshire, I, p. 148; II, pp. 114, 141, 202, 220; IV, p. 270.
47. *ibid.* vol. ii, p. 218.
48. Records of the Borough of Reading, vol. i, p. 445.
49. Bateson, Records of Leicester, vol. iii, p. 114.
50. McArthur, *English Historical Review,* vol. xv.
51. 39 Eliz. c. 12.
52. McArthur, *English Historical Review,* vol. xv.
53. Hist M. S. S. Com. Cd. 784, pp. 161-75.
54. Atkinson, Quarter Sessions of the North Riding of Yorkshire, lists of recusants, *passim.*
55. Willis Bund, *Kalender of the Sessions Rills of Worcestershire 1591 to 1643,* Part. II.
56. For details see Tawney, *The Agrarian Problem in the Sixteenth Century,* pp. 63-6.

57. Savine's article in Vinogradoff's *Oxford Studies in Social and Legal History*, vol. i, pp. 223-6.
58. Surtees Society, vol. xxxiii.
59. Lee, *A vindication of a regulated enclosure* (1656).
60. Winthrop's *Journal*, vol. i, p. 112 (1633); vol. ii, p. 228 (1645).
61. Hist M. S. S. Com. Cd. 784, pp. 322-3.
62. Roger Coke, *A discourse of Trade* (1670).
63. *Britannia Languens, or A discourse of Trade* (1680).
64. Hist M. S. S. Com. Cd. 784, f. 132 (Wiltshire 1656); see also Hamilton, Quarter Session Records of Devonshire from Elisabeth to Anne, pp. 163-4, for an order made in 1657 that 'Masterless persons should have Masters within a month'.
65. Pseudonismus, *Considerations Concerning Common Field and Enclosures* (1654).
66. Pseudonismus, *A vindication of the Considerations Concerning Common Field and Enclosures* (1656)
67. S. P. D. James I, vol. lxxx, No. 13 (quoted Unwin, *Industrial Organization in the Sixteenth and Seventeenth Centuries*, pp. 188-9).
68. Hist M. S. S. Com. Cd. 788, pp. 17, 44 (Lincoln), *Records of the Borough of Reading*, vol. ii, pp. 273, 357; vol. iii, pp. 7, 25.
69. *Victoria County History of Suffolk*, p. 259.
70. S. P. D. James I, vol. 80, No. 13 (1615), quoted Unwin, *op. cit.* appendix A, II.
71. S. P. D. Eliz., vol. 244, No. 126.
72. Harris, *Coventry Leet Book*, vol. i, p. 94. 'Oct. 24, 1424. Indenture between the master weavers and journeymen . . . and the journeymen may have the third part of the payment for weaving cloth, as well less as larger, which they weave with their masters, as they used to have.'
73. *ibid.* vol. ii, p. 271.
74. *ibid.* vol. iii, p. 640.
75. *ibid.* vol. iii, p. 689.
76. *Selected Records of the City of Norwich*, vol. ii, p. 106.
77. *Records of the Borough of Reading*, vol. iii, pp. 46-47, 252.
78. 1) *Records of Nottingham*, vol. v, pp. 259-60.
79. 2) S. P. D. Eliz., vol. 244, Nos. 126, 128, 129, 130.
80. Hist M. S. S. Com. Cd. 784, p. 162.
81. *ibid.* p. 168.
82. *ibid.* p. 94.
83. Camden Society, Reports of Cases in the Courts of Star Chamber and High Commission, Attorney-General V. Archer (see especially Laud's remarks); Attorney-General *v* Taylor and others (both these in the Star Chamber); also, before the Court of High Commission, the case of Mr Viccars of Stamford, a Puritan minister who adds overstrict opinions about usury to his other heterodoxies.
84. S. P. D. Charles I, vol. 202, No. 54. 'We doe not find upon our enquiry that the Statute for laborers and ordering of wages is deluded . . .'
85. Privy Council Register, Charles I, vol. v, p. 399. Quoted Leonard *op. cit.* p. 160.

86. Quoted Leonard, *op. cit.* p.162.
87. Privy Council Register, Charles I, vol. v, pp. 350-1.
88. S. P. D. Charles I, vol. 197, No. 72.
89. *ibid,* vol. 189, No. 40. The Justices' assessment runs as follows: 'Essex. An order made at our Meetinge at Halsted in the said countie the eight day of Aprill anno dmi 1631 by vertue of an order from the Lords of the Cownsell.

It is ordered and agreed uppon by us whose names are hereunder written, that the Saye makers within the towne of Sudbury in Suff. shall paye unto the spynsters for spynnings of every seaven knotts, one penny, and to have noe deduccon of their wadges, and that the keele wheron the yard is reeled to be a yard in length and not longer. And we doe further order, that for all the white sayes under five pounds weight the Saymaker shall give unto the weaver 12d the pound for the weavinge thereof, and for the Sayes that shall be above five pounds und under Tenne pounds to give 12d the pound abatinge 6d in the peece for the weaving thereof, and for the mingled Sayes conteyninge eight or nyne pounds nyne shillings, and soe proporcionally, as it shall conteyne more or less in weight. This our order to contynewe untill the fiftenth daye of Maye next ensuinge, Excepte from the Cownsell there shall be other order taken.

Tho. Wyseman R. Wareyn
Willi Maxey Ri. Skynner
Dra. Deane Beniamine Fisher'

90. Privy Council Register, Charles, I, vol. xiii, pp. 389-90.
91. *ibid,* p. 422.
92. Salkeld's Reports vol. ii, p. 442. Trin. 3° Anne. Cf. Blackstone, *Commentaries,* vol. i, pp. 426-8.
93. Somerset Quarter Sessions Records, vol. xxv, p. 66, No. 13.
94. Harleian Miscellany, vol. ii. Serjeant Thorp's Charge to the Grand Jury at York Assizes. March 20th 1648.
95. Hist. M. SS. Com. Cd. 784, p. 169.
96. *ibid,* pp. 322-3.
97. Somerset Quarter Sessions Records (Somerset Record Society, vol. xxviii).
98. Morris, *Records of Chester,* p. 367.
99. McArthur, *English Historical Review* vol. xv.
100. See Hutchins in *Economic Journal,* vol. x.
101. Hist. M. S. S. Com. Fifteenth Report Appendix, Part VIII, p. 139.
102. Morris, *op., cit.* p. 436.
103. McArthur, *loc. cit.*
104. I take the prices on which my index number is based from Steffen, *Studien zur Geschichte der englischen Lohnarbeiter.*
105. Eden, *State of the Poor,* vol. III, app. p. CVI.—An assessment for Lancashire. May 22, 1735. 'The said county being eighty miles in length, we think the more northern parts thereof ought not to demand so much, but be content with what the custom of the county hath usually been'.
106. Rogers, *History of Agriculture and Prices,* vol. VI, p. 694. '. . . Which afterwards, since these troubles, have been increased, and in the year 1655 were thus assessed . . .'

107. Warwickshire Quarter Session Records. [These statistics are of questionable accuracy. They do not correspond directly with the published wage assessment records, for which see S. C. Ratcliff and H. C. Johnson (eds.), *Warwick County Records,* vol. iv, *Quarter Sessions Order Book Easter 1657 to Epiphany 1665* (Warwick, 1938), and vol. v, *Orders Made at Quarter Sessions, Easter 1665 to Epiphany, 1674* (Warwick, 1939).—Ed.]
108. *Victoria County History of Lincolnshire,* vol. ii, p. 336 (1680).
109. *Victoria County History of Buckinghamshire,* vol. ii,p. 69 (1562).
110. Hamilton, Quarter Sessions Records from Elizabeth to Anne.
111. Atkinson, Quarter Sessions Records of the North Riding of Yorkshire, vol. i, p. 204.
112. Massingberd, Ingoldmells Court Rolls, p. 285.
113. Atkinson, *op. cit.* vol. i, pp. 27, 60, 105.
114. *Archaeologia,* vol. xi, p. 200.
115. *Victoria County History of Derbyshire,* vol. ii, pp. 182-3.
116. *Victoria County History of Buckinghamshire,* vol. ii, pp. 67-8.
117. Burn, *Justice of the Peace,* vol. iv, pp. 130-2.

THE CONDITION OF CHINA (1933)*

I appreciate the honour of being allowed to address you, but my gratitude is mingled with diffidence. Nor is the embarrassment inspired by the names of my predecessors diminished by reflection on the character of the theme which I have been so rash as to select. Chinese civilization is a subject to which specialists have devoted their lives. It would be absurd for an amateur who has spent less than eight months in China, and who neither reads her literature nor speaks her language, to attempt to follow in their steps. My remarks must be regarded, not as formulating conclusions, but as suggesting problems. They are the tentative hypotheses of a layman concerned to interpret to himself, and, if he can, to his fellow-countryman, a world which has excited his curiosity and won his affection.

That it is a world which needs interpretation few will deny. It is the common misfortune both of Europe and of China that, as a result of the circumstances in which continuous contacts between them were first established, European opinion, apart from a handful of *savants,* has been concerned less with the realities of Chinese life, than with the foreign interests affected by them. The West came to China, first as trader, then as missionary and educationalist, then as financier and concessionnaire. It has regarded her as a sphere of economic enterprise, as a field of cultural activity, as an occasion of international friction. It has rarely been interested in her as a civilization whose qualities, precisely because they are not ours, it is instructive to contemplate, and whose achievements lend lustre to a humanity which is our own. But a society, like an individual, reveals its secrets, if at all, only to disinterested appreciation, and to approach it as a problem is to make certain of misconceiving it. So, though naturally the issues most prominent in the minds of my audience are those suggested by the words Manchuria, Washington Treaties, Extra-

*The Fifteenth Earl Grey Memorial Lecture, Armstrong College, Newcastle upon Tyne, 13 March 1933.

Territoriality, Foreign Settlements and Concessions, it may not be uninstructive, I hope, to consider this evening, not the problems which arise from contact between China and the West, but the salient characteristics of China herself.[1]

The western estimate of these characteristics has undergone in the last two centuries a singular reversal. In the Age of Reason China was held up, not merely in the writings of satirists who used her as a foil to the vices of Europe, but in the sober records of travellers, as a pattern for imitation. She was the grand example of a powerful, yet peaceful, empire, which ranked the soldier lower than the peasant; recruited its public services, not, like contemporary Europe, by jobbery and the sale of offices, but by merit; and secured the advantages of government, while avoiding its evils, by basing authority not on force but on an ethical code of generally recognized validity and universal application.

It is curious to turn from eulogies of the political tranquillity and economic prosperity of China, such as those of the Portuguese missionary, Alvarez Semedo, who wrote with the empire of the Mings beneath his eyes, and the noise of the Thirty Years' War still in his ears, to later Western verdicts. To the nineteenth century, with its religion of change, the static character of Chinese civilization appeared, not an ornament, but an offence. What had been applauded as stability was now derided as stagnation, so that Chinese intellectual traditions and the Chinese order of life became to the West a synonym for petrifaction. Then, when the old régime was overthrown by the Revolution of 1911, and the Revolution was followed by twenty years of a confusion which is not yet ended, that indictment, without being withdrawn, was heightened by another. To the reproach of an irrational conservatism was added that of an equally irrational, and more ruinous, anarchy. The foreign observer who today seeks to follow from a distance the course of Chinese politics with the same friendly curiosity as he would bring to those of a neighbouring nation not infrequently finds, in spite of himself, his sympathies flag beneath an almost irresistible impression of futility, of violence, of a meaningless welter of unending chaos. Nor are authorities wanting to confirm him in his dillusionment with the assertion that the conditions which bewilder him are, not transitory or accidental, but the expression of innate characteristics, which only his ignorance has prevented him from discerning. China, he is assured by men whose experience entitles their opinions to respect, lacks the faculty of combining continuity with change which is the secret of growth. She is incapable alike of progress and of order. She has discarded what she should have retained, the imperial institutions which alone were suited to her. Except here and there, she has retained what she should have modified, the primitive economic organization which condemns her people to poverty. Whatever her virtues, she must be regarded as politically a pathological phenomenon. If her internal troubles, a source of misery to herself and of danger to the world, are to be cured, peoples of greater political aptitude must administer the treatment.

If the issues raised by that verdict affected only China herself, it would be a matter of a moment. Judged either by the quality of the individual life which it fosters, or by its cultural contributions—architecture, painting, and, I am told, though here I speak without knowledge, philosophy and literature—Chinese civilization is among the greatest of human achievements. It cannot be a matter of indifference to mankind that the society which has produced it should disintegrate. In reality, however, it is not only the future of China which is involved. A structure so vast, embracing between one fifth and one sixth of the human race, does not crumble without producing portentous reactions. The varying interpretations placed upon them by Europe at different dates are reflected in the phases through which its Far Eastern policy has passed in the last two generations. The unedifying scramble of the Powers for ports, points of vantage, and railway concessions, which disgraced the close of the last, and the opening of the present, century, was inspired by a not unfounded belief that the old China was falling to pieces. The reversal of that policy in 1922, when the nine signatories of the Washington Treaty bound themselves to respect 'the territorial and administrative integrity of China', was based on the assumption that the new China, if allowed time, would achieve an equilibrium for herself. The course taken by Japan in the last eighteen months has been justified by her spokesmen on the ground that

China cannot, except by a misleading metaphor, be described as a nation, that these people are incorrigible, and that the decision taken at Washington to allow them a breathing-space was inspired by sentimental illusions which a sane realism must discard. The hesitations of Geneva, if caused partly by the European situation, have partly also been due to a doubt whether conventional political formulae were applicable to China. A society so disorganized, it has been suggested, cannot demand to be treated as a responsible state; and, though that doctrine, if pushed to extremes, would appear to imply that members of the League [of Nations] can claim its protection only in proportion as they do not require it, it would be a mistake to underestimate the genuine embarrassment which caused it to be propounded. It is not the first time that a domestic breakdown has started a wave which has travelled round the globe. In a world which has the interdependence of an organism without its unity, the question whether the disorders of China are to be regarded as a transient fever or a permanent disease is not merely a Chinese, but an international, question.

That question must be approached in the light of the legacy which modern China has inherited. It is a legacy different, not merely in degree but in kind, from that of the West; and, in order to understand it, the categories native to a European, with his political conceptions derived from Rome and the Middle Ages, and his assumption that the pivots of history are the Mediterranean and the Atlantic, must be discarded as irrelevant. The note of Western civilization might be described, perhaps, as crisis and rejuvenation. It has hitherto displayed an extraordinary capacity, not merely for survival, but for renewal and regeneration. There has been no lack of crises in Chinese history. But in the past equilibrium was established, not by innovation, but by restoration. A dynasty might fall, but the cadre remained, and there is truth in the observation, made eighty years ago by a British official, that 'of all peoples . . . the Chinese are the least revolutionary and the most rebellious'. The watersheds in the story of Europe, where a new social order and system of ideas begin their course, if not wholly absent from that of China, are different in their chronology and less decisive in their results.

As an organized community, with a distinctive culture, the China of today was the contemporary of Egypt and Mesopotamia. Not only, if area and population be the test, is she the largest nation in the world, but she has possessed for a longer period than any other some of the essential characteristics of a single organism. She is an organism, however, of a peculiar kind, which has no modern western analogies. Societies develop only the aptitudes which they need; and China did not evolve a highly organized political system, because, until recently, she did not require one. Isolated on the west by mountain barriers, and on the east in contact with civilizations inferior to her own, with a vast, but homogeneous, territory in which no feudal potentates competed for allegiance with the Son of Heaven, China experienced neither the external pressure which in Europe shaped the State, nor the internal disorder which caused the West to worship Leviathan as the mortal God, who, if he drank the blood of strangers, delivered his chosen people from chaos. Her unity, like that of medieval Christendom, was the unity of a civilization, rather than of a political system. The centre of an empire, which dominated for a thousand years the politics of the far East, she was conscious, like Christendom, that she was not merely a State, but the embodiment of a spirit—an oasis of culture and light holding back the barbarism of the outer darkness—and, as in Christendom, the unity which she derived from an ideal did not preclude the occurrence of violent internal struggles. She was, and in larger measure still is, a society based not on law, but on personal relations. From the patriarchal family, governed by a parent who was a kind of monarch, to the Emperor, a monarch who was a kind of parent, she found her cement less in political authority than in the universal acceptance of a common ethical code—the Confucian philosophy—uniting, not the living alone, but the living, the dead, and those yet to be born in an undying community, and, though the words carry misleading associations, in a great edifice of education by which that code was perpetuated and diffused.

An English observer will not be suspected of exaggerating the importance of that aspect of life. The testimony of a British Consul,[2] who wrote a remarkable book on China in the fifties of last century, is, therefore, the more impressive.

The causes of the long duration of the Chinese as a single nation, he wrote, 'consist of three doctrines, together with one institution. The doctrines are: (1) That the nation must be governed by moral agency in preference to physical force (2) That the services of the ablest and wisest men are indispensable to good government (3) That the people have the right to depose a ruler who . . . gives cause to oppressive and tyrannical rule. The institution is the system of public service examinations'. Custom, not law, fixed the framework of existence. Ethics, not theology or science, gave life its meaning. Government consisted of little more than the preservation of order and the collection of taxes, for there was no continuous economic change involving continuous readjustment. Thus, instead of advancing on all fronts at once, China was at the same time both mature and retarded. Voltaire once remarked that 'France rules the land, England the sea, and Germany the clouds'. China, to a far greater degree than any European country, had the excellences and defects of a non-political society. The private virtues flourished, the public were atrophied. Precocious in culture, she did not grow the hard shell of material organization, which protects and sometimes stifles it. Her intellectual and aesthetic achievements were on one plane; her political and economic were on another.

Nor, so admirable and satisfying was her way of life, did change appear other than evil to be shunned. There are two famous letters by the great emperor Ch'ien Lung, which had as their occasion Lord Macartney's Commercial Mission of 1793. His reply to George III was couched in tones of patient condescension; his attitude to the products of Western industry was that of Queen Victoria to frivolity: 'We are not amused.' 'You, O King, live beyond the confines of many seas. Nevertheless, impelled by your humble desire to partake of the benefits of our civilization, you have dispatched a mission respectfully bearing your memorial. . . . The earnest terms in which it is couched reveal a respectful humility on your part which is highly praiseworthy . . . I do not forget the lonely remoteness of your isle . . . nor do I overlook your excusable ignorance of the usages of our Celestial empire. . . . Nevertheless, your petition cannot be entertained. . . . As your ambassador can see, we possess all things. Swaying the wide world, I have but one aim in view, to maintain a perfect governance, and to fulfil the duties of the state. . . . I set no value on objects strange and ingenious, and have no use for your country's manufactures. . . . It behoves you, O King, to respect my sentiments, and to display even greater devotion and loyalty in future, so that, by perpetual submission to our Throne, you may secure peace and prosperity for your country hereafter'. It has been justly remarked that no one can begin to understand China until he has acquired a perspective which makes these words seem, not fantastic, but reasonable. The unique and inimitable excellence of Chinese civilisation was as axiomatic to those who shared it as had been that of Rome, whose empire was narrower in extent and shorter in duration.

> Haec est in gremio victos quae sola reciept,
> Humanumque genus communi nomine fovit,
>
> Huius pacificis debemus moribus omnes
>
> Quod cuncti gens una sumus . . .

In spite of the profound contrast between the rulers of the East and of the West, the lines of Claudian, written when the Roman world was tottering, express not inaptly what till three generations ago China, the Middle Kingdom, stood for to herself and to the Far East.

A society in which government played so small a part could survive on two conditions. The first was isolation, the second the absence of catastrophic economic change. In the nineteenth century the fragile vase crashed against brazen vessels. Once more the barbarian broke in, this time from the south, bringing piece-goods and opium, and equipped with the gunpowder which the Chinese had discovered long before the West, but characteristically had used, not for the serious business of destruction, but to brighten life with fireworks. The old order collapsed, not merely, as in the past, in an anarchic interregnum between rival dynasties, but in principle and in essence. Its effects, however, remained—the absence of centralized authority, of the rule of law, of a tradition of political subordination—for they were wrought into the very texture of Chinese life.

They remained in an environment no longer static, but in motion. The opening years of the century saw a threefold revolution, political, economic and cultural. The long agony of the old régime had ended in 1911, with the expulsion of the Manchus. But the problem was not merely, as in Western revolutions, to capture political power, for such power did not exist. It was to create it. It was to unify a country larger than Europe, in which both the material and the psychological conditions of unity still remained to be created. The dynasty could be overthrown by a *coup d'état,* but a new order to succeed it could not be improvised. Though the Republic survived Yuan Shih-kai, the military adventurer financed by Western powers, he had time to plant on the country the swarm of generals who are the curse of China today. The result is an unorganized feudalism—private armies, private taxes, private justices, and private war. In a country without tolerable communications it can defy the central government, while modern weapons make it almost immune to the local rebellions which tamed the tyrants of the past.

The political transformation was accompanied by two others. On the one hand, the Industrial Revolution, which had been slowly advancing since the nineties, received a new impetus when the import of foreign goods was cut off by the war of 1914-18. Western capitalism, historically an alien importation, is still localized on the Eastern Coast, in the neighbourhood of the northern coalfields, on the great rivers and in the hinterland of Canton; but its competition is felt in regions not directly affected by it, while, in those which it has penetrated, it has undermined the traditional foundations of Chinese society. On the other hand, the mentality of the younger generation was profoundly affected by contact with Western ideas. In China, as in Europe, the intellectual renaissance had its source in the discovery of a culture long ignored or despised. To a generation born into a world visibly falling to pieces, the new knowledge seemed to whisper the magic word that could rebuild it. It was natural that the vogue of western science should be immense and its worship indiscriminate, that by 1906 there should be 12,000 students in

Japan and some 500 in America, and that even in 1930, in spite of over fifty universities established in the interval in China, there should be more than 5,000 students in foreign institutions. The effect of the New Learning was profound; but its light sometimes dazzled and bewildered as well as illuminated. To lift the load of the past, China required, not merely new technical devices and new political forms, but new conceptions of law, administration and political obligations, and new standards of conduct in governments, administrators and the society which produced them. The former could be, and were, borrowed; the latter had to be grown. One scheme of life, long accepted without question, had lost its prestige; its successor was too immature to occupy the vacant throne. The result was an interregnum, in which everything seemed possible and nothing certain.

Such, as I see it, is the background of modern China. In view of it, her condition should not give cause for surprise. Her political incoherence, which shocks Western observers, is a phenomenon analogous in kind to the internecine warfare of the West, which shocks the Chinese. It is the product of history and geography, and it is needless to invoke that ambiguous phantom, national character, to interpret her disorders, since simpler explanations are adequate to account for them. In population, area, and diversity of economic condition, China is to be compared, not with a single European nation, but with Europe as a whole. But the conditions which have caused Europe to be organized in a score of national states have, for good or evil, been absent from China. Hence problems which in the West are international, are in China domestic; breakdowns, which in the former result in wars between states, in the latter take the form of civil disturbance. To suppose that she is unique in her liability to such disturbances is equally an illusion. As a glance at the history of Europe is sufficient to prove, they are the characteristic, not of a country or people, but of a phase of civilization. Other societies have painfully emerged from it. If it still remains for China to do so, the first reason is her long isolation, the second its abrupt termination.

That is part of the truth, and an important part; but it is only part. Though many of the morbid phenomena of Chinese political and economic life have had their parallels in the West, there is a contrast of fundamental importance between her situation today and that of Europe in the past. In a world which is economically one, a society which goes its own pace cannot avoid being trampled on. Unlike the Europe of past centuries, modern China is in contact with nations in a different stage of development, which have small mercy for those whom they regard as laggards. In such circumstances it is not credible that the instability by which she has been racked during the last quarter of a century will for long continue. Either she will find an equilibrium for herself and evolve a government strong enough to maintain it; or she will be compelled, under one guise or another, to acquiesce in one imposed by foreign action. The intention of the policy adopted at the Washington Conference was to make possible the first. It was to secure China an interval in which, undisturbed by foreign intervention, she could set her house in order. The aim of Japan has now been shown to be the second. It is to convert the Eastern Provinces into a Japanese Protectorate, and from that vantage ground to dominate, the historic role of the north, the politics of China as a whole. Whether she fails of that object, or attains it, the crucial question is the condition of China south of the Wall. Both culturally and in racial composition Manchuria is Chinese to the core; of its 30,000,000 inhabitants, 27,000,000 are Chinese. While Japan does not colonize, the number of Chinese in Manchuria year by year increases, and the net immigration from China—immigration less returns—amounted for the seven years, 1923-9, to nearly 2,500,000. If Manchuria is detached from China, it will be because Japan commands the resources of an organized state, while China does not. If China acquires them, it is to her, not to Japan, that Manchuria will gravitate. The question is whether she will succeed in that task.

The problem is twofold. It is to modernize economic organization and establish political authority. And ultimately, since a nation cannot live politically in one age and economically in another, these two problems are one. The main influence in the economic progress of the West had been the transmission of new ideas, new technical methods, and new types of organization by imitation, rivalry, and actual migration. Till recently no such influence affected China. The isolation which protected her politically retarded her economic development. Unlike Europe, with its long and deeply indented coastline and two inland seas in the north and south, which made foreign commerce possible for all her regions and indispensable to some, the greater part of China was, and remains, difficult of access from the sea. Unlike Europe, with its multitudinous subdivisions, she did not feel the stimulus to innovation arising from the existence of numerous independent centres of economic energy. Her economic system, therefore, was less plastic and mobile than that of the West, and, over the greater part of the country, it survives unchanged. She remains what she was—a society of cultivators and craftsmen, on the fringe of which capitalist industry has been developing for rather less than half a century.

The latter movement is obviously of profound importance, but in scale it is still inconsiderable. The number of cotton-mills in China—about 130—is smaller than existed in England in 1795; the output of coal from modern mines is about 25,000,000 tons, perhaps equal to that of England in 1820; and, while there are some 2,000-3,000 other modernized undertakings, no estimate which I have seen puts the number of industrial wage-earners at more than 2,500,000. Of a population which may be estimated, perhaps, at about 450,000,000 some 70 per cent are usually thought to be peasants. Much of China is too rough, too dry, or too cold for cultivation; and, unlike the Europe of the Middle Ages, with which she is often compared, she possesses, except in Manchuria, and possibly in the north-west, no large unoccupied areas available for colonization. Hence population is crowded on the plains and waterways; in the valleys of the Yellow River and the Yantze, the plain of Chengtu in Szechwan and the Canton delta, it attains an almost urban density. As a consequence holdings have been subdivided to such a point that, when the government obtained figures in 1918, 36 per cent were found to be below 1½, and 62 per cent below 4½ acres. The intensity of cultivation which results from that situation has often been admired; and it is true that, a century and a half ago, the technique of Chinese agriculture was probably the most efficient in the world. But it is the agriculture of a pre-scientific age, which owes nothing to the discoveries that have revolutionized western farming in the course of the last century. The human cost at which its miracles are performed is appalling; for it is the output per man, not the output per acre, which determines the standard of life; and, while the latter, in the case of one crop—rice—is surprisingly high, the former is invariably low. When to the effects of this primitive productive technique are added the exploitation of the peasant by moneylenders and dealers; the existence, in parts of the country, of a vicious system of land-tenure; the absence of the resources needed to cope with droughts and floods; a system of communications so deficient that in the whole of China there are less than 50,000 miles of motor-road and less than 12,000 miles of railway, the poverty of the rural population is not surprising. There are districts in which its position is permanently that of a man standing up to his neck in water, so that even a ripple is sufficient to drown him.

Political organization rests on economic foundations; when the latter crumble, it crumbles with them. Many of the political phenomena which shock Western observers are the results less of political than of economic causes. Intermittent banditry—often a seasonal occupation— is in China, as in the Europe of the past, the natural resource of the peasant who cannot make a living from the land. Inflated armies survive partly because they offer a livelihood to men for whom no other exists, and to disband them would be to intensify the problem of rural congestion. Internal disunion, which is not incompatible with a profound consciousness of national identity, is to be expected in a country where difficulties of communication make it impossible for the Central Government to maintain regular contact with distant provinces or to strike swiftly at rebellious militarists. Famine, the feature of Chinese economic life of which the West hears most, has as its occasion a failure of crops due to drought or flood, but as its cause the primitive organization, and absence of surplus resources over daily needs, which turns the misfortune of individuals into a general catastrophe.

As far as the technical aspects of the matter are concerned, an improvement in the conditions of Chinese economic life is not, in my judgment, impracticable. It is not always remembered that, till little more than a century ago, the social problem of Europe, as of China today, was, not the wage-earner, but the peasant. There is no reason to suppose that the modernization of productive methods, the extension of roads and railways, the development of co-operative credit and marketing, the elimination of the worst types of land-tenure, and, above all, the diffusion of education—all of which, in spite of overwhelming difficulties, are slowly advancing—will not produce in China effects similar in kind, if slower in their operation, to those which resulted from them in the West. Nor is it to be expected that the process of equipping the country with modern technological resources will fail to continue. China is never likely to be industrialized in the same sense as Great Britain, Germany, or the United States. She has supplies of coal, which, though not conspicuously large, are adequate for some hundreds of years; but she is deficient in iron ore, and possesses, as far as is known, no considerable oil resources. Her development is likely to resemble that less of those countries than of France down to 1914. It will take the form of manufactures based, not on the production of a large output of iron and steel, but on taste and dexterity, and on such imports of machinery as are needed to supply requirements that cannot be met at home. Her Industrial Revolution is still in its first phase; but, in spite of the unfavourable conditions of the last decade, the advance made in the modernization of certain industries and regions has been extraordinary. In view of the intelligence of her population, and her valuable raw materials, it would be paradoxical to suppose that, given political stability, it will not proceed more rapidly in the future.

'Given political stability'—that condition is, of course, the central issue. Whether such a phenomenon as a nation endowed with political intelligence has ever existed is an interesting speculation; if it has, we can only regret, when we observe the world around us, that the nature of mankind has not permitted its survival. For the reasons which I have given, the view which ascribes the present troubles of China to some innate incapacity for political action seems to me superficial; nor do I share the opinion once expressed to me by a Chinese acquaintance that the mistake of the founder of the Republic was to found a Republic. The forms of the constitution are elaborate and unimportant. They are the product, partly of the genius of Dr Sun Yat-sen, who gave the revolution its doctrine and programme, partly of an American version of Western political theory, partly of the Russian example, partly of military exigencies. The reality is, on the one hand, the military power wielded by the commander-in-chief, General Chiang Kai-shek, who, till the end of 1931, was also president, and, on the other hand, a bureaucracy composed of officials largely educated in the West, particularly in America, and, though less often, in France. The Government of which it is the organ was established as the result of the drive north from Canton of the Kuomintang armies in 1927. It represents the victory of the right wing of the Kuomintang over the left. Part of its weakness, indeed, is that the social forces behind it consist predominantly of financial and commercial interests—bankers, merchants, and industrialists at the ports, the smaller bourgeoisie dependent on them, and the urban intelligentsia—who desire order and security, but are little interested in the issues, for example the land question, which most intimately affect the mass of the population.

In judging this Government's achievements, it is necessary to remember that it has been in existence for less than six years; that it assumed power at a time when the country had already been distracted for more than a decade by the struggles of rival generals; that it has had to face two civil wars; and that, at the moment when it could hope to settle down to the tasks of peace, its plans were shattered by the Japanese invasion. Its record is naturally a chequered one, but it includes successes as well as failures. In the sphere of international policy it has recovered two leased territories, customs autonomy, and postal rights, and has negotiated treaties on a footing of equality with foreign powers. It has carried through, amid almost overwhelming difficulties, important financial reforms, including the consolidation and simplification of taxes, the establishment of a Central Bank, and a more effective supervision of the financial methods of the provinces. Before the Japanese attack imposed a new strain upon its scanty resources, it had established a Central Planning

Department—the National Economic Council—which was to prepare and give effect to plans of economic development. Nor, in estimating what has been accomplished, should attention be confined to measures initiated at Nanking. The new China which is struggling on to its feet is the creation, not of the Central Government, but of a national movement of reconstruction affecting every side of life, in which thinkers, like Dr Hu Shih, the father of the intellectual renaissance, social reformers, like Dr James Yen and his colleagues, who are bringing education to the peasants, and Provincial and Municipal Authorities, have all played their part. One example must suffice. In 1910, China possessed no public system of Primary and Secondary Education and less than half a dozen Universities. Today she has some nine million children in public Primary schools, something over half a million in Secondary schools, and, if account is taken, as it should be, of institutions which, though financed from private funds, are recognized by the government, no less than 33,000 students in 59 Universities. Whatever the defects of her educational system, no admiration can be too great for the enthusiasm thrown into developing it. To have built it up in less than a generation, in the midst of civil disorder, international complications, grave financial stresses, and the recurrent calamities of flood and famine, is an extraordinary achievement. Not all European countries would have been capable of it.

If progress depended on intelligence alone, the future of China would give little cause for apprehension. But it depends also on the existence of an environment which permits ideas to be applied with continuity and system. That environment, over large parts of the country, has still to be created. The view expressed by some foreigners—the view that, in order to escape from disorder, China requires to be broken into smaller units—does not seem to me plausible. The result of such a policy, could it be applied, would be an eternity of civil war, but its application is impossible. Economically, as in the matter of customs and railways, China for all her diversity of conditions, is one. Politically, she is treated as one by foreign Powers. In culture and spirit, she has possessed for many centuries a unity more profound than that of some nations whose governmental machinery is more highly centralized.

On a broad view, the possibilities before her appear to be three. The first is that she should become, under one disguise or another, a Japanese protectorate, and that Japan, having given notice to the West—the real meaning of her policy—to leave Far Eastern politics to the Far East, should proceed, like past invaders, to control China from the north. The second is that the Communist regions of the south—already the nucleus of a great state with a population of, perhaps, some 75,000,000—should succeed in securing control of the Yangtze valley, and compel Nanking to come to terms with them. The third is that the present régime, or one resembling it, should achieve stability, and gradually carry out the unification of the country.

Which of these possibilities is realized depends partly on China herself, partly on the policy pursued by other Powers. The first may temporarily succeed, as at present appears likely; in so far as it does, China will cease to have an independent foreign policy, and her internal reconstruction, for example in the vital matter of communications, will be carried out, if at all, only with the sanction, and under the supervision of, Japan. On a longer view, however, I regard the Japanese design of using China as a stepping-stone to an Asiatic empire as doomed to failure. China has absorbed and civilized many barbarians. Her resisting power is as great as her striking power is small, and the strain of attempting to master her would ultimately, it may be suspected, prove intolerable. It is not easy to say what exactly the Chinese version of Communism means. My own guess is that it has its economic roots in the land question—it is significant that its hold is strongest in those areas where the system of land-tenture was particularly vicious—and that, while it is organized and led by political missionaries, its affinities are less with the doctrinal Communism of the West than with a medieval *Jacquerie.* Since the grievances behind it are acute, it can be met only, not by force, but by measures to remove the causes producing it. The gravest error of the present régime—an error due partly to circumstances beyond its control, but partly also to the character of the interests on which it rests—has been its failure to take seriously the necessity for drastic measures to improve the life of the peasants. Until such measures are carried through, both the material and the psychological conditions of political stability will continue to be absent.

On the methods to be adopted, a foreigner must speak with diffidence. But, whatever régime may be in power at Nanking, two general considerations will remain relevant. The first is that China is too vast, and, in the absence of adequate communications, too amorphous and unmanageable, for it to be possible for all parts of the country to advance together. What is required is a region which, like Prussia and Piedmont in the Europe of the nineteenth century, will serve as a basis where reform can mobilize its forces, and spread new standards of public spirit and good government by the influence of its example. That region must be found, in the first place, in the group of provinces nearest the capital, which economically and culturally are the heart of modern China. It is by making these provinces a model of order and efficiency—by concentrating its resources, instead of dispersing them—that a government, whatever its colour, is most likely in the long run to win the prestige which will enable it to assert its authority in provinces now hostile or indifferent. The gravest weakness of Chinese politics, in the second place, like that of European countries till less than a century ago, is the absence of efficient administration and, indeed of any adequate idea of what administration implies. In the West there are means without ends, in China ends without means. The legislative output is enormous; the complications of Departments voluminous and instructive. Mountains of paper are accumulated, but the wheels do not turn, or turn too slowly. Here again, however, such is the swiftness of the Chinese intelligence in seizing ideas at first unfamiliar that this weakness had only to be remarked for efforts to be made to correct it. Distracted though it has been by internal difficulties and by the blows of foreign enemies, the Chinese Government has found time to co-operate with advisers put at its disposal by the League to assist in the organization of flood prevention and famine relief, the improvement of agriculture and transport, and the development of the services of Public Health and Education. It is significant that it has this year asked that a European official shall be sent to aid it in creating an efficient

Civil Service.

A Government does not invite foreigners to take part in arranging for their own deception. Such efforts to build a modern state should dispose of the suggestion that Chinese talk of reconstruction is fundamentally insincere. Their result will depend, not only on herself, but on the policy of Western powers. It was my lot to spend in China the three months immediately following the incident at Mukden which supplied the pretext for the Japanese attack; to observe the astonishing self-restraint shown by the Chinese in the face of almost intolerable provocation; and finally to see the Government, which has staked its credit on the intervention of the League of Nations, collapse when its reliance on the Covenant proved to have been misplaced. It was at that time the opinion of experienced observers that, had the League acted with decision at once, before the civilian authorities in Japan had been reduced to impotence by what was, in effect, a military *coup d'état,* it would have been possible to arrest the army's adventure. By what may yet prove to have been the most costly blunder made since 1919, the moment when preventive action was possible was allowed to slip. It is still not too late for the League to frustrate the Japanese object of forcing China into negotiations with herself to the exclusion of other Powers; to place on record that Japan had committed a breach of the covenant of the Kellogg Pact and of the Treaty of 1922; and, by the use of financial pressure, to make Japan feel the economic consequences of defying world opinion. But, though it is possible that Japan could have been prevented from seizing the Eastern Provinces of China, she cannot now be expelled from them. As far as Manchuria is concerned, the issue is for the immediate future closed.

If, however, Manchuria is for the time being lost, the necessity of aiding China south of the Wall to create an ordered state is, alike for her sake and for that of the world, only the more urgent. In providing such assistance the League, if the Powers will allow it to function, may play a beneficent part. Its task will neither be easy, nor, in view of the attitude of Japan, unaccompanied by risks, though risks not comparable, in my judgment, to those involved in allowing China to disintegrate, and—an almost inevitable consequence if that process continues—to become the battleground of rival Powers. Our answer to the question whether it should be undertaken will depend partly, at least, on our estimate of the value to mankind of the culture which may either be preserved or be further undermined. It is inevitable, perhaps, that a Western observer should see more of the weak than of the strong points of China, especially if his attention has been concentrated on the problems presented by her primitive economic organization and still unstable political system. But he must be, I think, more than ordinarily superficial if he remains unmoved by the appeal of the qualities—a respect for individuality, a belief in the things of the spirit, a preference of qualitative excellence to mechanical efficiency—of which those weaknesses are the defect. Such an attitude to life is not among the failings to which the West is most prone. It is worth while, it seems to me, to aid the nation representing it to make its contribution to civilization.

NOTES

1. Readers sufficiently interested to pursue the subject further are recommended to begin by reading the following works:

Pearl S. Buck, *The Good Earth* and *Sons* (Methuen).
Lionel Curtis, *The Capital Question of China* (Macmillan & Co.).
Owen Lattimore, *Manchuria Cradle of Conflict* (The Macmillan Company New York).
Arthur N. Holcombe, *The Chinese Revolution* (Harvard University Press).
J. B. Condliffe, *China Today, Economic* (World Peace Foundation, Boston).
R. H. Tawney, *Land and Labour in China* (George Allen & Unwin).

2. T. T. Meadows, *The Chinese and their Rebellions* (1856).

AN OCCUPATIONAL CENSUS OF THE SEVENTEENTH CENTURY (1934)*

I

Occupational statistics on any considerable scale are, before the nineteenth century, scarce. The figures on which the present article is based are, apart from estimates, the most comprehensive known to us.[1] They relate to the occupations of men between 20 and 60 years of age in the county of Gloucestershire in the year 1608. As far as we are aware, they have not previously been used for the purpose of economic history; but, after we had begun tabulating them, we were shown, by the kindness of Mr Raggatt, a study by him of the Gloucestershire clothing industry in which he has made use of the figures showing the number and distribution of textile workers. We have accordingly refrained from discussing in detail more than a few of the questions as to the organization of the textile industry which are suggested by them.

The source from which our material is taken consists of a reprint,[2] published in 1902, of a manuscript in the possession of Lord Sherborne. The headings prefixed to the entries for each of the five divisions of the county explain the purpose of the document. The first, which relates to the City of Gloucester, runs as follows: 'The names and surnames of all the able and sufficient men in body fitt for his Majestie's service in the warrs, within the City of Gloucester and the Inshire of the same, wherein are contayned the City of Gloucester and the Hundreds of Dudstone and Barton Regis, with their ages, parsonable statures and armours, viewed by the Right honorable Henry, Lord Barkley, Lord Lieutenant of the said city and the county thereof, by direction from his Majestie in the month of September, 1608.' The document is, therefore, a Muster Roll. Its occasion was the demand of the Government for a list of men in the county of Gloucestershire and City of Gloucester capable of bearing arms, and its practical

**Economic History Review*, v (1934), pp. 25-64. By A. J. and R. H. Tawney.

character as a compilation made for military purposes is maintained throughout. The age of the persons appearing in it is indicated by numbers after their names showing whether it is 'about twenty', 'about forty', or 'between fifty and three score'.[3] Each name is followed by a letter showing the branch of the service for which its bearer is physically best fitted. Women, and men physically unfit for duty, are included in the list when, though unable to serve in person, they can provide arms. Apart from the weapons owned by individuals, those for which a tithing or parish is collectively responsible are in some cases, though not all, inserted at the end of the lists of persons in it. Finally, in the case of some hundreds, a piece of information not directly germane to the matter in hand is added, in the shape of the abbreviation 'sub' after the names of such persons as are assessed to subsidies.[4]

Muster returns were demanded at frequent intervals under Elizabeth and the first two Stuarts, and a considerable number of them have been printed. The military value of information as to the physical characteristics and occupations of recruits is obvious. One does not set weavers or haberdashers to dig trenches or mind horses, if miners, quarrymen, and carters are to hand; and the quips at Feeble, the woman's tailor, with which Falstaff delighted Mr Justice Shallow, show that, if he had no intention of doing the job properly, he knew how it should be done. It would not have been surprising, therefore, if the Government had made a practice of requiring that occupations, as well as mere names, should be listed by the authorities responsible for making returns. In fact, however, it does not appear to have done so, either in 1608 or on other occasions; though other examples of returns compiled in the same form as that under consideration may exist, only one,[5] and that a very meagre specimen, is at present known to us. For the information given for Gloucestershire in 1608 we are indebted, it seems, not to any belated outburst of official zeal for military efficiency, but to the insatiable curiosity of a Gloucestershire worthy, the learned, lovable, pedantic John Smyth of North Nibley.

To those acquainted with that instructive and charming book, *The Lives of the Berkeleys,*[6] Smyth needs no introduction. He was not a great man, but he lived in a great age; and his humanity, his versatility, his inexhaustible gusto, carry a breath of the air in which the heroes were bred. Born in 1567, he entered the service of the Berkeleys as a boy of seventeen, to attend the nine-year-old son of Henry, Lord Berkeley. After studying at Oxford and the Middle Temple, and acting for a year as steward of the household of Lord Berkeley, he became steward of the Hundred and Liberty of Berkeley in 1597. He acted as legal adviser, man of business, and confidant of the family till his death in 1641.

To judge by such of Smyth's papers as remain and are accessible, his duties were not light; but he carried them lightly. He was a practical farmer,[7] wise in the ways of Cotswold sheep, and selling his own as far afield as London; was a person of some importance in the public life of the county, whose support it was worth while to canvass when candidates were being considered;[8] and himself sat for Midhurst in 1621. But while law was his profession and farming his hobby, it was scholarship that had his heart. The Antiquarian Society had been founded in 1572, though only to be suppressed in 1604, and Smyth was one of a mighty line. He knew the muniments of Berkeley Castle as few, it is probable, have known them since; and, when in London on business, snatched odd hours for work in the Tower.[9] His labours were prodigious, even for a day when there were giants in the land. When, in his old age, he counted the twenty-six volumes which he left to a posterity so thankless as to have printed only three of them, he uttered, for all his ardour, a faint groan. What had induced him to go through with it? Not the artless vanity of D'Ewes, nor the frigid malice of Prynne, but pleasure, merely pleasure. 'A continued delight of forty yeares haled mee alonge.'[10]

It was a delight, not only in the hard knots of feudal tenures and lawsuits lasting two hundred years,[11] but in the scene around him. Smyth was of the scholars, not always the worst, who 'would rather hear the lavrock sing than the mouse cheep'. One amiable feature of the unlovely nationalism of his age was an enthusiasm, not only for England, but for its provinces. It was a devotion to local peculiarities which smelt of the soil, and the mention of which evoked a loved picture—Kentish hop-fields; hedges gay with fruit trees in Worcester and Hereford; Devonshire seen from the sea; the wall of the Cotswolds looking west to the Severn; the country folk of Cheshire, blameless as the Ethiopians, 'very gentle and courteous, ready to help and further one another . . . especially in harvest how careful of one another!'[12] Such features were dwelt on with affectionate pride by men to each of whom his own 'country'—to speak their language—was not an administrative area, but, as Michelet said of France, a kind of person; or cited by geographers to heighten their portrait of a rich and varied society, commanding within its own borders the means of ample and generous life.

This provincial patriotism, which gave us between 1570 and 1640 the first vivid descriptions of the regions of England, was with Smyth a passion. His lines were cast in pleasant places and he wished the world to know it. At the end of a lifetime spent in a struggle to prevent his patrons making the fortunes of moneylenders, they remained to him, not amiable country gentlemen with an eye for a horse, but the descendants of Vikings. Of Gloucestershire he wrote—almost in the manner of his namesake, the Captain, describing Virginia for the benefit of shareholders—as a land blessed by Providence above all others; of the hundred of Berkeley—for his devotion increased as its object contracted—as the most fortunate region of a fortunate county; of Nibley, his home, as the very eye of the Eden.

If there is something to be said for the first doctrine, the two last are absurd; but, in spite of these eccentricities, Smyth's evidence is good. He was a shrewd man of business and an admirable recorder of facts—methodical, accurate, and candid, when his knowledge gave out, in admitting ignorance. His connexion with Lord Berkeley made it natural that, when the latter became Lord-Lieutenant, Smyth should stand at his elbow. Partly because all information about Gloucestershire was grist to his mill; partly because he was an inveterate note-taker, who recorded the proceedings of politicians[13] and sheep with impartial precision; partly, perhaps, through a mere habit of doing thoroughly whatever he did, he found in the dull business of preparing a muster return an opportunity for sociological investigation too tempting to be missed. So, instead of scamping the job, as it was commonly scamped elsewhere, he asked, or told his clerks to ask, questions not in the book, and had the answers written down. The result was the lists which form the basis of this article.

II

The first point to be considered is: How complete are the figures? Was the whole county covered, or did part of it escape attention? The procedure followed in making the return is partially indicated by Smyth in the description given in the list which he made of his works: 'Three books in folio containinge the names of each inhabitant in this county of Glouc., how they stood charged with Armour in A.6to Jacobi. And who then was the lord or owner of each Manor or Lordship within the County; which you may call my Nomina Villarum'.[14] The manor, that is to say (or, in the case of boroughs, the borough), was taken as the unit, and the persons liable to serve were listed under it. Apart from the City of Gloucester and Borough of Cirencester, there are 28 hundreds and about 400 manors.[15] Were any areas omitted?

The answer to that question seems to be in the negative. Bristol did not appear in the return; but, with that exception, the whole county, including its sixteen[16] boroughs, was covered by it. It is true, of course, that a manor was primarily not a territorial, but a jurisdictional, unit, and that the number of actual or reputed manors somewhat exceeded that given by Smyth. What he did, when one village was divided between several manors, was to describe it by the name of the principal one, and to group all the inhabitants under that, ignoring the distinction between manors and sub-manors or members of manors. The effect was to make manors coincide more nearly with villages, and parishes than would otherwise have been the case. Since his object was not to throw light on the respective rights of different lords of the tenurial obligations of different groups of tenants, but to secure a complete list of individuals in a given area, his inquiry lost nothing by this procedure, and gained a good deal in simplicity and compactness. Only a very minute acquaintance with the county could enable it to be said with certainty that no hamlet existing in 1608 has been omitted; but, in the few districts where we have been able to test the return by local knowledge, its accuracy has been confirmed.

Granted that the return is complete geographically, how complete is the list of individuals contained in it, and how fit is it to be used for statistical purposes? As the basis of an occupational census, it has several defects, some of which consist in omissions, some in ambiguities of statement. The most important are five.

First, the return is not exhaustive.[17] As the prevalent attitude to direct taxation shows, a high sense of duty to the State was not among the virtues of the age; on the subject of military service in particular, the sentiments of the plain man were those of Mouldy and Bullcalf. Hence, as Smyth himself notes,[18] a considerable number of persons who ought to have given in their names failed, or refused, to do so. There is no reason to think that such evasion was more prevalent among workers of one kind than among those of another, so that it does not affect the proportions employed in different occupations. But the figures throughout are *minima.*

Second, in the case not only of the 135 women, but of a substantial proportion of the 19,402 men[19] appearing in the return, no occupation is stated. As far as a small number of these—109, or ·5 per cent—are concerned, the reason is that they were 'unable in body', and presumably did not work. In the case of the remainder, amounting to 11·5 per cent of the total, that expanation is not given. Either, when questioned as to their occupation, they did not answer, or the clerks concerned with particular hundreds were careless. Such persons of unspecified occupation number in all 2,247,[20] leaving 17,046 men for whom some information as to occupation or social status is given.

Third, of these 17,046, a group of 1,962, 11·5 per cent, consists of persons described merely as 'labourers', and another 283, or 1·7 per cent, of persons described merely as 'servants' without the occupation of their employer being stated.

Fourth, there are 619 individuals, or 3·6 per cent of the reduced total of 17,046, of whom the only account given is that they are sons or brothers of persons engaged in this or that occupation.

Finally, though we have used the word 'occupation', some of the descriptions—knight, esquire, gentleman, mayor, constable, tithingman—relate, not to gainful employments, but to social or official status. Of the persons placed by the return in these categories some might equally well, on strictly economic grounds, have appeared in others. Many gentlemen, for example, depended for their incomes on farming land, whether of their own or taken on lease, and some were probably clothiers; nor is it to be supposed that the mayors of the tiny boroughs of Newnham and Wickwar managed to live by their offices. Thus a social, or official, cuts across an economic, classification.

These defects[21] are undoubtedly serious. They are stated here once for all; and, if they are not emphasized below on each occasion that particular figures are cited, it is for reasons of space, not that their gravity is underestimated. The least important are the last two. Apart from the knights, esquires, and gentlemen, the fifth affects only some twenty persons;[22] and, while it would have been preferable to be told how many of the gentry were themselves farmers or industrialists, it is not without interest to know the number of individuals in the small ruling class of the county. Among persons returned as sons and brothers, of whom the former greatly predominate, more than half occur in the families of agriculturists, and three-quarters in those of agricultural and textile workers combined. They have been assigned to the occupations followed by their relatives.

In dealing with labourers of unspecified occupation we have proceeded, we must admit, somewhat arbitrarily. Those outside the three largest towns, Gloucester, Cirencester, and Tewkesbury, have been placed under agriculture, while the small number—6·6 per cent of the whole group—within those towns have been assumed to be engaged in some non-agricultural employment. This classification is, doubtless, not satisfactory; and for one part of the county, it is likely, we think, to be definitely misleading. The number of coalminers and ironworkers in the Forest of Dean appearing in Smyth's lists is so small that it seems to us probable that some workers in these categories were entered as labourers,[23] a procedure which was the more natural because a good many of both had some other occupation and were not employed in the industries in question throughout the year. With that exception, persons appear normally to have been described as labourers only when there was no specific occupation, other than agriculture, to which they could be assigned. In view of that fact, and of the character of the surrounding population, the error involved in treating labourers outside the three largest towns as employed in agriculture does not seem likely to be large.

A somewhat similar difficulty arises in the case of some of the persons described as servants. They fall into three categories—servants employed by masters whose occupation (husbandman, clothier, miller, and so on) is stated; servants of knights, esquires, gentlemen, and similar classes of persons; servants of whose employers' occupation or status no indication is given. Those in the first group have been placed under the occupations of their employers; those in the second have been classed as household servants; the third have been entered separately, as servants the nature of whose employment is not stated. That arrangement, again, is clearly open to criticism; some of those classed as household servants, for example, were undoubtedly farm servants.[24] The difficulty is due partly to the character of an economic system under which the sharp modern line between domestic service and agricultural or industrial employment did not exist, so that, as in the statute of 1563, workmen were described indifferently as labourers or servants; partly to a failure on the part of Smyth and his clerks to insist on precise statements. The group most affected by the latter fault, that consisting of persons described as 'servants' without any clue being given as to their employers, is not, however, large. They amount to only 1·7 per cent of the persons appearing below in Table XII.

The other two *lacunae* mentioned above are more embarrassing. The first, that caused by evasion, obviously impairs the value of the figures as a basis for estimating the population of the county. They were used for that purpose a century later by the historian of Gloucestershire, Sir Robert Atkyns,[25] who compared them with those produced by a religious census taken under Charles II, and argued that the results of the two inquiries agreed; but, though not uninstructive, they require to be handled with caution. Their second great weakness—the fact that about one in nine of the names has no description attached to it—is equally serious. If there were reason to think that the places for which information is scanty or absent were also places in which particular occupations were represented more strongly than on the average, the incompleteness of the return would invalidate conclusions as to the relative importance of different branches of industry. We think it does invalidate them to some, but not to any very great, extent. It is probable, for example, that the number of men engaged in retail trade and miscellaneous crafts is somewhat understated, since it happens that a hundred[26] which included part of the suburbs of Gloucester, and in which these occupations might be expected to have a larger number of members than in more rural districts, is that containing the largest number of persons of unstated occupation. On the other hand, the highly industrialized parts of the county lay within clearly defined boundaries, and, of the other six hundreds[27] in which persons of unstated occupation exceed one-sixth of the men returned, none is in areas marked by an unusual predominance of any industry other than agriculture. If, therefore, the occupations of the men in these hundreds were more fully stated, the result would probably be somewhat to increase the percentage of the population engaged in agriculture; but, apart from that, it is unlikely that the economic complexion of the county as a whole be substantially altered.

III

So much by way of explanation; next for the figures themselves. If they may be regarded, in spite of their obvious defects, as a rough approximation to the truth, they throw light on certain aspects of the economic life of an important, and probably more than ordinarily prosperous, part of England in the early seventeenth century, in particular (i) the proportion of persons engaged in different occupations and industries; (ii) the distribution of the population and the relative size of the units in which it was grouped; (iii) the relative number of employers, independent producers, and wage-workers. Some of these points are touched on in the following pages. The number of separate occupations listed in the return is large. For reasons both of economy and of convenience, therefore, workers have been grouped below by industries, not by particular crafts.[28]

(i) *The Industrial Classification of the Population*

As already stated, the total number of individuals in Smyth's list, exclusive of lords of manors and women, is 19,402, of whom 109 are men disabled in body, and 2,247 are other men between 20 and 60 of whom no description is given. There remain 17,046 men of 20 to 60 whose occupation or social status is indicated. The number and proportion of these in different industries, or (as in the case of knights, esquires, gentlemen, and servants not more specifically described) different social groups, are set out in Table XII, first for the three towns with a male population aged 20 to 60 of over 340, then for the county exclusive of the towns in question, and finally for the county as a whole. As explained above, persons described merely as labourers have, except in the case of the three largest towns, been treated as engaged in agriculture, and sons and brothers have been assigned to the occupations of their relatives. When a servant's occupation is indicated, he has been placed under the appropriate industry; otherwise he appears among household servants or servants of unspecified occupation. To see the number of servants in different industries, and to compare them with the number of employers, the reader must consult, not this table, but Table XV.

Before considering the figures relating to the county as a whole, it is worth while to glance at the three towns. Tiny though they seem, Gloucester, Tewkesbury, and Cirencester were, apart from Bristol, much the largest centres of population in Gloucestershire.[29] If men unable in body and those of unspecified occupation be included, Gloucester returned 562 men. Tewkesbury 455, Cirencester 350; a total of 1,367 compared with 18,035 in the rest of the county. If these figures may be taken as an approximate indication of the distribution of the population, 93 per cent of it lived outside

Table XII
Number and Proportion of Males aged 20-60 in different industries

	Gloucester, Tewkesbury, and Cirencester		*County exclusive of Gloucester, Tewkesbury, and Cirencester*		*Total*	
	Number	*Per cent*	*Number*	*Per cent*	*Number*	*Per cent*
Agriculture and Estate Service	48	3·9	7,835	49·5	7,883	46·2
Fishing, Mining, and Quarrying	3	·2	187	1·2	190	1·1
Textiles	135	11·0	2,502	15·8	2,637	15·5
Leather-work	59	4·8	142	·9	201	1·2
Making of Articles of Dress	188	15·3	1,073	6·8	1,261	7·4
Woodwork	72	5·8	603	3·8	675	4·0
Building	28	2·3	318	2·0	346	2·0
Metal-work	73	5·9	493	3·1	566	3·3
Making of Food and Drink	83	6·7	300	1·9	383	2·2
Dealing and Retail Trade	237	19·3	478	3·0	715	4·2
Transport	40	3·2	238	1·5	278	1·6
Miscellaneous Occupations	25	2·0	38	·2	63	·4
Gentry, Professional, and Official	78	6·3	441	2·8	519	3·0
Servants, household	22	1·8	893	5·7	915	5·4
Servants, unspecified	10	·8	273	1·7	283	1·7
Labourers, non-agricultural	131	10·6	—	—	131	·7
Total	1,232		15,814		17,046	
Unable in body	1		108		109	
Other men of unstated occupation	134		2,113		2,247	
Grand Total	1,367		18,035		19,402	

the three towns in question, and 7 per cent in them.

It is sometimes suggested that, apart from a few great cities, the seventeenth-century town was still largely agricultural. As regards many of the smaller boroughs—a term of legal, not economic, significance—the statement is, doubtless, true; in Chipping Campden, for example, 30 per cent, and in Winchcombe 39 per cent, of the men whose occupations are stated were engaged in agriculture. In the case of the towns under consideration it requires to be qualified. The composition of their population suggests that they had an economic character of their own, which made them something other than large villages. In the first place, however intimate their dependence on farming, they contained few farmers or farm labourers,[30] and a negligible number of miners and fishermen. In the second place, the proportion of their inhabitants employed in every industry except textiles—a significant exception—was higher than in the rest of the county. Workers in metal, wood, leather, and the building trades accounted for nearly one-fifth of their adult male population whose occupation is stated, as against just under one-tenth in the latter, and makers of articles of dress 15·3 per cent, as against 6·8 per cent. The proportion engaged in transport was also noticeably higher.

Though, however, these towns were not agricultural, neither were they industrial, centres. That they did not act as powerful magnets, attracting manufacturers from the surrounding regions, is shown by the fact that in the case of only three of the groups represented in the table did they contain as much as one-fifth of the male workers in the county as a whole. Those groups were dealing and retail trade—their largest single industry—food and drink, and working in leather. The first employed almost exactly one-fifth of the townsmen whose occupation is stated, as compared with 3 per cent in the remainder of the county, and the three together 30·8 per cent, as compared with 5·8 per cent.

It was the prominence in the towns in question of these three employments which was the special characteristic of their economic life. They were primarily, that is to say, not manufacturing, but finishing and distributing centres which had gathered round them rather more that the ordinary number of workers in other industries. They handled such products of the surrounding regions as required to be worked up, supplied the agricultural districts with wares that could not be produced locally, and served as a link between them and the distant world of London. Thus Gloucester, to take the largest of the towns as an example, contained 9 brewers, 15 maltsters, 18 tanners and curriers, and 10 sadlers, who offered a market for barley, hops, and hides; while its 34 mercers, 16 drapers, 20 tailors, 23 shoemakers, 11 glovers, and 5 haberdashers, together with the 18 servants employed by them, can hardly have made a living by clothing its own population. Each of the two other large towns had certain features of its own. At Tewkesbury, for example, 33 men (7·6 per cent) were engaged in transport, mostly by water, as against negligible numbers at Gloucester and Cirencester;[31] Cirencester had 18·1 per cent of its men engaged in textiles, compared with 10·7 per cent at Gloucester and 6·3 per cent at Tewkesbury; while at both Cirencester and Tewkesbury the tradesmen aristocracy of mercers and drapers was less strongly represented than at Gloucester. In all three, however, the basis of their economic life was the same. It was to serve as a market and source of supply for the agricultural districts.

In the county as a whole, and still more in the county exclusive of the three largest towns, much the most important industry was, of course, agriculture. Next to agriculture came textiles, and then, at a long distance, the making of articles of dress, household service, the wood-working trades, the metal trades, dealing and retail trade and building. The workers employed in the first two amounted to a little less than two-thirds of the men whose occupations are stated, and those in the last six to just under one quarter. As explained above, it is probable that the number of miners and ironworkers is understated, but materials for correcting the figures do not seem to exist.

It is needless to emphasize the contrast between these figures and those of the present day. As would be expected, a far larger part of the working force was concentrated on meeting such primary needs as food, shelter, and clothing. Apart from that obvious point, the figures call attention to certain features of the economic life of the early seventeenth century which would not, perhaps, have been so readily anticipated. The most noticeable are three: the relative unimportance of transport and building;[32] the large proportion of textile workers; and the fact that agriculture, in spite of its preponderance, employed only about half of the adult male population. We confine ourselves, for reasons of space, to a consideration of the third point.

Agricultural workers amounted in 1921 to 26·2 per cent of the male population over 12 in the Rural Districts of Gloucestershire. In 1608 they formed, according to our return, 49·5 per cent of the males of stated occupation between 20 and 60 in the county, exclusive of Gloucester, Tewkesbury, and Cirencester, and 46·2 per cent if the latter be included. It will be noticed that, while over nine-tenths of the population represented lived outside the three largest towns, only about one half of those whose occupations are indicated were stated to be employed in agriculture. It may be observed in passing that the only other return of a comparable kind, though on too small a scale for much reliance to be laid on it, suggests that in another region, which, unlike Gloucestershire, was not specially pre-eminent as a textile district, the relative importance of agriculture was only slightly greater than in Gloucestershire. In the ten hundreds of the eastern division of Northamptonshire agricultural workers, even when all the labourers and half the servants of unspecified occupation are added to them, amounted in 1638 to only 58 per cent of the total number listed.[33]

Such figures suggest a somewhat wide distribution of industries other than agriculture. That point is illustrated in the following two tables. Table XIII shows the number of industries and craftsmen for each unit of population, exclusive of Gloucester, Tewkesbury, and Cirencester.

As would be expected, the number of different industries per manor, and the percentage which craftsmen form of the population, tend to increase with the size of the unit. Even in the smallest, however, the proportion of craftsmen is not negligible; in the larger it is not far short of half the adult male population.

Table XIV omits, in addition to Gloucester, Cirencester, and Tewkesbury, those manors (26 in number) for which less

Table XIII
Number of Industries per Manor

Manors[34] in which there are returned	*Number of Manors*	*Number of industries[35] represented per Manor*		*Number of Craftsmen[36] per Manor*	
		Range	*Average No*	*Average No*	*Average %age*
under 10 men	26	From nil to 3	0.5	0.6	10.3
10-19 "	75	" " " 5	1.2	2.0	15.1
20-29 "	84	" " " 5	1.8	3.1	12.9
30-39 "	58	" " " 7	2.8	6.8	19.1
40-49 "	39	" 1 " 6	3.3	8.8	20.7
50-59 "	27	" nil " 7	3.7	14.5	26.7
60-69 "	17	" 1 " 7	3.8	19.7	31.0
70-79 "	19	" nil " 8	5.1	19.7	26.9
80-89 "	7	" 1 " 7	5.0	21.3	25.2
90-99 "	7	" 4 " 8	6.0	28.5	30.0
100-119 "	17	" 1 " 9	6.5	48.9	44.8
120-149 "	12	" 4 " 8	5.3	61.6	48.2
150-199 "	12	" 4 " 8	6.5	67.1	40.6
200-220 "	2	6 & 7	6.5	45.5	21.0
Total number of Manors	402				

than 10 men were returned, and those (9 in number) for which the occupations of over 75 per cent of the men are unstated. It divides the remaining 367 into three groups, small, medium-sized, and large, and sets out the number of manors (a) in which under 25 per cent, 25 per cent and under 75 per cent, 75 per cent and over, were engaged in agriculture; (b) containing one or more representatives of fourteen occupations other than agriculture.

It will be seen that in 8·4 per cent of the manors no craftsmen were returned. In 11·7 per cent of them under one quarter of the men were stated to be employed in agriculture; in 60·8 per cent between one quarter and three quarters; and in 27·5 per cent three quarters or over. Of the non-agricultural occupations those widely dispersed were tailoring, wood-working textiles, metal-working,[37] building, milling, butchering, and shoemaking. Each of the first four was represented in more than half of the manors with 30 to 79 men. Nearly two manors out of three possessed one or more tailors, more than

Table XIV

Number of Craftsmen per Manor

No of Manors containing one or more

	Total No. of Manors	No. of Manors in which no craftsmen are returned	Miners	Textile Workers	Workers in Leather	Tailors	Shoemakers and Cobblers	Glovers	Workers in Wood	Builders	Workers in Metal	Maltsters and Brewers	Millers	Bakers	Butchers	Innkeepers
1. *Small Manors (where from 10 to 29 men are returned)*																
(a) Under 25 per cent* engaged in agriculture	4	1	—	3	—	2	1	1	1	1	—	—	—	—	—	—
(b) 25-74 per cent engaged in agriculture	79	5	3	30	4	38	5	4	36†	27	24	—	17†	3	4	4
(c) 75 per cent and over engaged in agriculture	69	23	1	12	1	14	4	1	15	5	11	—	6	—	1	—
	152	29	4	45	5	54	10	6	52†	33	35	—	23†	3	5	4
2. Medium-sized Manors (where from 30 to 79 men are returned)																
(a) Under 25 per cent engaged in agriculture	23	1	4	20	6	18	9	5	15	10	10	2	10	6	11	2
(b) 25-74 per cent engaged in agriculture	105	1	12†	71	18	80	26	13	76	42	67	†2	33	13	33	16
(c) 75 per cent and over engaged in agriculture	30	—	2	18	1	18	3	1	14	11	14	1	3	2	2	2
	158	2	18†	109	25	116	38	19	105	63	91†	5	46	21	46	20
3. Large Manors (where 80 or more men are returned)																
(a) Under 25 per cent engaged in agriculture	16	—	2	14	9	14	12	9	13	12	13	—	4	8	10	7
(b) 25-74 per cent engaged in agriculture	39	—	9	39	18	40	28	12	38	25	38	6	20	11	30†	15
(c) 75 per cent and over engaged in agriculture	2	—	—	2	—	2	1	—	1	1	1	—	1	—	—	—
	57	—	11	55	27	56	41	21	52	38	52	6	25	19	40†	22
Grand Total	367	31	33†	209	57	226	89	46	209†	134	178†	11	94†	43	91†	46

*i.e. of those whose occupations are stated.

†These figures would in each case be increased by one if sons or brothers were included, e.g., if a village were reckoned as containing a craftsman in which no woodworker is returned but only the son or brother of a woodworker.

one out of two possessed textile workers, and more than one out of two woodworkers. As the figures show, it was naturally the small units which were most exclusively agricultural. Of those with 30 men or over only two returned no craftsmen.

There is reason to think that the figures in Table XII do not understate the proportion of the population engaged in agriculture.[38] If that view is correct, some conventional pictures of what is called pre-industrial England may require to be modified. Parts of it, at least, would appear to have been more industrialized than such accounts suggest. In reality, rural society in the early seventeenth century was, at any rate in Gloucestershire, somewhat highly differentiated. It was by no means exclusively, and in certain important areas was not even predominantly, an agricultural society. Agriculture and industry were inextricably intertwined. Not only corn and cattle, but corn, wool and cloth, and even, in some districts, corn, coal and iron, were almost joint products. Many families, from the gentry to the humblest peasants, were almost equally interested in farming and manufacturing, and the surplus yielded by one readily found its way into the other. In such circumstances, histories of the former which disregard the latter are necessarily misleading.

Space does not permit us to illustrate in detail this interlacing of interests, but a single example may sharpen the outlines of the picture. It happens that in 1608, the year of our return, the large manor of Bisley, which was then in the hands of the Crown, was surveyed.[39] Bisley, its principal village, lies on the edge of the tableland overlooking the westernmost valley but one of the Cotswolds, much of which, including the stream at the bottom, then formed part of the manor. According to Smyth's figures, it was somewhat highly industrialized; of the 140 adults of whom he gives particulars, 41, including labourers, were engaged in agriculture, 63 in textiles, and 36 in other occupations. The investment of capital which was the corollary of the prominence of the clothing industry has left its traces on the survey. The latter shows that, in addition to two quarries and three cornmills, Bisley possessed in 1608 six[40] fulling-mills, four dye-houses, and fourteen rack-rooms, and that 29 of its 106 tenants held 'water-courses', or rights of water needed in the manufacture of cloth. Clearly, in such a case—and Bisley, though an important textile centre, was not the most important—rural society and agricultural society were by no means equivalent expressions.

(ii) *The Geographical Distribution of Industries*

Were different occupations distributed more or less evenly throughout the county, or did they tend to concentrate in particular areas? For certain of them the figures are too small to be significant, unless they confirm a tendency known on other grounds to exist.[41] In addition to agriculture and textiles, the making of articles of dress, woodworking, dealing, and retail trade are represented in all the hundreds, and building in all but one, the exception being the very small hundred of Tyboldstone, with a high percentage of men of unstated occupation. Particular occupations within these industries show a preference for particular localities[42]; but, as far as the last five of them are concerned, there are, apart from that, few signs of any strong tendency to local specialization. The industries in which significant variations in the regional distribution of workers are found are mining and quarrying, certain—though not all—branches of the metal-working trades, agriculture, and textiles.

We do not venture to attempt any account of the economic geography of Gloucestershire, but certain points deserve attention. The percentage of men of stated occupation engaged in different hundreds in the four industries in question is shown in the Table on p. 240 and the accompanying map. As has already been explained, the figures for mining and quarrying are unsatisfactory.[43] Such as they are, they indicate that nine tenths of the men concerned were found in two regions. The first consisted of three of the five Forest hundreds, St. Briavels, the Duchy of Lancaster, and Botlow. The second and larger was the three hundreds of Langley and Swineshead, Pucklechurch, and Barton Regis, near the southern boundary of the county. They included Kingswood Forest (the centre of what became later the Bristol coalfield), which was stated by Norden,[44] when he surveyed it under James I, to produce a small, but increasing, output. The largest group of workers in the metal trades were smiths, who numbered, with servants, apprentices, and relatives, 430 out of 566. These, as would be expected, were somewhat widely dispersed, few villages of any size being without one.[45] In another branch of the metal trades there was some local specialization. The iron ore of the Forest of Dean had been worked since, at any rate, the Roman occupation; and, though the number of ironworkers is understated in Smyth's return, owing, probably, to the fact that some of those engaged in smelting were classed as labourers, that district had an exceptionally large proportion of metal-workers. The hundred with the largest number was St. Briavels, which possessed 92, over 10 per cent of the men in the hundred whose occupation is stated, while this and two other Forest hundreds[46] had together 130, or between one fifth and one quarter of all in the county. The large number of metal-workers in these hundreds was due, not to the heavy iron industry, only six iron-founders and their servants being assigned to them by Smyth, but to the fact that together they contained all the 54 nail-makers in the county.

Agriculture was everywhere the largest single industry, but the proportion of men engaged in it varied widely in different parts of the county. In six hundreds they accounted for over two thirds of those whose occupations are stated, in ten for under two thirds and over half, in eleven for under half and over one third, and in one for under one third. While the six hundreds in which they formed over two thirds were remote from each other, they were situated in the main near the frontiers of the county. They lay, that is to say, with one exception, off the wolds, or where the wolds begin to rise from the lower land. Observers, then and later, were struck by the contrast between the economy of the hill regions and that of the vales; corn was grown in both, but the speciality which went with it in the former, where sun and drying winds play havoc with pasture, was sheep, and in the latter cattle.[47] Some faint trace of these differences appears in the figures. It is not chance, perhaps, that half the 93 shepherds are found in two hundreds[48] in the heart of the wold country, and the contemporary reputation of the hundred of Berkeley for pre-eminence in 'the state and eminency' of the yeomanry[49] derives some confirmation from the return. But to reveal varieties of farming methods a more precise classification of occupations would be required than that given by Smyth.

What his evidence does prove with some clearness is the strong tendency to local concentration shown by the textile industry. Its stronghold was the steep western escarpment of the Cotswolds and the valleys at its foot. Five hundreds[50] had more than a quarter of their male workers engaged in the industry, and these five hundreds included just over three quarters of the textile workers in the county. The principal reason for the density of the textile population in this region was the configuration of the western Cotswolds. On the one hand, considerable parts of them are too steep to be farmed, so that long belts of woodland intervene between the cornland on the top and the pasture and meadow in the valleys. On the other hand, with the technique prevailing in the seventeenth century, that feature was an industrial asset of some importance.

There have been, not one, but at any rate two, industrial revolutions in England; and thc first, like the second, had its occasion in the utilization of a neglected source of power. As Mr Kinvig[51] has shown, it was less Cotswold wool than Cotswold water-power which made the Gloucestershire clothing industry. Owing to the smallness of the catchment areas, the streams in the west of the county are, with the possible exception of the Stroudwater, smaller than in the east; but they are numerous and rapid.[52] Hence the west, with water-power at its door, took a step towards specializing in manufactures, while the rest of the county remained predominantly agricultural. The textile workers in Smyth's return were concentrated, in fact, in those districts where, apart from his evidence, their concentration was to be expected. Further, water-power determined the localization, not only of the industry as a whole, but of particular sections of it. It was little, if at all, required for weaving; it was indispensable to fulling, tucking, and dyeing. Hence the first was more widely dispersed than the three last. Nearly three quarters of the tuckers were settled in three hundreds,[53] and four fifths of the fullers in one.[54] Finally, water-power in the seventeenth century had in a small way the same influence in attracting and maintaining a relatively dense population as the coalfields were to acquire in the nineteenth. The five hundreds with the highest percentage of textile workers are approximately equal in area to the eight hundreds with the highest percentage of agriculturalists, but their population was half as much again (5,908 men as against 3,872).

(iii) *The Relative Numbers of Employers and Employed*

What proportion of the men whose occupations or status are recorded were independent producers,[55] with or without hired labour, and what proportion were employees? The answer given to that question is important; it will determine whether, in the generation before the Civil War, England is to be regarded as predominantly a society of peasant farmers, small masters, and *travailleurs isolés,* or as containing large proletarian elements. The problem is not merely a statistical one; Smyth's figures throw light on it, but they require, if misconception is to be avoided, interpretation and explanation. In particular, for the reasons given below, it must not be assumed that there were no employed persons other than those definitely placed by him in that category. With that warning, to some of the applications of which we recur later, we begin by setting out in tabular form the bare facts as to the number of servants, apprentices, and labourers described as such in the return.

It will be seen that the total number of persons entered as servants, apprentices, and labourers was 4,728, of whom over three quarters were found in two employments, agriculture and the service of the gentry.[56] The great preponderance of employees in agriculture, as compared with other occupations, is due partly to the fact that we have placed under agriculture all labourers, except those in Gloucester, Cirencester and Tewkesbury. Even however, if the labourers are excluded, and attention is confined to persons returned as servants, it remains true that agriculture and the service of the gentry account for two thirds (67·2 per cent) of the total. Textiles employ 4·8 per cent of the employees in the table, including labourers, and 8·2 per cent of the servants and apprentices alone. With one exception—servants of unspecified occupation—the relative number of employees found in other groups is almost negligible.

These figures have some utility as fixing a minimum. Not less, at any rate, than one in four of the men returned were employees. That fact by itself, however, does not carry us far.

TABLE XV
Number and Proportion of Servants, Apprentices, and Labourers in Different Industries

	(i)	(ii) Number returned as				(iii)	(iv)
	Total in group (exclusive of sons and brothers)	*Servants*	*Apprentices*	*Labourers*	*Total*	*Percentage of (ii) to (i)*	*Percentage of employees in each group to total number of employees*
I. Agriculture and Estate Service	7,500	965	1	1,831	2,797	37·3	59·1
II. Fishing, Mining, and Quarrying	186	2	—	—	2	—	—
III. Textiles	2,555	220	9	—	229	8·9	4·8
IV. Leather Work	197	32	—	—	32	16·2	·7
V. Making of Articles of Dress	1,231	89	5	—	94	7·6	2·0
VI. Woodwork	656	41	5	—	46	7·0	1·0
VII. Building	336	11	3	—	14	4·2	·3
VIII. Metal-Work	548	57	8	—	65	11·9	1·4
IX. Making of Food and Drink	372	27	—	—	27	7·2	·6
X. Dealing and Retail Trade	697	79	—	—	79	11·3	1·7
XI. Transport	269	10	—	—	10	3·7	·2
XII. Miscellaneous	62	4	—	—	4	6·4	·1
XIII. Knights, Esquires, Gentry, and their Servants	1,180	750	—	—	750	63·5	15·8
XIV. Professional and Official and their Servants	102	43	—	—	43	42·1	·9
XV. Servants to Women	122	122	—	—	122	—	2·6
XVI. Servants, unspecified	283	281	2	—	283	—	6·0
XVII. Labourers, non-agricultural	131	—	—	131	131	—	2·8
Total	16,427	2,733	33	1,962	4,728		

It is evident that some pains were taken to ascertain whether an individual was or was not in service—naturally enough, since the point might be of practical importance to the military authorities—and there is no reason to think that they were not generally successful. But the question which is of economic significance is not merely how many persons worked under a contract of service, but how many were employees, as distinct from independent producers, whether technically servants or not. That question cannot be completely answered by means of the table.

The difficulty arises, not primarily from possible errors of description, but from the nature of the facts to be described. It is due to the character of the economic organization of the age. The truth is that the attempt to draw a sharp line between wage-earners and independent producers is for the early seventeenth century—and, indeed, much later—an anachronism. A wage-earning class was in process of formation, but it was not yet fully formed. In many, perhaps most, occupations, wage-labour was an occasional or subsidiary expedient, rather than the unquestioned basis of economic organization; nor is it always easy to distinguish the wage-contract from relations of another kind, for example between buyer and seller, creditor and debtor, or even landlord and tenant. Much labour on farms, for example, which in England is now done by a definite class of lifelong wage-earners, was then done by men whose primary concern was with their own holdings, or by the sons of peasants who expected to obtain one. The remuneration, again, of many shepherds, miners, fishermen, and sailors was, in part or whole, of a kind which can hardly be described as wages. Weavers, if in effect the employees of the clothier from whom they received orders, were not wage-earners in the same sense as the servants engaged by him, and were sometimes themselves employers.

The uncertainties caused by these conditions must not be exaggerated. They are most serious in the textile industry, owing to the prevalence of the putting-out system; and they occur also in other industries, for example fishing, and mining, where groups sometimes worked together on 'shares' or 'lays'. In the majority of occupations, where sub-contracting, if it occurred at all, was the exception, they are not important. It remains true, however, that conditions were too different in different industries for a generalized account to be other than misleading. the most useful course is to examine briefly the more important occupational groups,[57] with a view to suggesting the limits, at any rate, within which a solution of the problem must fall.

(a) *Agriculture.*—In the case of agriculture, the distinction between independent producers and employees is reasonably clear. The largest groups among the former consisted of yeomen and husbandmen. The latter were composed, in the first place, of (i) servants of yeomen and husbandmen, (ii) shepherds, estate workers, and certain miscellaneous agricultural workers employed either by the yeomen and husbandmen or by the gentry, (iii) labourers outside the towns of Gloucester, Cirencester, and Tewkesbury. The number in each of these categories was as in Table XVI.

TABLE XVI
Independent Producers and Employees in Agriculture

Independent Producers (exclusive of of sons and brothers)		*Employees*	
Yeomen	927	Servants to yeomen	387[58]
Husbandmen	3,774	Servants to husbandmen	437
Farmers or graziers	2	Shepherds	93[59]
		Husbandmen servants	87
		Estate servants	31[60]
		Miscellaneous	18[61]
		Labourers	1,831
Total	4,703		2,884

It will be seen that the 4,703 yeomen and husbandmen[62] were entered in the return as employing 824 servants. There was one yeoman's servant to every 2·4 yeomen, and one husbandman's servant to every 8·6 husbandmen. The difference accords with the fact that it was the more substantial farmers who were commonly described as yeomen. In addition to the persons returned as servants to yeomen and husbandmen, there were, if the labourers outside Glouceser, Tewkesbury, and Cirencester be assigned to agriculure, 2,060 other employees. Of these, some, no doubt, worked for well-to-do yeomen; others, for example the various estate servants, must have been principally employed by the gentry. Further, the gentry themselves were frequently engaged in farming, and are returned as employing a considerable staff of servants. Finally, the return includes 283 servants of whose employments no indication is given. If these were divided between agriculture and other industries in the same proportions as the rest of the men listed, then approximately one half should be assigned to agriculture.

To complete the picture, therefore, it is necessary to allow for these additional groups. Knights, esquires, and gentlemen (exclusive of sons and brothers) numbered 430, and their servants 750. It is not possible to state what proportion of the former were themselves engaged in farming. If it had been the case that all of them were, together with half their own servants, and half of those unspecified, then the total number of independent producers and employers in agriculture would have been approximately 5,100, and the total number of agricultural employees about 3,300. Even if it be assumed that only half the gentry were directly interested in agriculture, the number of independent producers and employers would still remain, in proportion to the employees, surprisingly large.[63]

It would be absurd to press these figures far. On the other hand, they may fairly be said to indicate the limits within which hypothesis is profitable. Two conclusions are suggested by them, which are at once reasonably certain and not without importance.

The first is the relatively large number of employees in the service of the gentry. If only those persons who are described as servants be taken into account, the number of servants (agricultural and non-agricultural) per employer among the knights, esquires, and gentry was 1·7. If, as is perhaps more reasonable, not only the 69 husbandmen servants stated to be employed by the gentry, but also the estate servants, half the shepherds and miscellaneous agricultural workers, and a quarter of the labourers, be treated as in their employment, the figure is 3·1. Owing to the large number of servants whose occupation and employers are not stated, a complete picture of the scale of the gentry's establishments cannot be given. The following figures of the distribution among different employers of those servants of the gentry whose employers are stated are, therefore, *minima:—*

TABLE XVII
Servants of Knights, Esquires, and Gentlemen[64]

	Total servants		*Total servants*
1 has 32 servants	32	3 have 8 servants each	24
1 ,, 25 ,,	25	4 ,, 7 ,, ,,	28
1 ,, 15 ,,	15	7 ,, 6 ,, ,,	42
2 have 13 ,,	26	22 ,, 5 ,, ,,	110
2 ,, 12 ,, ,,	24	22 ,, 4 ,, ,,	88
5 ,, 11 ,, ,,	55	26 ,, 3 ,, ,,	78
4 ,, 10 ,, ,,	40	49 ,, 2 ,, ,,	98
1 has 9 ,,	9	74 ,, 1 ,, ,,	74

The number of employers and servants in this category varied widely from village to village. A good many manors had no resident gentry, and some gentry had no servants described as such; while on other manors gentlemen's servants were numerous. One may take as an example the hundred of Slaughter. Of its 22 manors 9 had no gentry[65] or gentlemen's servants; 3 had 1 gentleman apiece, but in each case without persons stated to be their servants; in the remaining 10 manors there were 14 gentlemen, of whom 5 had 1 servant each, 2 had 2 each, 1 had 3, 2 had 4 each, 1 had 7, 1 had 8, 1 had 10, and 1 had 25. In the case of the last four[66] manors the total numbers of men returned were 28, 33, 34, and 83 respectively. When from a quarter to a third of the adult male population, even apart from any labourers employed, were in the service of a single individual, the social influence of the gentry is not surprising. Such conditions were not uncommon. Manors are even found where five sixths and, in one case, actually the whole, of the men returned were the servants of one gentleman.[67]

The second conclusion suggested by the figures is the small part which wage-labour played in the agricultural economy of seventeenth-century Gloucestershire. In the case of the yeomanry and husbandmen, as in that of the gentry, the scale of undertakings, measured by the number of servants employed, varied considerably. The 824 servants whose employers are stated were distributed as follows:

TABLE XVIII
Servants of Yeomen and Husbandmen

(a) Yeomen	Total Servants	(b) Husbandmen	Total Servants	(c) Yeomen and Husbandmen combined	Servants Combined Total
1 has 8 servants	8	1 has 5 servants	5	1 has 8 servants	8
1 ,, 5 ,,	5	1 ,, 4 ,,	4	2 have 5 ,, each	10
8 have 4 ,, each	32	8 have 3 ,, each	24	9 ,, 4 ,, ,,	36
17 ,, 3 ,, ,,	51	40 ,, 2 ,, ,,	80	25 ,, 3 ,, ,,	75
63 ,, 2 ,, ,,	126	324 ,, 1 ,, ,,	324	103 ,, 2 ,, ,,	206
165 ,, 1 ,, ,,	165			489 ,, 1 ,, ,,	489
255 Total	387	374	437	629	824

For the majority of this group (672 yeomen and 3,400 husbandmen) no servants are returned. The figures are, again, *minima;* but the scale of the establishments of this section of the rural population must, on any showing, have been small. The yeomen and husbandmen in the return are more that ten times as numerous as the gentry; but, as employers of labour, they stand at the opposite pole from them. If only the workers entered as their servants be taken into account there were 5·7 independent producers to every employee; if half the shepherds, miscellaneous agricultural workers, and those servants of unspecified occupations who have been classed under agriculture, together with three-quarters of the labourers, be also assigned to them, the figure is still as much as 2. It would appear, therefore, that in the group of yeomen and husbandmen the independent producers must, on almost any view, have outnumbered the wage-workers by at least two to one, and probably by considerably more.

The picture which emerges from these figures is confirmed by a good deal of other evidence. It is one of a system of family farms worked with the aid of relatives—more than half[68] the sons and brothers in the return are those of yeomen and husbandmen—and only to a small extent with hired labour. That situation, and its significance for economic life and policy, cannot here be discussed. It was, however, of fundamental importance, especially when related to two other factors in the economy of the age—the smallness of the population and the abundance of land available for settlement. The conditions of large parts of seventeenth-century England were, in fact, still semi-colonial. The result was that it was easy for the small man to get a holding; that wage-labour, being scarce, was in a strong position; and that, since the largest group in rural society consisted, not of wage-workers, but of peasant farmers, the critical issues of the age were those, not of wages, but of land-tenure and credit. The modern contrasts and parallels are too obvious to be pointed out.

(b) *Industrial occupations other than Textiles*—In the remaining industries other than textiles, which raises special problems, the number of employees is small. The following Table sets out the number of servants returned for the principal crafts in seven industrial groups, together with the number of masters stated to employ one or more servants. It must be remembered (i) that, since twenty was the lower age limit of the return, only a small number of apprentices were included in it, (ii) that possibly half the 283 servants of unspecified occupation should be assigned to non-agricultural employments.

As explained on page 232, the figures of servants in the Table are *minima*. Even, however, if the servants whose occupation and employers are not stated were assigned to the industrial groups represented in it, the outlines of the picture would not be much changed. It is one of a multitude of one-man businesses, with a few larger concerns employing less than half a dozen journeymen.

The groups with the highest proportion of servants are leather-work, metal-work, dealing and retail trade. The largest employers were 2 innkeepers, each of whom had 5 servants, and 3 other innkeepers, a tanner, a shipwright, and a mercer, each of whom had 4. The fact that some mercers had as many servants as the largest industrialist outside the textile industry is, perhaps, characteristic. It was commerce and finance which yielded most of the substantial fortunes, and merchants, rather than manufacturers, who formed the aristocracy of the middle classes. The small number of servants in the wood-working and building trades arouses suspicion, but it is not really surprising. The total number of wage-earners was, doubtless, larger than the number entered as servants, since some of the labourers were probably employed in building,

TABLE XIX
Servants in Trade and Industry

	(i) Total number in group exclusive of son and brothers	(ii) Number returned as servants[69]	(iii) Number of Masters Employing				
			5 Servants	4 Servants	3 Servants	2 Servants	1 Servant
Leatherwork							
Tanners and Curriers	159	29	—	1	1	5	12
Sadlers and Collarmakers ..	38	3	—	—	—	—	3
Making of articles of dress							
Tailors	690	35	—	—	—	2	31
Glovers	143	10	—	—	—	2	6
Shoemakers	381	48	—	—	3	10	19
Woodwork							
Carpenters[70]	448	31	—	—	1	5	18
Shipwrights	29	6	—	1	—	—	2
Coopers	86	5	—	—	—	2	1
Wheelwrights	25	3	—	—	—	1	1
Building							
Masons, Stonelayers, and Roughlayers	210	11	—	—	—	1	9
Slaters, Tilers, and Glaziers ..	105	3	—	—	—	—	3
Metalwork							
Ironfounders	10	3	—	—	1	—	—
Wiredrawers, Pewterers, etc. ..	24	6	—	—	—	2	2
Nailers	54	15	—	—	2	3	3
Smiths	415	38	—	—	1	3	29
Making of food and drink							
Millers	165	19	—	—	—	2	15
Maltsters	72	1	—	—	—	—	1
Brewers	17	3	—	—	1	—	—
Bakers and Cooks	118	4	—	—	—	—	4
Dealing and retail trade							
Merchants	4	3	—	—	1	—	—
Drapers	31	1	—	—	—	—	1
Mercers	131	19	—	1	3	1	4
Butchers	267	15	—	—	—	1	13
Vinters and Innkeepers ..	158	39	2	3	—	2	13

and the industry could draw at certain times of year on agricultural workers. But there were few, if any, larger contracts to be executed, and it is difficult to see from what source a demand could have come to make it possible to find employment for any considerable staff of wage-workers. In such circumstances, the condition of the industry was what, in regions remote from large centres of population, it still remains. Its typical figure was not the operative, but the jobbing craftsman.

(c) *Textiles.*—The group which, after agriculture and the service of the gentry, contained the largest number, though not the largest proportion, of persons entered as servants was that composed of textile workers. Not only, however, was textiles by far the most important manufacturing industry; it is also that for which any satisfactory statement of the relative number of employees and independent producers is most difficult to make. It will be well to begin with the facts as given by the return. They are as in Table XX. In addition there were a small number of workers in certain allied trades, viz.:—4 ropers, with 2 servants and an apprentice; a knitter; a bone-lace maker; and an embroiderer.

It will be seen that persons entered as servants or apprentices numbered 226 out of a total male textile population (exclusive

TABLE XX
Servants in the Textile Industry

	(i) *Number returned*	(ii) *Servants to (i)*	(iii) *Apprentices to (i)*	(iv) *Total*
Clothiers[71]	207	98[72]	2	307
Tuckers	230	26	1	257
Fullers	95	2	1	98
Dyers	36	11	—	47
Woollen Weavers	1,703	79	4	1,786
Silk Weavers	12	—	—	12
Shearmen	10	—	—	10
Miscellaneous[73]	26	2	—	28
	2,319	218	8	2,545

of sons and brothers) of 2,545, or 8·9 per cent. Rather less than half of them were employed by clothiers, just over one third by weavers, and over one tenth by tuckers. Judged by the number of servants, the scale of most businesses was small. The largest clothier had 10, two others 6 each, and two 3 each; none of the rest had more than 2, and the majority had none. Among the other groups, one dyer had 4 servants, one 3, and two 2 each. One tucker had 3 servants, and three tuckers had 2. Of the weavers eleven had 2 servants each, and fifty-five had 1.

These figures are useful as far as they go. Among the clothiers there were, no doubt, some considerable capitalists; but the preponderance of clothiers without servants, combined with the fact that the sons and brothers of some of them were stated to be weavers, suggests that such men were the exception, and that the majority, whether themselves weaving or not, differed little from the manual workers in economic and social position. Hired servants, however, were only one, and not the most important, element in the working force of the industry. What we should wish to know is not merely the number of persons returned as in service, but the relative numbers of employers and employed.

A satisfactory answer cannot be given to that question. Clothiers giving out work may reasonably be regarded as employers; most of the fullers, tuckers, and dyers who executed their orders can hardly, however, be described as their employees. A few individuals among them were hired wage-workers[74]; but there is nothing to indicate that the majority were not in business on their own account, and, though that cannot be proved, it is probable that they were. Somewhat the same is true of the weavers. They included workers in very varying positions, from small masters employing one or two servants to peasants doing a little weaving at odd moments. We do not know what proportion, if any of them, worked directly for customers, and what proportion to the order of clothiers. Even in the latter case, however, though their dependence for work upon the clothier must often have been almost complete, they do not appear to have been regarded as the employees of the latter in the same sense as his hired servants. They remained, in form, not wage-workers, but independent producers.

This feature of the textile industry is, of course, a commonplace. Its effect is that, since the wage-contract was not the basis of organization, the relations of the industry cannot be expressed in terms of employer and wage-earner. More serious is the impossibility of stating whether any of the weavers worked directly for the market. In the absence of information on that point, all that remains are the bare figures. If, as seems to be held by most historians, the clothiers are to be regarded as the fly-wheel of the industry, then 207 clothiers found work for (in addition to their own servants) rather more than eight[75] times that number of weavers, and a little over twice the same number of tuckers, fullers, dyers, shearmen, miscellaneous textile workers, and their servants. In that case, the number of workers employed per clothier, though it seems small to modern eyes, is in reality large. It is higher, not only than in some Prussian industries in the middle of the nineteenth century, but than in some British industries even in 1871, a good many French industries in 1901, and the vast majority of Chinese industries for which figures are available at the present day.[76] The assumption, however, that all, or nearly all, work was given out by the clothiers, though it is suggested by a good deal of other contemporary evidence,[77] is not susceptible of proof. If, as is possible, there were many weavers who worked, not for clothiers, but for customers, the picture of a large body of craftsmen dependent on a small hierarchy of clothiers must be correspondingly modified.

For most sides of economic life statistical evidence is so scanty before the day of the Political Arithmeticians, that there is a temptation, when it exists, to make too much of it. History is too subtle a business for the last word on any subject to be said by figures. They are valuable to those who know enough of the social background of an age to be able to interpret them; to others they are a snare. Even to the first they more often suggest problems than supply solutions. The gaps and ambiguities in our material must have struck every reader, and it is needless to repeat the warnings already given on that point. When due allowance, however, has been made for these deficiencies, it remains true, we think, that Smyth's return throws into relief certain characteristics of the economy of the region covered which deserve consideration. That is all we should claim for it.

The principal features on which attention has been concentrated in the preceding pages are three; the wide distribution of employments other than agriculture, and the large proportion of the population engaged in them; the somewhat high degree of specialization obtaining in parts of the county; and the smallness of the proletarian elements in the population compared with the large numbers of the *petite bourgeoisie.* The last of these features, which was as significant for the political as for the economic life of the seventeenth century, we should have expected; for the first we were not prepared. Whether they were specially pronounced in Gloucestershire, or were present in much the same measure throughout the country, is a question which can be decided only be a study of the life of other regions. As far as we know, no thorough search has been made to ascertain whether the sensible procedure of giving the occupations of men capable of bearing arms was followed on other occasions and in other counties. Perhaps some reader may be sufficiently interested in the result of Smyth's labours to make the investigations needed to answer that question.

APPENDIX

TABLE XXI
Classification of Occupations

	(i) *Number returned*	(ii) *Servants to (i)*	(iii) *Apprent-ices to (i)*	(iv) *Sons or brothers of (i)*	(v) *Total*
I. Agriculture and Estate Management					
Farmers, Graziers	2	—	—	—	2
Yeomen	927	386	1	144	1,458
Husbandmen	3,774[78]	437	—	225	4,436
Shepherds[79]	90	3	—	—	93
Estate workers[80]	29	2	—	2	33
Labourers, probably agri-cultural	1,831	—	—	10	1,841
Other agricultural workers[81]	18	—	—	2	20
Total	*6,671*	*828*	*1*	*383*	*7,883*
II. Fishing, Mining and Quarrying					
Fishermen	17	—	—	1	18
Miners, Colliers, Coaldrivers	156	2	—	3	161
Quarry and Allied Workers[82]	11	—	—	—	11
Total	*184*	*2*	—	*4*	*190*
III. Textiles					
Yarnseller	1	—	—	—	1
Woolworkers[83]	8	2	—	—	10
Clothiers[84]	207	98	2	25	332
Clothworkers, Clothmakers, Feltmakers	17	—		—	17
Weavers	1,442	61	4	38	1,545
Broadweavers	251	14	—	11	276
Other Woollen Weavers[85]	10	4	—	1	15
Silk Weavers	12	—	—	—	12
Tuckers	230	26	1	6	263
Fullers	95	2	1	1	99
Dyers	36	11	—	—	47
Shearmen	10	—	—	—	10
Others[86]	7	2	1	—	10
Total	*2,326*	*220*	*9*	*82*	*2,637*
IV. Leather Work					
Curriers[87]	17	1	—	—	18
Tanners	113	28	—	1	142
Sadlers	26	2	—	3	31
Collarmakers	9	1	—	1	10
Total	*165*	*32*	—	*4*	*201*

	(i) *Number returned*	(ii) *Servants to (i)*	(iii) *Apprent-ices to (i)*	(iv) *Sons of brothers of (i)*	(v) *Total*
V. Making of Articles of Dress					
Tailors	655	31	4	19	709
Glovers	133	9	1	2	145
Shoemakers[88]	333	48	—	9	390
Others[89]	16	1	—	—	17
Total	*1,137*	*89*	*5*	*30*	*1,261*
VI. Working in Wood, etc					
Sawyers	21	—	—	—	21
Carpenters, Joiners	410	25	5	10	450
Millcarpenters, Millrights	7	1	—	—	8
Shipcarpenters, Shipwrights	23	6	—	4	33
Turners	17	—	—	1	18
Coopers[90]	81	5	—	—	86
Wheelers, Wheelwrighs	22	3	—	4	29
Others[91]	29	1	—	—	30
Total	*610*	*41*	*5*	*19*	*675*
VII. Building and Works of Construction					
Masons, Freemasons[92]	199	9	2	6	216
Slatters and Tilers	92	1	1	4	98
Thatchers	9	—	—	—	9
Glaziers	10	1	—	—	11
Others[93]	12	—	—	—	12
Total	*322*	*11*	*3*	*10*	*346*
VIII. Metal Work					
Ironfounders and Metalmen[94]	7	3	—	—	10
Wiredrawers	8	3	—	—	11
Cutlers	23	—	—	—	23
Goldsmiths	2	—	—	—	2
Pewters and Tankard makers	10	3	—	3	16
Nailers	39	14	1	—	54
Smiths[95]	377	31	7	15	430
Tinkers	7	—	—	—	7
Pinmakers	5	1	—	—	6
Others[96]	5	2	—	—	7
Total	*483*	*57*	*8*	*18*	*566*
IX. Making of Food and Drink					
Millers	146	19	—	5	170
Maltsters	71	1	—	3	75
Brewers	14	3	—	—	17
Bakers	103	3	—	3	109
Cooks	11	1	—	—	12
Total	*345*	*27*	—	*11*	*385*

	(i) *Number returned*	(ii) *Servants to (i)*	(iii) *Apprent-ices to (i)*	(iv) *Sons or brothers of (i)*	(v) *Total*
X. Dealing and Retail Trade					
Merchants	1	3	–	–	4
Badgers, Chapmen and Pedlars[97]	40	1	–	1	42
Drapers[98]	30	1	–	–	31
Haberdashers	12	–	–	–	12
Mercers	112	19	–	2	133
Butchers	252	15	–	7	274
Innkeepers, Vintners and Victuallers	119	39	–	8	166
Dealers in other foods[99]	10	–	–	–	20
Chandlers	20	–	–	–	20
Barbers	13	–	–	–	13
Others[100]	9	1	–	–	10
Total	*618*	*79*	–	*18*	*715*
XI. Transport (Road and Water)					
Carriers, Carmen[101]	49	5[102]	–	2	56
Loaders	6	–	–	–	6
Sailors	183	4	–	7	194
Boatmen, Watermen[103]	21	1	–	–	22
Total	*259*	*10*	–	*9*	*278*
XII. Miscellaneous and Unidentified Occupations					
Workers in Paper and Cardboard[104]	13		–	–	14
Cardmakers	9	–	–	–	9
Limeburners	8	–	–	–	8
Salters	5	–	–	–	5
Other Miscellaneous[105]	7	1	–	–	8
Unidentified Occupations[106]	16	2	–	1	19
Total	*58*	*4*	–	*1*	*63*
XIII. Gentry, Professional and Official					
Knights, Esquires and Gentlemen	430	–	–	27	457
Professional[107]	38	–	–	3	4
Official[108]	21	–	–	–	21
Total	*489*	–	–	*30*	*519*
XIV. Servants, Household and Unspecified					
Servants to Knights, etc	–	750	–	–	750
Servants to Professional	–	39	–	–	39
Servants to Official	–	4	–	–	4
Servants to Women	–	122	–	–	122
Servants to Unspecified	–	281	2	–	283
Total	–	*1,196*	*2*	–	*1,198*

		(i) *Number returned*	(ii) *Servants to (i)*	(iii) *Apprent- ices to (i)*	(iv) *Sons or brothers of (i)*	(v) *Total*
XV.	Labourers in Three Largest Towns[109]	*131*	–	–	–	*131*
	Total whose occupation is given	–	–	–	–	*17,046*
XVI.	Unable in body	109	–	–	–	109
XVII.	Occupations Unstated	2,247	–	–	–	2,247
	Grand Total	–	–	–	–	*19,402*

MAP OF GLOUCESTERSHIRE

TABLE OF MAP

Hundreds[110] *in which*	*No. of Hundreds*	*Names of Hundreds*
66% or more of men of known occupation are engaged in Agriculture.	6	Tewkesbury[111] (70·6%), Hembury (69·3%), Deerhurst (69·1%), Rapsgate (68·5%), Crowtherne and Minty (68·4%), Tyboldstone (67·5%).
50% and under 66% are engaged in Agriculture.	10	Botlow (63·2%), Dudstone and Barton Regis (63·1%), Langley and Swineshead (62·9%), Cleeve (59·9%), Westminster (59·3%), Wesbury (58·8%), Kiftsgate (58·7%), Slaughter (54·2%), Brightwelsbarrow (53·4), Pucklechurch (50·4%).
33% and under 50% are engaged in Agriculture.	11	Duchy of Lancaster (49·5%), Bradley (48·9%), Cheltenham (48·9%), Gromboldsash (44·4%), Barton Regis (44·3%), Thornbury (44·3%), Whitstone (44·3%), Bledisloe (39·7%), Berkeley (38·3%), Bisley (35·3%), St. Briavels (35%).
25% and under 33% are engaged in Agriculture.	1	Longtree (29%).
33% and under 50% are engaged in Textiles.	3	Longtree (45·2%), Bisley (39·4%), Berkeley (37·9%).
25% and under 33% are engaged in Textiles.	2	Whitstone (31·6%), Gromboldsash (28%).
10% and under 25% are engaged in Textiles.	5	Cirencester (18·1%), Thornbury (15·1%), Barton Regis (13·8%), Gloucester (10·7%), Pucklechurch (10%).
5% and under 10% are engaged in Textiles.	10	St. Briavels (7·9%), Duchy of Lancs. (7·1%), Brightwelsbarrow (6·8%), Borough of Tewkesbury (6·3%), Henbury (5·8%), Langley and Swineshead (5·6%), Cheltenham (5·5%), Botlow (5·4%), Bledisloe (5·2%).
10% and under 25% are engaged in Coalmining.	1	Barton Regis (11·2%).
1% and under 10% are engaged in Coalmining.	3	Langley and Swineshead (7·4%), Pucklechurch (5·5%), St. Briavels (4·1%), Duchy of Lancs. (1·9%), Botlow (1·8%).
2% and under 10% are engaged in Iron-working (excluding Smiths).	2	St. Briavels (7%), Gloucester (5·4%), Bledisloe (3%), Wesbury (2%), Borough of Tewkesbury (2%).

NOTES

1. We are deeply indebted to Miss M. E. Bulkley, who has not only given us invaluable help in preparing the statistical material used, but has assisted us throughout with advice and criticism. We should also like to express our gratitude for the kindness of Mr Roland Austin, Librarian of the City of Gloucester, who gave us every facility in examining the valuable collection of Smyth MSS in the Gloucester Public Library.

2. *Men and Armour for Gloucestershire in 1608,* compiled by John Smith, London, 1902.

3. The expression 'about twenty' might include some persons under that age; but Smyth elsewhere *(A Description of the Hundred of Berkeley,* ed. by Sir John Maclean as vol. iii of *The Berkeley Manuscripts,* 1885, pp. 44, 55, etc.) makes it clear that twenty was in fact the lower limit. It may be added that in other muster returns the lower age limit appears to be normally 16.

4. Smyth states that the return contains this information. In fact, however, there are some hundreds, e.g. Dudstone and Barton Regis, St. Briavels, and Wesbury) for which it is not given.

5. S.P.D. Ch. I, Case E, no. 15: 'A List of enrollment of untrayned men of able bodyes within the East Division of the Co. of Northampton fitt for H.M. service in the Wars, 1638.'

6. John Smyth, *The Lives of the Berkeleys,* ed. Sir John Maclean as vols. i and ii of *The Berkeley Manuscripts,* 1883. For a brief account of Smyth's life see 'The Berkeley Manuscripts and their author, John Smyth', by J. H. Cooke, in *Bristol and Glos. Arch. Trans.,* vol. v, 1880-81, pp. 212-21.

7. Smyth of Nibley MSS. (Gloucester Public Library), no. 16064, contains an account of the 'gaynes and charges' of Smyth's sheep-farming business. The receipts for 26 June 1622, show 73 lambs, 1 ram, 15 ewes, and 11 wethers sold at Smithfield for £38 15s. 8d.; for 23 July 1622, 110 lambs, 16 ewes, and 14 wethers sold at Smithfield for £37 3s. 10d.; for 12 June 1623, 84 lambs, 28 ewes, and 8 wethers sold at London for £34 6s. 5d.; and for 11 July 1623, 123 lambs, 10 wethers, and 34 ewes sold at London for £47 13s. 2d.

8. Smyth MSS., vol. ii, p. 89 (Sir Maurice Berkeley to John Smyth, 12 December 1639).

9. Smyth, *Lives of the Berkeleys,* vol. ii, p. 440.

10. Smyth, *A Description of the Hundred of Berkeley,* p. 34.

11. 'And thus ended that *trita et vexata questio,* that old, intricate and perplexed title, as it was usually in all courts called, that had continued the space of 192 years, from the 5th of King Henry the fifth to the seaventh of King James, between the heires generall and the heirs male of this noble family; wherein, besides more than fower times the value of the inheritance of the lands, that had by both parties in that longe tract of time been spent, the bloud of divers eminent persons on both sides had been spilt'. (Smyth, *Lives of the Berkeleys,* vol. ii, pp. 332-3).

12. D. King, *the Vale-Royall of England; or the County Palatine of Chester illustrated,* 1656.

13. Smyth's diary of the Parliament of 1621 is in the Brit. Museum, Add. MSS., 34121. It covers the sessions February to June and November to December, 1621.

14. Smyth, *A Description of the Hundred of Berkeley,* p. 412.

15. We put the number at 402, exclusive of Gloucester, Cirencester, and Tewkesbury (see Table II, p. 40); but it is possible that a few places which have been counted as parts of the same manor may have been separate manors.

16. Fourteen according to Smyth, who did not enter as boroughs Chipping Campden and Stow-on-the-Wold.

17. The procedure employed in collecting information is not stated. The words prefixed to the return—'the names and surnames of all the able and sufficient men . . . viewed by Henry, Lord Berkeley . . . in the month of September 1608'—appear to imply that the individuals concerned appeared in person. As it is hardly credible that they should have presented themselves at any one place, it is to be presumed that Lord Berkeley or his officers held sessions in different parts of the county. There is, however, no statement to that effect.

18. Smyth (*A Description of the Hundred of Berkeley,* p. 9) refers to 'many that made default in this hundred and appeared not'. If there were defaulters in the hundred of Berkeley, it is probable that there were many more in other parts of the county. It may be added that only three clergymen appear in the return, though the servants of fourteen are listed.

19. The lords of manors appearing directly under the name of each manor have here and elsewhere been excluded. Among them were the Crown—the largest owner of manorial property—cathedral chapters, colleges, and a few women. Of the remainder, several were absentees who did not reside in Gloucestershire, while a number owned more than one manor. The names of lords are valuable as showing the distribution of manorial property among different owners, but many of them cannot properly be included in the population of the county.

20. The percentage of men for whom no information as to occupation or social status is given is as follows:— Under 5 per cent in the 3 hundreds of Thornbury (where the exact figure was 2·3 per cent), Langley and Swineshead (3·1), and Berkeley (4·1); between 5 and 10 per cent in the 10 hundreds of Henbury (5·0), Botlow (6·1), Barton Regis (6·4), Wesbury (6·5), Duchy of Lancaster (7·8), Pucklechurch (7·8), Rapsgate (7·9), Bisley (8·7), Gromboldsash (8·9), and St. Briavels (9·5); between 10 and 15 per cent in the 8 hundreds of Tewkesbury (10·4), Whitstone (10·9), Bledisloe (11·4), Longtree (11·4), Kiftsgate (12·2), Deerhurst (13·3), Cheltenham (13·9), and Bradley (14·1); between 15 and 20 per cent in the 3 hundreds of Slaughter (17·0), Crowtherne and Minty (17·5), and Cleeve (17·6); between 20 and 25 per cent in the 2 hundreds of Brightwelsbarrow (21·8) and Westminster (23·9); between 30 and 35 per cent in the 2 hundreds of Tyboldstone (30·4) and Dudstone and Barton Regis (33·4). In the borough of Cirencester and City of Gloucester the percentages unstated were 8·6 and 15·3.

21. Ambiguity of nomenclature should, perhaps, be added as a sixth defect. When it is uncertain under which industrial group a particular

occupation should be placed, it has been classified as miscellaneous. Some terms which appear obscure in print are clear to anyone who knows the local pronunciation; but certain others continue to baffle us (e.g. 'bedor', 'furnkeeper', 'sadser', 'tewgorer', 'torn-maker'). These last have also been placed in the miscellaneous group. They number in all 16.

22. Viz.: 2 mayors, 4 chamberlains, 1 sergeant, 10 constables, 1 tithingman, 1 clerk of parish, 1 apparitor, 1 bellman.

23. This appears to us the more probable because of the large number of persons in the Forest of Dean entered as labourers. In the hundred of St. Briavels they numbered 151 out of the 951 men (15·8 per cent), in Wesbury 102 out of 463 (22 per cent), in Bledisloe 52 out of 378 (13·7 per cent). The labourers in these three hundreds accounted together for one-sixth of the total number in the county, exclusive of Gloucester, Cirencester, and Tewkesbury. Against this view must be set the fact that labourers are not specially numerous in the other group of mining hundreds, Langley and Swineshead, Pucklechurch, and Barton Regis, which supplied workers to the Bristol coalfield. We can only suppose that, either through greater care on the part of the clerk or through some local difference of nomenclature, persons were entered in the latter case as miners who in the former were entered as labourers.

24. In some cases this is definitely stated. Thus as Sapperton the 24 servants of Sir Henry Poole are divided in the return into two groups, of which one consists of 15 'gentlemen and yeomen servants', and the other of 9 'husbandmen servants', and at Dodington the 14 'menyall and household servants' of Mrs Codrington are divided into 8 yeomen and 6 husbandmen. The same is done at some other places. As, however, no uniform procedure appears to have been observed, we have thought it better to classify the servants of knights, esquires, and gentlemen as household servants. For a further discussion of the point, with reference to the number of servants in agriculture, see below pp. 50-2.

25. Sir Robert Atkyns, *The Ancient and Present State of Gloucestershire,* 2nd ed, 1768, p. 22. He estimates from 'the return made from the several dioceses in the reign of Charles II' that the 'able men' in the county then numbered 'about 22,000', and continues: 'This number agrees with the muster taken by Henry, Lord Berkeley of all the able men in the county in the sixth year of King James I, which was performed with great industry and exactness.' The return to which he refers was a census of 'Conformists, non-conformists and papists' in the province of Canterbury taken in 1676 (Salt MSS. 2112, and no doubt elsewhere), which gave the total population over the age of 16 in the diocese of Gloucester as 67,285. If—which is improbable—males between 20 and 60 formed in 1608 the same proportion of the total population of the county as in 1921, then, on the basis of Smyth's figures (admittedly incomplete), the population of Gloucestershire at the first date would have been approximately 85,000. As it was stated to be 250,723 in 1801, a figure round about 100,000 nearly two hundred years before is, perhaps, not unplausible. But such questions are too intricate to be discussed in a footnote

26. Dudstone and Barton Regis.

27. See note 22.

28. For a more detailed classification of occupations, see Table XXI at end of essay.

29. The next largest centres of population were the following:—

	(i) Total men returned	(ii) Men whose occupation is stated	(iii) Percentage of (ii) engaged in agriculture
Bitton and Hanham	209	205	53
Minchinhampton	178	144	22
Cheltenham	170	165	32
Painswick	170	152	37

A census taken in Bristol in 1607 showed that it then had a population of 10,549 persons (Nicholas and Taylor, *Bristol Past and Present,* p. 273).

30. Even if half the group classified in Table XII as 'Labourers, non-agricultural' be transferred to 'Agriculture and Estate Service', the number of persons engaged in the latter still only amounts to 9·2 per cent of the men of known occupation in the three towns.

31. 1 at Gloucester and 6 at Cirencester.

32. There is reason to think that the small number of transport and building workers returned is due primarily, not to defects of enumeration specially affecting workers in these industries, but to the fact that in both a good deal of work was done, not by specialists, but as a by-employment, e.g., by the employees of farmers and other producers, who in Smyth's return would appear as servants, and by amateurs who built their own cottages, as is still sometimes done, with a little expert help from a mason and the assistance of neighbours. But space does not allow us to argue the point.

33. S.P.D. Ch. I, Case E, no. 15. The total number listed was 1,031, of whom 278 were returned as engaged in agriculture, 263 as labourers, and 115 as servants. Workers engaged in the cloth industry numbered only 37.

34. Including boroughs other than the three mentioned above.

35. The industries included are textiles, leather-work, making of articles of dress (tailoring, glove-making, and shoe-making are here counted as separate industries), woodwork, building, metal-work, paper and cardboard-making.

36. The figures in this and the following Table are *minima,* since in most manors there are some men whose occupations are not given. Of the 31 manors for which no craftsmen are returned it can be said with certainty of only 7 (all manors) that they are entirely agricultural. The others all contain some persons of unstated occupation.

37. The wide distribution of metal workers is due to the fact that there were smiths in most considerable villages. Apart from them, the metal industries were somewhat highly concentrated. See pp. 221-2.

38. As has been pointed out, some of the 750 servants of the gentry (see Appx., Table XXI) were so employed, as were also some of the 122 servants of women; and the same is likely to have been true of the 283 servants of unspecified occupation. If it be assumed that half of each of

these groups was employed in agriculture, the effect is to increase the proportion which agricultural workers formed of the total population from 46·2 to 49·6 per cent. Against that, however, must be set the facts (i) that all the 1,831 labourers outside Gloucester, Cirencester, and Tewkesbury have been assigned to agriculture, (ii) that, as explained above, there were almost certainly more miners and ironworkers in the county than appear in the return, and probably also (since the hundred with the largest number of men of unspecified occupation included part of the suburbs of Gloucester) more craftsmen and dealers. It may be added that, even if three quarters of such men in the six other hundreds where they exceed one sixth of those listed were assigned to agriculture, the result would be to add only 361 men to the agricultural population.

39. Misc. Bks. Augm. Off., vol. 394, ff. 78-126.

40. Or seven. In addition to those mentioned above there was one mill whose use is unspecified, but which was probably a fulling-mill.

41. E.g. nearly all the 194 sailors, 22 boatmen, and 18 fishermen are in hundreds bordering, or within easy reach of, the Severn or one or other of the two Avons.

42. E.g., 21 out of 71 maltsters lived, for reasons unknown to us, in a single village, Marshfield, in the hundred of Thornbury, 16 in the Borough of Tewkesbury, and 15 in the City of Gloucester; 23 out of 146 millers are found in the hundred of Berkeley, and 53 in the four hundreds of Berkeley, Tewkesbury, Gromboldsash, and Langley and Swineshead, where there is abundant water; 77 out of 333 shoemakers occur in two hundreds, 47 in Berkeley and 30 in Tewkesbury, of the latter of whom 26 lived in the borough.

43. See p. 224. The miners, including 2 servants and 3 sons or brothers, numbered 161, the workers in and about quarries 11.

44. S.P.D. Jas. I, vol. lxxxiv, no. 46, printed in H. T. Ellacombe, *The Parish of Bitton,* 1881-3.

45. Of the whole 402 manors 187, and of the 159 manors with 40 men or more 115, contained one or more smiths.

46. Bledisloe and Wesbury.

47. 'The lowe and fat groundes doe yeild . . . abundance of pasture for kyne and oxen . . . and in the hilly part, where the ground is dryer and the grasse shorter, it feedeth innumerable numbers of sheep' (Smyth, *The Hundred of Berkeley,* p. 4). Marshall *(Rural Economy of Gloucester,* 1796) divided the county into eight regions, of which he described in detail three, the Vale of Gloucester, 'equally abundant in grass and corn', the vale of Berkeley, 'a grassland dairy country', and 'the Cotswold hills, an upland arable district', largely interested in sheep. 'For generations', writes Professor Hanley of the wold country north of Cirencester, 'it has been concerned chiefly with corn-growing and the breeding of livestock, mainly sheep, the land being that so frequently referred to by agriculturalists as 'sheep and corn land'. The proportion of permanent grass on the cultivated land is low, and confined mainly to valleys'. *(Memoirs of the Geological Survey, England and Wales, The Country round Cirencester,* 1933, pp. 94-5).

48. Kiftsgate and Slaughter.

49. Smyth, *op. cit.* p. 5. In three hundreds yeomen were over 20 per cent of the whole agricultural population (excluding sons and brothers), in five under 20 and over 15, in nine under 15 and over 10, in eight under 10 and over 5, in three under 5. Berkeley, with the largest number (134), had the fifth largest percentage, 18·3.

50. Longtree (45·2 per cent); Bisley (39·4 per cent); Berkeley (37·9 per cent); Whitstone (31·6 per cent); Gromboldsash (28 per cent).

51. R. H. Kinvig, *The Historical Geography of the West Country Woollen Industry* (Geographical Teacher Reprints, No. 10, 1916). See also L. D. Stamp and S. H. Beaver, *The British Isles,* 1933, pp. 445-447.

52. 'Many hundreds, even thousands, of springs breake forth at the sydes, knees and feete of those hills, begettinge divers delicate small rivers, neither knowing want of water in sommer nor so increasinge their chanell in winter, that the trade of clothinge, which heere aboundeth, is neither in drought nor wett wether hindred: A principall cause of the multitude of tuckmills and fullinge mills, which heere abound' (Smyth, *The Hundred of Berkeley,* p. 4).

53. Whitstone, Bisley, and Longtree.

54. Berkeley.

55. We use this expression in the sense of the French *chefs d'exploitation,* for which there appears to be no exact English equivalent.

56. Including women.

57. Sons and brothers have in all cases been omitted.

58. Including 1 apprentice.

59. Including 1 flockman and 3 servants to shepherds.

60. Viz.: 6 bailiffs; 12 keepers, rangers, warreners, fowlers, and 2 servants of these; 1 woodman; 10 gardeners.

61. Viz.: 1 hayward; 11 seivgers; 6 horse-riders, horse-coursers, and horse-drivers.

62. The word 'husbandmen' was sometimes used to mean servants in husbandry, for example in some wage-assessments; and in Smyth's return 91 persons are entered as 'husbandmen servants', 69 of whom were employed by knights, esquires, and gentlemen, 1 by a parson, 17 by women, 2 by yeomen, and 2 by husbandmen. It was ordinarily used, however, unless accompanied by words of qualification, to describe the smaller landholders, as distinct from yeomen, on the one hand, and labourers, on the other, though it must be remembered that the holdings of such men were often insufficient to afford a living, and that they eked it out by part-time work for wages. The 91 'husbandmen servants' have been classed in Table V as servants, not as husbandmen.

63. The servants of knights, esquires, and gentlemen definitely stated to be engaged in agriculture number 69. But no uniform practice is followed in the return, and in the case of the great majority of manors no distinction was made between servants in husbandry and other servants. It seemed better, therefore, to make the larger allowance for servants given above. It is probable that one half is an underestimate of the proportion employed part or full time in agriculture.

64. In addition 32 servants were employed by 14 clergymen—17 by one,

2 each by two, and 1 each by eleven.

65. i.e. except the lord of the manor, who, as explained above, might often be an absentee, and has not been counted.

66. Nether Swell, Broadwell, Maugersbury, and Sherborne.

67. Farmcote and Postlippe.

68. 369 out of a total of 619.

69. Including apprentices.

70. Includes 7 millcarpenters and millwrights, and 1 servant.

71. Including 2 clothmen.

72. Including 8 fullers, 1 tucker, and 1 clothworker.

73. Viz.: 2 wool-drivers, 1 wool-dryer, 2 wool-winders, 1 wool-worker, 2 wool-dyers, 1 yarn-seller, 8 cloth-workers or cloth-makers, 9 felt-makers.

74. See note 72.

75. There were 8·6 weavers (including weavers' servants) per clothier and 2·1 tuckers, fullers, dyers, shearmen, and miscellaneous textile workers, including their servants.

76. For Prussia, sec J. H. Clapham, *The Economic Development of France and Germany,* pp. 84-5; for Great Britain, Clapham, *An Economic History of Modern Britain,* vol. ii, pp. 117-19; for France, E. Levasseur, *Questions ouvrières et industrielles en France sons la troisième République,* pp. 274-5; for China, R. H. Tawney, *Land and Labour in China,* pp. 109-15.

77. Thus, to give one example, the mayor of Gloucester, describing in January, 1625/6, the alleged decline of the textile industry, writes of 'the excessive number of poore, chiefly occasioned by the decay of clothinge, wherein this city and county have much suffered more that other parts, there being nowe not above two or three clothiers, and those men of mean ability, whereas wee have heretofore hadd more than twenty men of good estates who have kept great numbers of poore on worke' *(Hist. MSS. Com., Twelfth Report,* Appx., pt. IX, p. 476).

Notes to Table XXI

78. There are also 87 'husbandmen servants', included under household servants (Class XIV).

79. Includes 1 flockman.

80. Viz. 6 bailiffs, 12 keepers, rangers, warreners, and fowlers, 1 woodman, 10 gardeners.

81. Viz. 11 seivgers, 6 horse-riders, horse-coursers, and horse-drivers, 1 hayward.

82. Viz. 2 quarriers, 2 millstone-hewers, 6 grindstone-hewers, 1 holliar.

83. Viz. 2 wooldrivers, 1 wooldryer, 2 wooldyers, 1 woolworker, 2 wool-winders.

84. Includes 2 clothmen.

85. Viz. 4 fustian weavers, 5 coverlet weavers, 1 tabberer (carpet-weaver?).

86. Viz. 4 ropers, 1 knitter, 1 bonelace maker, 1 embroiderer.

87. Includes 1 furrier.

88. Includes 20 solemakers, 7 cobblers and cosiers.

89. Viz. 12 hatters, 2 hosiers, 2 pointmakers. The servant is servant to a gartermaker.
90. Includes 5 hoopers.
91. Viz. 2 carvers, 3 bowyers, 2 fletchers, 8 basket-makers, 5 trencher-makers, 3 shovel-makers, 3 hive-makers, 2 lattice-makers, 1 sleigh-maker.
92. Includes 3 stonelayers and 1 roughlayer.
93. Viz. 5 plasterers and pargeters, 4 painters, 3 paviors.
94. Includes 1 bell-founder.
95. Includes 5 blacksmiths and 3 farriers.
96. Viz. 4 braziers, 1 plumber.
97. Includes 1 broker to husbandman.
98. Includes 3 woollen drapers and 1 linen draper.
99. Viz. 7 fishmongers, 1 grocer, 1 cheesemonger, 1 pearmonger.
100. Viz. 5 apothecaries, 3 stationers, 1 ironmonger.
101. Includes 1 raddle carrier and 1 fish carrier.
102. Includes 2 servants to son of carrier.
103. Includes 4 trowmen.
104. Viz. 5 papermen, 4 parchment-makers, 3 cardboard-makers, 1 book-binder.
105. Viz. 2 potters, 2 bottle-makers, 1 starch-maker, 1 saltpetreman, 1 loiterer.
106. Viz. 4 warburners, 2 staymakers, 2 tewgorers, 2 bedors, 1 tornmaker, 1 furnkeeper, 1 ganger, 1 keeper of corslane, 1 pamer, 1 sadser.
107. Viz. 5 chirurgeons and surgeons, 2 physicians, 1 toothdrawer, 6 schoolmasters, 1 usher, 1 scholar, 2 barristers, 1 attorney-at-law, 3 clergymen, 5 scriveners, 9 musicians, 1 drummer, 1 harper.
108. Viz. 2 mayors, 4 chamberlains, 1 sergeant, 10 constables, 1 tithingman, 1 clerk of parish, 1 apparitor, 1 bellman.
109. Viz. Gloucester, Tewkesbury, and Cirencester.
110. Including the three large towns, Gloucester, Tewkesbury, and Cirencester, which are treated as separate entities. Other towns are included in the hundreds in which they are situated.
111. *i.e.,* the hundred of Tewkesbury exclusive of the borough.

INDEX